Turkey's New World

Changing Dynamics
in Turkish Foreign Policy

Edited by

ALAN MAKOVSKY and SABRI SAYARI

The Washington Institute for Near East Policy

© 2000 by The Washington Institute for Near East Policy

Published in 2000 in the United States of America by The Washington Institute for Near East Policy, 1828 L Street NW, Suite 1050, Washington, DC 20036.

Library of Congress Cataloging-in-Publication Data

Turkey's new world : changing dynamics in Turkish foreign policy/ edited by Alan Makovsky and Sabri Sayarı.
     p.   cm.
    Includes bibliographical references and index.
    ISBN 0-944029-43-4 (pbk.)
    1. Turkey—Foreign relations—1980–   2. Turkey—Foreign economic relations.   I. Makovsky, Alan, 1950-   II. Sayarı, Sabri.
DR477. C445 2000
327.561—dc21   00-043711
                                                       CIP

Cover design by Alicia Gansz.
Additional cover art by Equator Graphics, Inc.

The Editors

A lan O. Makovsky is a Senior Fellow and director of the Turkish Research Program at The Washington Institute for Near East Policy in Washington, D.C. Makovsky has written widely on both Turkish and Middle Eastern affairs, as well as U.S. regional policy concerns. He joined The Washington Institute in 1994 after eleven years in the U.S. State Department, where he served in a variety of capacities, including division chief for southern Europe in the Bureau of Intelligence and Research, political advisor to the Turkey-based Operation Provide Comfort, and advisor to the Special Middle East Coordinator.

S abri Sayarı is the executive director of the Institute of Turkish Studies (ITS), a private, non-profit educational institution based at Georgetown University that promotes scholarly research on Turkey in American universities. Dr. Sayarı also teaches at Georgetown University's School of Foreign Service and currently serves as the chair of Turkish Area Studies at the U.S. State Department's Foreign Service Institute. He has published widely on Turkish politics, including issues related to democratization, political parties, the politics of economic reform, and foreign policy.

Table of Contents

Acknowledgments   xii
Preface   ix
Note on Turkish Pronunciation   xi
Map   xii

Introduction
  by Alan Makovsky and Sabri Sayarı   1

Reflections on the Atatürkist Origins of Turkish
  Foreign Policy and Domestic Linkages
  by Andrew Mango   9

Economic Issues in Turkish Foreign Policy
  by William Hale   20

Turkey and the Muslim Middle East
  by Kemal Kirişçi   39

Turkish Policy toward Israel
  by Meliha Benli Altunışık   59

Turkish Policy toward the Balkans
  by Şule Kut   74

Turkish–Russian Relations: From Adversity
  to 'Virtual Rapprochement'
  by Duygu Bazoğlu Sezer   92

Turkish Policy toward Central Asia
  and the Transcaucasus
  by Gareth M. Winrow   116

Turkish Policy toward Greece
  by Tozun Bahcheli   131

Turkey and the Cyprus Question
  by Clement H. Dodd   153

Turkey and the European Union
  in the Post–Cold War Era
  by Atila Eralp   173

U.S.–Turkish Relations
 by George S. Harris   189

Beyond 'Bridge or Barrier': Turkey's Evolving
 Security Relations with the West
 by Ian O. Lesser   203

Contributors   222
Index   225

Acknowledgments

Virtually all the chapters in this volume developed from papers presented at five seminars on Turkish foreign policy organized by The Washington Institute for Near East Policy in 1997-98. (An additional essay by Gareth Winrow was added after the seminars.) The seminars were made possible only through the very generous support of The Smith-Richardson Foundation of Westport, Connecticut. Known for its low-key approach, Smith-Richardson has been associated with many first-class foreign-affairs-related projects over the years, and we were honored by their confidence and by the opportunity to work with their personnel, especially program officer Nadia Schadlow.

Crucial additional funding for the fifth seminar, on Turkey's relations with the West, was provided by the United States Information Service offices of the U.S. embassies in Turkey, Greece, and Germany. We are deeply grateful to public affairs counselors Helena Finn in Ankara, T.J. Dowling (acting) and Arlene Jacquette in Athens, and David Arnett in Berlin both for deeming our project worthy of a place in their ever-scantier budgets and for their substantive suggestions regarding the seminar agenda.

In addition to the authors and co-editors, several others participated in the discussions in the seminars and offered valuable suggestions, rich insights, and thought-provoking debate. These include Oya Akgönenç, Bulent Aliriza, Bülent Aras, Ekavi Athanassopoulou, Sencer Ayata, Mahmut Bali Aykan, Hüseyin Bağcı, Henri Barkey, Fuat Çalışır, Oğuz Çelikkol, Van Coufoudakis, Theodore Couloumbis, Metehan Demir, Nadir Devlet, Cem Duna, Selim Egeli, Şükrü Elekdağ, Asım Erdilek, Sedat Ergin, Andrew Finkel, Graham Fuller, Paul Goble, Thomas Goltz, Jean-Marie Guehenno, Şükrü Gürel, Talat Halman, Famil Ismailov, Charles Jenkins, Paul Jureidini, Bahadir Kaleağası, Ali Karaosmanoğlu, Ibrahim Karawan, Dimitris Keridis, Hakan Kırımlı, Sami Kohen, Fehmi Koru, Martin Kramer, Ömer Kürkçüoğlu, Gün Kut, Barry Lowenkron, Heath Lowry, Carol Migdalovitz, Malik Mufti, Vitaly Naumkin, Selim Oktar, Ümit Özdağ, Soli Özel, Erdal Oztürk, Necdet Pamir, Daniel Pipes, Hugh Poulton, Harold Rhode, Philip Robins, John Roper, Özdem Sanberk, Mahmood Sarioghlam, Robert Satloff, Martin Sletzinger, Udo Steinbach, Seyfi Taşhan, Maria Todorova, Alexandre Toumarkine, Dimitrios Triantaphyllou, Baran Tuncer, Hasan Ünal, Ross Wilson, James Wolfe, and Paul Wolfowitz. Advice from Keith Weissman and Birol Yeşilada in the post-seminar phase of production of this book was also most useful.

Our diligent copy editor Bob Greiner did a superb job with this volume, even while handling with aplomb two demanding co-editors. The Washington Institute's director of publications, Monica Neal Hertzman, made crucial contributions as preparations for publication neared the home stretch. When she left the Institute to pursue opportunities elsewhere, publications associate Alicia Gansz was punctilious and tirelessly dedicated in seeing the project through to completion. We thank all three of them for their help.

We also wish to thank The Washington Institute's executive director Robert Satloff for his backing of the project and the staff of The Washington Institute for tireless work that facilitated the seminar proceedings and the subsequent volume. Edward Finn, James Green, Niyazi Günay, Yola Habif, Laura Hannah, Rebecca Medina, Michael Moskowitz, Levent Onar, Benjamin Orbach, Yoav Schlesinger, Sulay Öztürk, and Liat Radcliffe made particularly valuable contributions. Yonca Poyraz-Doğan was indispensable. As seminar organizer, she handled much of the seminar planning and contact with participants, as well as all the logistics, and she did so with a rare and admirable combination of thoroughness, intelligence, grace, and good cheer. We are most indebted to Yonca.

Preface

One of the most important developments of the past decade, for both the Middle East and neighboring regions, has been the emergence of Turkey as a regional power. As Alan Makovsky and Sabri Sayarı point out in their Introduction, several factors have enabled Turkey to transform itself from a staid political actor into a more assertive one: more prosperity, a stronger military, weaker neighbors, and a broadening of foreign policy priorities that saw Ankara build up its ties with the Turkic states of the former Soviet Union and, dramatically, with Israel.

Nowhere have the new dynamics of Turkish foreign policy been more evident than in the Middle East. The late President Turgut Özal's decision to align Turkey firmly with the U.S.-led war against Saddam Husayn's Iraq in 1991 marked a turning-point for Turkey in the region. Since that time, Turkey has been involved in numerous initiatives in the Middle East—although sometimes more to fend off danger than to cultivate opportunity. As part of its fight against the separatist Kurdistan Workers' Party (PKK), Turkey has several times sent its forces into northern Iraq, which the PKK has used as a staging-area. In autumn 1998 it warned Syria to end its support for the separatists and to expel PKK leader Abdullah Öcalan; fearful of Turkey's superior might, Damascus quickly complied.

Its role as a crucial Middle East actor has naturally made Turkey a focus of interest for The Washington Institute for Near East Policy. Turkey is the only nation in the world that borders three countries on the State Department's list of "state-sponsors of terrorism": Iran, Iraq, and Syria. Moreover, Turkey's relationship with Israel has reinforced its credibility in the region; indeed, it probably explains the late Syrian president Hafiz al-Asad's ready surrender to Turkish threats in 1998. Turkey's relations with Israel presently consist of several dimensions in addition to security, including trade, tourism, and a vigorous intellectual exchange through universities; and in 1999, Israel emerged as Turkey's leading export market in the Middle East.

As the following essays illustrate, Turkey is indeed a "pivotal state" par excellence, and uniquely so. In November 1999, President Clinton declared that "at Turkey . . . Europe and the Muslim world can meet in peace and harmony." Turkey is the only Muslim-majority state in the Western alliance and the only Western ally in the Islamic Conference Organization. The United States has strongly backed Turkey's bid for membership in the European Union, and it sees this secular, democratic, pro-Western country as a role model for the Islamic world.

Turkey's policy approaches to neighboring regions have an important impact on U.S. policy not only in the Middle East but elsewhere. Richard Holbrooke aptly remarked that Turkey "stands at the crossroads of almost every issue of importance to the United States on the Eurasian continent." Indeed, Turkey has been central to countless U.S. policy initiatives over the past decade. In addition to the Gulf War and Operation Northern Watch, Washington and Ankara have been partners in NATO, the Middle East peace process, Bosnia, Kosovo, energy transport plans in Azerbaijan and Central Asia, and counter-terrorism efforts.

For all these reasons, it is important that Americans learn more about this strategically crucial nation. It is hoped that this book of essays by regional experts, covering the kaleidoscopic concerns of Turkish foreign policy, will enlighten U.S. foreign-policy students, scholars, afficionados, and professionals alike about one of the world's most important emerging powers.

Fred S. Lafer   Michael Stein
President   *Chairman*

Note on Turkish Pronunciation

In the following text, Turkish proper nouns, Turkish books and articles, and the occasional Turkish word or phrase are rendered in (it is hoped) proper Turkish spelling. The one exception to this rule is "Istanbul." Because of the familiarity of this spelling to English-language readers, we have elected to represent it here without the Turkish "İ" except in footnotes, where it is cited as a place of publication or as part of a title.

For those unfamiliar with Turkish, a few points may be useful. Turkish is primarily a phonetic language; unlike English, all Turkish consonants and most vowels letters are pronounced the same way at all times. Most Turkish letters are found in the English alphabet and pronounced roughly like their English counterparts—b as in *boy*, d as in *dog*, s as in *sit*, a as in *father*, e as in *lend*, u as in *plume*, etc. A list of exceptions and additions follows:

c—pronounced as the *j* in *jet*

ç—pronounced as the *ch* in *chug*

g—pronounced always as a "hard *g*," as in *girl*

ğ—unvoiced; tends to elongate the preceding vowel

j—pronounced as the French *j*

ş—pronounced as the *sh* in *shirt*

I/ı (upper case/lower case)—pronounced as the second vocalized vowel in *battle*, usually rendered phonetically as a schwa (ə) in English

İ/i (upper case/lower case)—generally pronounced as the short *i* in *fit*

ö—pronounced as the same letter in German

ü—pronounced as the same letter in German

In spelling the names of the authors in this volume, we have deferred to individual preference, of course.

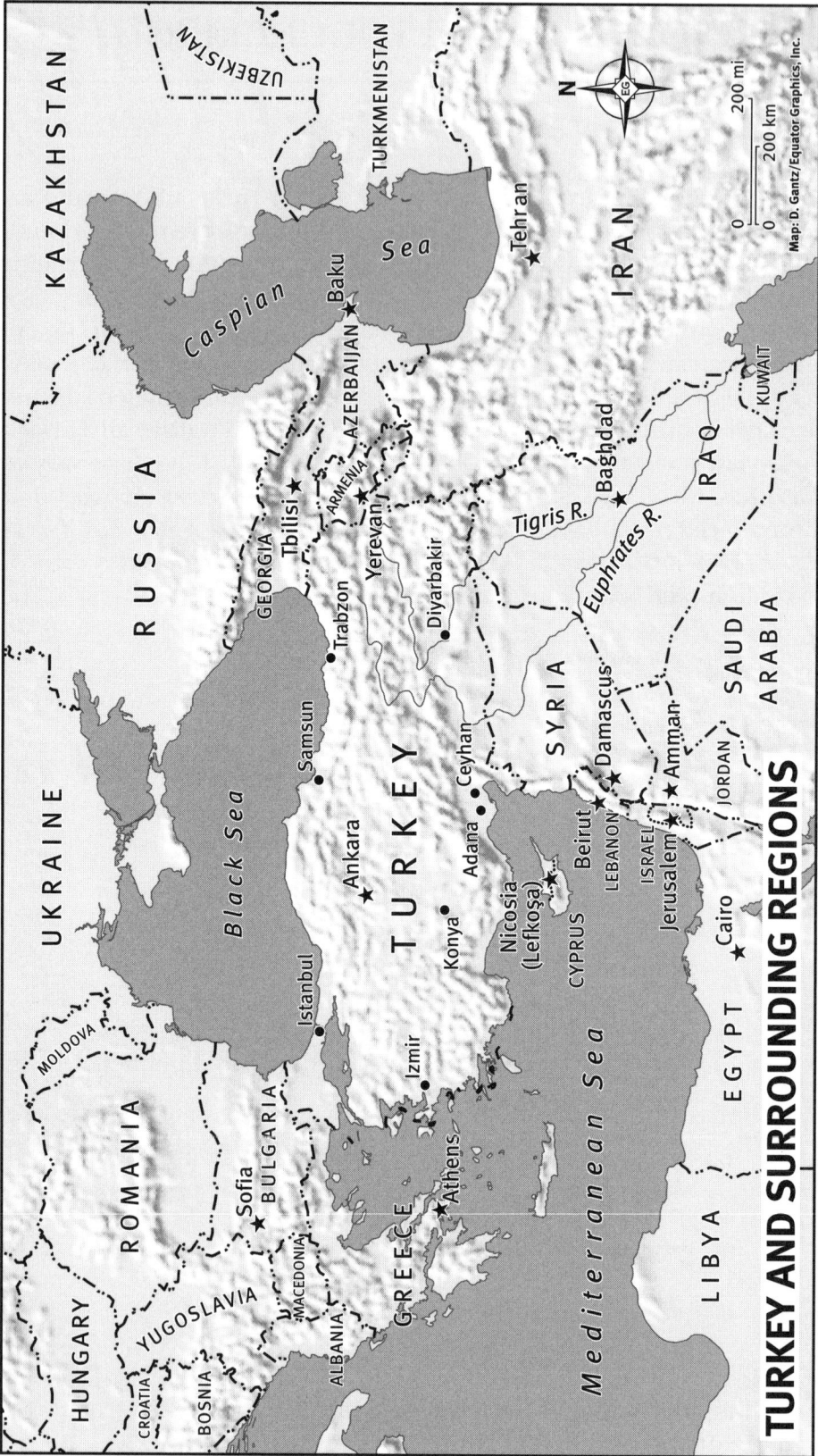

TURKEY AND SURROUNDING REGIONS

KAZAKHSTAN

UZBEKISTAN

TURKMENISTAN

N

EG

200 mi

200 km

0

0

Map: D. Gantz/Equator Graphics, Inc.

Caspian Sea

Tehran ★

IRAN

Baku ★

AZERBAIJAN

RUSSIA

ARMENIA

Tbilisi ★

Yerevan ★

Diyarbakir ●

Baghdad ★

Tigris R.

IRAQ

Euphrates R.

KUWAIT

GEORGIA

Trabzon ●

Samsun ●

Black Sea

Ankara ★

T U R K E Y

Adana ●

Ceyhan ●

SYRIA

Damascus ★

Amman ★

JORDAN

SAUDI ARABIA

Beirut ★

LEBANON

ISRAEL

Jerusalem ★

Cairo ★

UKRAINE

Istanbul ●

Konya ●

Izmir ●

Nicosia (Lefkoşa) ★

CYPRUS

Mediterranean Sea

EGYPT

LIBYA

MOLDOVA

ROMANIA

Sofia ★

BULGARIA

MACEDONIA

GREECE

Athens ★

HUNGARY

YUGOSLAVIA

ALBANIA

CROATIA

BOSNIA

Introduction

During 1997 and 1998, the Washington Institute for Near East Policy organized a series of seminars in Washington, D.C., to examine changing dynamics and trends in Turkish foreign policy. The decision to organize the seminars was prompted by the realization that Turkish foreign policy in the post-Cold War era was passing through one of its most crucial and volatile periods since the founding of the Turkish Republic in 1923.

During the long Cold War era, Turkish foreign policy was restricted to just a few basic, if difficult and crucial, questions: how to ward off the Soviet threat, how to protect Turkish interests vis-à-vis Greece and Cyprus, and how to maintain and strengthen ties with the United States and NATO. Slightly less pressing but still important were questions of how to further Turkey's integration with Western Europe and, during the latter part of the Cold War, how to defend against terrorism supported by neighbors like Syria, Iraq, and Iran. These issues were problematic, rendered more complicated in combination. As the U.S. arms embargo of Turkey in the mid-1970s bears witness, managing relations with Cyprus and Aegean rival Greece while building bilateral ties with Washington were goals not always easily reconciled.

Turkey's foreign policy challenges during the Cold War were high-risk, posing existentially threatening dangers, even in addition to the threat of nuclear annihilation shared by all NATO allies. Thousands of Turks died in political violence and terrorism in the late 1970s, with Turkey apparently targeted for destabilization by the Soviets.

On the other hand, the Cold War also imposed a certain amount of order, regularity, and predictability. Stalin's claims on northeastern Turkey and the Turkish Straits in the immediate aftermath of World War II definitively sealed the era of Turkish-Soviet friendship established by Atatürk and Lenin and pushed Ankara toward alliance with the West. By the mid-1950s, however, Ankara and Moscow had established a modus vivendi, at least at the overt level, that would last throughout the Cold War. U.S. support for Turkey and Turkish membership in NATO were instrumental in deterring the Soviet Union's aggressive intentions. Turkey's long border with the Soviets and its short one with their Warsaw Pact ally Bulgaria remained quiet. At no point during the Cold War, with the possible exception of the Cuban Missile Crisis in 1962, did direct hostilities with the Soviet Union or the Warsaw Pact appear imminent.

1

During the Cold War period, Turkey's regional environment also displayed far more stability than it does today. The Caucasus and Central Asia were firmly under the control of Moscow. The Balkans were largely tamed by Tito's firm rule in Yugoslavia and by Cold War discipline. Middle Eastern neighbors were then, as they are today, a source of instability but unlikely to incite open warfare. However unsavory some of these neighbors' behavior, Ankara usually courted them—partly out of weakness, partly to encourage trade, and usually in the forlorn hope that Turkish support for the great Arab cause, the Palestinians, would be repaid in Arab support for the great Turkish cause, Cyprus.

Today Turkey, like the United States, faces no existential threats but its neighborhood, even if no longer cowering under the threat of nuclear war, is more complicated than ever. Turkish officials who spent entire careers trying to steer their nation's foreign policy through the challenges of the Cold War era are no doubt amazed at the mounting number of regional problems their heirs face today. Turkey plays a direct role in at least seven different, if overlapping, regions: Western Europe, the Balkans, the Aegean and the Eastern Mediterranean, the Middle East, the Caucasus-Caspian complex, Central Asia, and the Black Sea. This post-Soviet world is still rife with threats to Turkey but it presents opportunities as well—economic relations with Russia, a hub for energy distribution, new regional cooperation schemes, and perhaps even membership in the European Union. The removal of the Soviet Union's influence from the Arab world has given more flexibility to Turkey's Middle Eastern policies, enabling Ankara to pursue close relations with Israel, to deploy air and ground forces in northern Iraq against the ethnic Kurdish separatist organization, the Kurdistan Workers Party (PKK, by its Kurdish initials), and to issue an ultimatum forcing Syria to expel the PKK's leader Abdullah Öcalan (as happened in 1998)—all without fearing that a tussle with a Soviet client might produce a conflagration with the patron.

Changing Dynamics

The Washington Institute's primary focus, as its full name implies, is U.S. policy in the Near East, which, by the Institute's definition, includes Turkey. Our interest in exploring the changing dynamics in Turkish foreign policy was stimulated by the growing role Turkey has come to play in U.S. foreign policy during the 1990s. More and more, Turkey is emerging in world affairs as a true regional power and a pivotal state.

Powered by a growing private sector, the Turkish economy experienced dynamic growth during the 1990s. Militarily, Turkey has acquired the rudiments of an effective modern conventional fighting force, thanks primarily to co-production (with the U.S. firm Lockheed Martin) of more than two hundred F-16 fighter jets and acquisition of nearly one thousand M60 tanks. Simultaneously with the burgeoning of Turkey's power, most of Turkey's neighbors have declined in strength. Of those that pose potentially the most immediate security problems for Turkey—Russia, Iran, Iraq, and Syria—all have seen their economic and military fortunes sink in the 1990s. Greece, Turkey's neighbor and NATO ally, probably also deserves inclusion in any list of Turkey's most immediate security threats. Although it does not fit the pattern of a declining power, Greece has a much smaller population base (11 million) than does Turkey (63 million) and thus probably would find it difficult indefinitely to maintain parity with Turkey's growing strength. Such a calculation may partly explain Greek motives for the rapprochement with Turkey that blossomed in late 1999.

As Turkey has become stronger and its neighbors weaker, Turkish officials have gained the self-confidence to break out of their traditionally passive foreign policy (to which the 1974 Cyprus intervention was a rare exception). Turkey was the first state to recognize the independence of all the former Soviet states, and it did so even before the formal collapse of the Soviet Union. Ankara has not succeeded in establishing a full-blown Turkish "sphere of influence" in the Turkic states of the former Soviet Union, as initially had been envisioned. However, it has established the basis for greater influence in the region with relatively significant trade relations, energy projects, people-to-people efforts, and a near-annual Turkic summit. Its initiation of close ties with Israel was path-breaking for a state that traditionally had deferred to Arab sensitivities, at least in its overt policies. In the 1990s, Ankara also actively engaged in regional multilateral efforts, as an important participant in the Arms Control and Regional Security group in the Middle East multilateral peace process and as the creator and implementer of ideas such as a Balkan peace-keeping force and a Black Sea Economic Cooperation Zone. At the same time, Turkey's relations with the European Union, though rocky throughout most of the decade, took important steps forward with the completion of a customs union arrangement in 1995 and the EU's formal acknowledgment of Turkey's candidacy for full membership in 1999.

As the Cold War wound down, many Turks fretted that their nation would no longer hold much value for the United States and the West, its once-tense Soviet and Warsaw Pact borders no longer lines of confrontation. Some in Washington policy-making circles initially shared that assessment, but not for long. Turkey's geostrategic stock soared as its role in the 1991 Gulf War and in post-war U.S. efforts to contain Saddam Husayn's Baghdad regime made Turkey once again crucial to a high-priority U.S. foreign policy objective. Other post-Cold War developments have strengthened those ties. Washington moved closer to Turkey's views on the plight of Bosnian Muslims and the uncertainty of Russia's long-term stability and regional intentions. The U.S. also embraced the idea that Turkey should be the outlet for an "east-west energy corridor" transporting the energy riches of the Caspian Sea via a route that would exclude Russia and Iran, thereby enhancing the independence of states like Azerbaijan and Turkmenistan and linking them more closely with the West.

The United States is a global power that values Turkey primarily for geostrategic reasons. Washington's concerns about Balkan instability, Russia's future direction, Iranian fundamentalism, Iraqi aggression, and the durability of the Middle East peace process all reinforce the interest of U.S. policy-makers in Turkey. The Washington Institute's seminars, like this book, were intended to increase understanding about Turkey's relations with all its regions at a time when such systematic study is of increasing importance to U.S. foreign policy.

Foreign-Policy Decision-Making

In addition to formal papers, the seminars generated presentations and debate about the foreign-policy-making process in Turkey and Turkish attitudes toward key foreign policy issues. Participants generally agreed that foreign-policy-making in Turkey remains largely the purview of an elite.

One long-time Turkish diplomat, now retired, spoke of a classic "tripod" that traditionally shaped Turkish foreign policy, consisting of the foreign ministry, the prime minister, and the military. The foreign ministry runs day-to-day foreign policy and serves as a major source of expertise on issues that concern Turkey's international relations. The prime minister is a key political actor in the foreign-policy-making process but the involvement and influence of Turkish prime ministers in shaping their country's relations with the world have varied significantly according to the intensity of their interest in foreign affairs. For example, Bulent Ecevit has always been keenly interested in international politics, whereas Süleyman Demirel gave far more attention to domestic affairs when he served as prime minister in the 1960s and 1970s.

The military, of course, is often a dominant player in Turkish foreign policy. Institutionally, it exercises its influence primarily through the National Security Council (NSC), half the members of which are military leaders. Much of the military's authority derives from its moral leadership, particularly when military and security (including domestic security) issues are at stake, and from its ability to intimidate, based on its historic interventions in Turkish politics. It is widely assumed, for example, that the military takes the lead in decisions regarding Turkish policy in northern Iraq and the fight against the PKK.

Most of the seminar participants agreed that the classic "tripod" model of foreign policy has been modified since the early 1980s, with the presidency emerging as a fourth major pole of decision-making. In part, this is a consequence of the 1982 constitution, which increased the powers of the presidency. It also reflects changes in the mission of the NSC, whose powers, and the powers of the president as its chairman, were enhanced by a law enacted in 1983. If the importance of these changes did not become immediately clear, it may be because of the relatively low-profile manner in which the first president under the 1982 constitution, former military chief Kenan Evren (president from 1982 to 1989), conducted the office.

The possibilities for the president to play an activist role in foreign-policy-making became clear during the presidencies of Turgut Özal (1989 to 1993) and Demirel (1993 to 2000). As politicians who vaulted from the prime ministry to the presidency thanks to their parties' parliamentary voting strength, Özal and Demirel publicly broke the mold of the "above-parties" presidency that took hold after the 1961 constitution, when the office was largely ceremonial and invariably held by retired military men. Özal did not hesitate to assert foreign policy leadership as president. He notably engineered Turkey's support for the United States-led Gulf War against Saddam Husayn, virtually brushing aside the reluctance of the Turkish military and the antiwar sentiments of the Turkish public.

Demirel as president took a somewhat more traditional approach. Unlike Özal, he did not initiate bold foreign policy departures. Nevertheless, he was often a crucial focal point of foreign-policy decision-making. Over time, Demirel took on more clearly defined roles, taking the lead in Turkey's relations with the states of the Caucasus and Central Asia as well as with Black Sea neighbors Romania and Bulgaria. He was also widely credited with bringing bureaucratic coherence to Turkey's policies toward Caspian Sea energy pipelines.

Parliament is rarely a player in foreign policy. Its foreign relations committee, still in relative infancy, exerts no meaningful influence over day-to-day policy. Parliament does have a role in certain extraordinary situations. Specifically, parliamentary approval is constitutionally required to declare war, commit Turkish troops abroad, or allow foreign troops to use facilities in Turkey. However, these parliamentary prerogatives are likely to be invoked only rarely and mainly in circumstances in which the decision is a foregone conclusion. Moreover, in such urgent situations, parliament is likely to take its cue from the government leadership, as it did in January 1991, when, after some hand-wringing, it passed a "war powers act" granting the government authority to permit U.S. fighter jets to use Turkish territory in the war against Iraq.

Parliament ostensibly has played a central role in prolonging the existence of Operation Provide Comfort (OPC), the Turkey-based, U.S.-led air operation that has enforced a "no-fly" zone in northern Iraq almost since the end of the Gulf War. (It was renamed Operation Northern Watch (ONW) in 1997.) Although the issue provoked heated debate for several years, parliament renewed the unpopular OPC/ONW's mandate every six months. But the manner in which it did so—every party voted for OPC's renewal when in government and voted against it when in opposition—suggested that governmental coalition parties in parliament were simply deferring to the strong recommendations of state authorities.

Despite its formally assigned responsibilities, parliament had no part in determining the conduct of war against the PKK, including decisions to carry the hostilities across an international border into northern Iraq. Similarly, parliament was on the sidelines in fall 1998 when Turkey threatened Syria with military action in response to Damascus's support of the PKK. Had Turkish authorities decided to follow through with an attack, the decision most likely would have been driven by the military. It is doubtful that a declaration of war would have been requested or that parliament would have been meaningfully consulted.

Much of Turkish foreign-policy decision-making is shrouded in secrecy. Still, it can be safely said that the emergence of a stronger presidency and National Security Council over the last two decades of the twentieth century has increased the number of poles in Turkey's "multipolar" decision-making apparatus. The primary reference points now seem to be the presidency, prime ministry, and military, with the foreign ministry nevertheless still an important player. Which takes the lead in a crisis seems to be a matter of personality, political circumstance, and the issue at hand.

Public Opinion

There has been relatively little polling of popular Turkish attitudes toward foreign policy issues. Available data from survey research suggest Turks collectively are not very interested in foreign-policy-making or Turkey's international relations. In a survey conducted in mid-1997 by the Istanbul-based Strateji/MORI company (and presented at one of the seminars), 57 percent of Turks declared themselves "not interested" in foreign policy, and only 23 percent said they were "interested." (For university graduates, the figures were almost reversed, 62 percent "interested" and 16 percent "not interested.")

This response as to general interest in foreign policy may not accord, however, with feelings about specific "national pride" foreign policy issues, such as Cyprus or Greece, where emotions can run high. Turkish Cypriot leader Rauf Denktaş's popularity in Turkey has long been seen as a factor limiting Ankara's diplomatic maneuverability on the Cyprus question. Public sentiment was a crucial factor in the Turkish government's decision in late 1984 to take up the cause of the Bulgarian Turks, objects of a "Bulgarification" campaign that included mosque-closings and forced adoption of Slavic names. The initial reflex of the characteristically cautious Cold War-era government in Ankara was to avoid involvement, so as not to interfere in the internal affairs of a neighbor, even when those affairs directly affected the fortunes of fellow Turks. Led by the media, public opinion simply turned Turkish policy around in this instance. Probably embarrassed over its initial reticence, Ankara changed tacks, leading a campaign to draw international attention to the Bulgarian Turks' plight.

Public sentiment was also a determining factor in Turkish responses during the Imia-Kardak crisis, a near-clash with Greece over a small islet in the Aegean in January 1996. The incident that precipitated the crisis, the running aground of a Turkish fishing boat on an islet of contested sovereignty, was handled quietly for a full month. It did not become a "crisis" until word of the problem leaked into the media. As the crisis mounted, Turkish television offered live shots of Turkish warships at sea heading toward the island. The Imia-Kardak crisis underscored the growing importance of the media in mobilizing public opinion and influencing the stands of Turkish governments on key foreign policy questions—a trend likely to gain importance in an era of sophisticated television technology.

Nevertheless, the ability of Turkish foreign policy elites to manage public opinion is mostly intact. Despite the unpopularity of Operation Provide Comfort, Turkish governments consistently renewed its lease without paying any clear political price. Likewise, in the aftermath of PKK leader Öcalan's capture and revelations that Greece had been protecting him in its embassy in Nairobi, Kenya, the Turkish government chose to cool popular anti-Greek sentiments rather than fan them. That reaction eased tensions surprisingly rapidly and helped pave the way for rapprochement. The widely reported responsiveness of mainstream media to governmental importuning on issues deemed important to national interest is no doubt an important element in the government's ability to manage public opinion.

The essays in this volume are intended to review and analyze the changing dynamics in Turkish foreign policy in the post-Cold War period. Andrew Mango sets the historical framework with his essay that examines the Atatürkist origins of foreign policy and the role of ethnicity since the founding of the Republic. William Hale's chapter provides an evaluation of Turkey's international economic relations in the 1990s. New trends in Turkey's regional relations are analyzed by Duygu Bazoğlu Sezer (Russia), Gareth Winrow (Central Asia), Şule Kut (Balkans), Tozun Bahcheli (Greece), Clement C. Dodd (Cyprus), Kemal

Kirişçi (Arab world and Iran), and Meliha Benli Altunışık (Israel). The last three chapters of the book focus on Turkish ties with the West, which remain Ankara's top foreign policy priority: George Harris examines Turkey's relations with the U.S., Ian Lesser reviews problems and prospects concerning Turkey's role in Western security issues, and Atila Eralp discusses the evolution of Turkish-European Union relations. It should be noted that the authors extensively revised their papers to take into account the suggestions and exchanges of views at the seminars, as well as developments in Turkish foreign policy since the seminars were held in 1997-98.

Taken together, the essays in this volume illustrate a post-Cold War Turkish foreign policy that is increasingly bold, multi-directional, and— as Turkey becomes a more prosperous, militarily formidable power among neighbors mostly in decline—less predictable. The editors hope the insights offered in the following pages will contribute to understanding of those dynamics.

Alan Makovsky and *Sabri Sayarı*
Washington, D.C.
June 2000

Andrew Mango

Reflections on the Atatürkist Origins of Turkish Foreign Policy and Domestic Linkages

Turkey's position in the world is undergoing a reassessment. As old certainties are questioned, views are expressed which only recently would have appeared heretical or even absurd. Thus a 1997 survey of Turkey published by the London *Financial Times* quotes a European diplomat in Ankara as saying, "We can accept a Moslem state [in the European Union] but not a Kemalist one." The newspaper's Ankara correspondent wrote that "Kemalism set a backward rural nation on the road to becoming a modern state. However, as Turkey has developed, so the limitations of [Kemal] Atatürk's legacy have become more apparent."[1] However, in another article in the survey, the correspondent quotes U.S. secretary of state Madeleine K. Albright as saying, "We feel it vital that Turkey remain a secular state."[2] Secularism is an essential part of Atatürk's legacy, which is embodied in the present-day Turkish Republic.

The need to reassess Turkey's world position and the confusion that this reassessment engenders derive from the crisis—in its original meaning of "time for decision"—through which Turkey is currently passing. It is a political crisis, not just in the sense of a government crisis but in the wider meaning of a crisis in governance. The political system which developed in Turkey after World War II is unable to provide the public administration that Turkish society requires in order to make progress. Decisions have to be made to address this failure.

Kemalist Principles

The political crisis had little effect on foreign policy until the July 1996 advent to power of a coalition with the Islamist *Refah* (Welfare) Party (RP) as senior partner and the center-right *Doğru Yol* (True Path) Party (DYP) as junior partner. Turkish foreign policy had remained remarkably consistent since its formulation by Mustafa Kemal—later known as Kemal Atatürk—in the midst of the War of Independence (1919-23) that preceded the founding of the Turkish Republic. Turkish foreign policy developed in line with changes in the world but remained true to the goal set by Atatürk: the use of the world power balance for defense of the full independence and territorial integrity of the Republic.[3] However, as Mustafa Kemal said in a long briefing to journalists in 1923 when the Lausanne peace conference was deadlocked, "The foundation of foreign policy is a strong domestic policy, a strong domestic administration and domestic organization. Domestic policy and foreign policy must always be linked."[4] Now it is the failure in domestic political arrangements that threatens the traditional consistency of Turkish foreign policy and confuses foreign observers.

The uncertainty, however, should not be exaggerated. Parliament's endorsement of an avowedly Islamist prime minister in July 1996 may have constituted a break in political history, but there was no break in the development of Turkish society, whose expectations remained congruent with traditional Kemalist foreign policy. Mustafa Kemal said in 1923 that the most sensible policy was "to remain in [these] lands, inhabited by people of the same culture and the same race, and to achieve organic growth and civilization within them."[5] A few months later, opening the first economic congress in Izmir, he made his oft-quoted remark that military victory is transient unless crowned with economic success. Drawing attention to Turkey's deplorable economic state, he stressed the disproportion between its geographical extent and its small population. This made it all the more important that education should impart technical knowledge and aim toward economic progress.[6] Turkey is estimated to have lost four million people in World War I, and by the end of the War of Independence in 1923, only a quarter of its cultivable land was being worked.[7] Nationalists saw population increase as a priority. In 1923 Mustafa Kemal said that, if necessary, foreign experts would be invited to advise on social and health measures to promote growth in the population, which he estimated at eight million. He went on:

> We must also bring in people of the same race and the same culture as ourselves who have found themselves outside the national frontiers and we must increase our population by ensuring a prosperous life for them in this country. If it proves possible to bring them in from Russia, we shall do so. But, in my view, all the Turks in Macedonia and western Thrace should be transferred here, and we should give up any thought of mounting expeditions to return to Europe.[8]

Atatürk thus saw the Turkic peoples of the Soviet Union and the Turks (and other Muslims) in the Balkans primarily as sources of immigrants. The War of Independence was fought to keep under Turkish rule all territory controlled by Ottoman armies on October 30, 1918, when the armistice with the Allies was signed. In December 1921, while the war was still in progress, Mustafa Kemal argued for a realistic foreign policy and denounced both pan-Islamism (unity of all Muslims) and pan-Turkism (unity of all Turkic-origin peoples) as inappropriate goals. "The actions which have brought the nation to the foot of the gallows have their origin in illusions and emotions," he declared. The Turks, he went on to say, had never actually implemented pan-Islamic or pan-Turkic ideologies, and the threat to do so had increased the number and pressure of their enemies.

> Let us return to natural, to legitimate limits. Let us recognize our limitations. As a nation we want an independent life. And for this alone are we willing to sacrifice ourselves.[9]

Foreign Policy and the Kurdish Question

However, giving up expansionism and irredentism did not eliminate the ethnic factor from domestic or, by implication, foreign policy. In a six-hour address to the people of Izmir in February 1923, nine months before the proclamation of the Republic, Mustafa Kemal declared,

> There is one basic [ethnic] element which has established the state of Turkey. But there [are] other elements which have joined their endeavors and their fates to that of the basic element. . . . Some of them profess different faiths . . . like, for example, our Jewish fellow-citizens.[10]

In 1923 Mustafa Kemal and his followers had no inhibitions about mentioning Kurds, although they always insisted that Turks and Kurds formed an indivisible entity. Speaking to journalists in 1923, he argued that Kurds were spread all over the country, that they were present in a mass only in limited areas, and that to draw a frontier to satisfy Kurdish nationalism (*Kürtçülük*) would destroy Turkey and the Turks. The term "people of Turkey" included the Kurds. In accordance with the 1920 constitution, however, Kurds could exercise autonomy only in districts where they were in the majority.[11] This passage was removed from the text of the speech when it was published later, just as the reference to provincial autonomy was dropped when a new constitution was adopted in 1924. When the Republic was proclaimed in 1923, an article was added making Turkish the official language of the state.[12]

Mustafa Kemal's words in 1923 about other ethnic groups joining the "basic" Turkish community are reflected today by liberals who describe their country as "an ethnic mosaic." However, not all elements in the mosaic have held equal importance or presented an equal danger to the country's unity. During the War of Independence, only two ethnic groups—Circassians and Kurds—caused major trouble for the Turkish nationalists. Both were internally divided. Among the Circassians, opponents of Turkish nationalism were quickly defeated by its supporters. A Circassian national congress held under Greek occupation in Izmir failed to make any impression.[13] Turkish nationalists also were able to defeat their opponents among the Kurds, with help from Kurdish allies represented in the Turkish Grand National Assembly (parliament) in Ankara. But the Kurds were more numerous than the Circassians. They were indigenous to the country, rather than refugees, and their tribal divisions were stronger than those in other Anatolian ethnic communities. They lived astride the new frontiers, and their relationship with the state presented more problems than that of the Circassians, who, as refugees, owed their new life to the Ottoman Turkish state.

Because of their tradition of seeking putative foreign protectors, the Kurds presented an immediate foreign policy problem to the Republic's founders. As the War of Independence began, the Turkish nationalist commander in northeastern Anatolia, General Kazım Karabekir, had little difficulty in preventing an alliance between Kurds and Armenians, as the latter could realize their territorial claims only at the expense of the former.[14] But Mustafa Kemal and his supporters feared that in the southeast some Kurds might succumb to "British incitement" in favor of an independent Kurdistan.[15] Military action by Turkish nationalists neutralized disloyal Kurds in territory not under British occupation. On the other hand, Kurds in the British-occupied province of Mosul continued to endanger nationalist Turkey. As Mustafa Kemal explained in 1923,

> Mosul is very valuable for us. First, there are round it oil wells which constitute an unlimited source of wealth. Secondly, there is the equally important question of Kurdishness. The British want to set up a Kurdish government there. If they do so, this idea will spread to the Kurds inside our borders. To prevent this, the border must be drawn further south. However, are we to continue the war if we do not receive Mosul? . . . We cannot regain Mosul by waging war.[16]

His refusal to contemplate war with Britain led to the cession of Mosul to British-mandated Iraq in 1926. The relevant treaty between Turkey, Britain, and Iraq provided that they would refrain from any political contact with tribal leaders across the border and prevent hostile activity in border areas.[17] Nevertheless, the Turkish prime minister İsmet İnönü warned the British ambassador that "so long as any large number of Kurds are included in [Iraq], the Turkish government would have perpetual trouble on [its] eastern provinces and trouble would arise automatically, however loyally the British authorities might act as neighbors."[18] In fact, the cooperation of the British and the royalist regime in Baghdad contained the Kurdish danger in northern Iraq until the fall of the Iraqi monarchy in 1958.

After the treaty, Kurdish nationalist exiles from Turkey moved to French-mandated Lebanon, where they planned a Kurdish rebellion near Mount Ararat on the border with Soviet Armenia and Iran.[19] Its suppression led in 1932 to a rectification of the Turkish-Iranian bor-

der.[20] The treaty Turkey had signed with Iran in 1926 already provided
for cooperation against "criminal activities" by Kurdish tribes.[21] There
was a similar provision in the 1937 Saadabad Pact between Turkey,
Iraq, Iran, and Afghanistan.[22]

After World War II, Turkey feared that the Soviet Union would exploit Kurdish nationalism. The short-lived Kurdish republic of Mahabad
in Iran was formed with Soviet help in 1946. In the same year, the Iraqi
Kurdish leader Mustafa Barzani was given asylum in the Soviet Union.[23]
In 1975 Barzani's rival, Jalal Talabani, formed the Patriotic Union of
Kurdistan (PUK) in Syria,[24] then Moscow's closest ally in the Middle
East. Between 1955 and 1958, Turkey sought to contain Soviet intrigues
through the Baghdad Pact, which the Kurds naturally opposed as they
had the Saadabad Pact.[25] After the dissolution of the Baghdad Pact following the Iraqi revolution, Turkey sought and at times achieved understanding with Iraqi regimes on averting the danger that Kurdish
nationalism presented to both countries.[26]

The danger posed by Kurdish nationalism has thus always been present
in the minds of Turkish diplomats. But the measures outlined above were
sufficient to render it a minor preoccupation of Turkish foreign policy until the insurgency of the Kurdistan Workers Party (known by its Kurdish
initials PKK) was launched in 1984. Founded in 1978, the PKK moved its
headquarters to Syria and Lebanon after the 1980 Turkish military coup.[27]
It then concluded a cooperation agreement with the Armenian terrorist
organization Armenian Secret Army for the Liberation of Armenia
(ASALA), which targeted Turkish diplomats throughout the world.[28] Born
in the Marxist student undergrowth in Ankara and grown in the rich com-
post of Middle Eastern terrorism, the PKK developed into a major international terrorist organization and acquired value in the eyes of Turkey's
adversaries. Sustained by them—directly by Syria and, presumably, indirectly by Syria's allies, the Soviet Union and Iran—and financed also by its
own efforts among Kurds in Western Europe (and, according to Turkish
authorities, by extortion and drug trafficking), the PKK presented a major
problem for Turkey's security forces.

Turkish diplomacy worked tirelessly to deprive the PKK of facilities abroad. At the same time, the general behavior of the security forces
and other Turkish authorities in counterinsurgency operations caused
difficulty in relations with Western democratic countries. Facing constant criticism from Western liberal opinion (and its not necessarily liberal prompters) and prodded to accommodate Kurdish national
sentiment, Turkish governments demanded support of their anti-PKK
operations as a test of friendship. Although other factors and interests
also determined Turkey's relations with foreign countries, the Kurdish
issue—spearheaded by the PKK—became a major irritant and an important trump card in the hands of Turkey's adversaries.

Despite the February 1999 capture of PKK leader Abdullah Öcalan, Turkish troops remain in action in southeast Turkey and across the border in northern Iraq. Cross-border operations have been carried out in concert with Massoud Barzani's Kurdistan Democratic Party (KDP), which controls the area immediately south of the Turkish border. Such activities may well lead to the consolidation of Barzani's fiefdom. But even if this fiefdom owes its existence to Turkish power, that existence will keep alive the idea of Kurdish self-rule.

There would seem to be only two ways in which Turkey can manage the Kurdish issue over the long term. The first is to secure common action by all states in which Kurds live. This policy worked as long as Western influence was paramount in the Middle East. In recent years, Turkish ministers and officials made countless visits to Damascus, Baghdad, and Tehran, and the foreign ministers of Turkey, Syria, and Iran held regular meetings. But a common policy to control the Kurds did not emerge. One attempt was made by Islamist prime minister Necmettin Erbakan. Choosing Iran for his first foreign visit as prime minister in August 1996, Erbakan, accompanied by two generals, declared that Turkey and Iran would cooperate against terrorism.[29] But it was not long before Turkish military authorities pointed out that the PKK continued to enjoy facilities in Iran, and in May 1997 Erbakan's minister of state Abdullah Gül admitted that Iran was helping the PKK.[30] Erbakan's aim to solve or at least contain the Kurdish issue on the basis of Muslim brotherhood clearly failed. As for a nonreligious understanding among the four key countries, the prospects appear exceedingly slim.

A second way would be a return to the early formulation of Turkey as a country of Turks and Kurds. In a letter to the fugitive Young Turk leader Talat Paşa in February 1920, Mustafa Kemal said his movement "aimed at preventing the partition of Turkey, as delimited by the national borders of Turks and Kurds."[31] This definition disappeared in the major effort of Turkish nation-building. On December 8, 1925, following the suppression of the Shaikh Said revolt, the Turkish education ministry published a circular banning the use of ethnic terms such as "Kurd," "Laz," "Kurdistan," and "Lazistan," describing them as injurious to Turkish unity.[32] Only in recent years was this ban eventually disregarded.

The process of adjustment to the "Kurdish reality"—the term used by then-Prime Minister Süleyman Demirel when he visited southeastern Turkey in 1991—will perforce be slow. In the meantime, management of the Kurdish problem remains a major preoccupation of Turkish foreign policy in the pursuit of its primary aim, securing Turkey's territorial integrity. However, as it responds to domestic pressures, Turkish diplomacy has to perform yet another function, namely, supporting economic progress in the southeast. An appreciation of these pressures is essential to an understanding of Turkish foreign policy and to a proper evaluation of the ethnic factors affecting it.

Prosperity and Ethnic Politics

Mustafa Kemal's 1923 decision to place economic progress atop the national agenda was adopted to a remarkable degree by the Turkish people, collectively and individually. Knowledge of the disparity between Turkey and wealthy countries also gave rise to jealousy, conspiracy theories, and ideological justifications for underdevelopment. But the ethic of achievement is still the stronger feeling, sustained as it is by material advances which, though uneven, have bettered the lives of most Turks. In a recent comment on the artificiality of the political game, columnist Doğan Heper described the country's real agenda as "to grow, to get rich, [then] to become a regional power."[33] Turkey is predominantly a country of hopeful achievers. Its business is business.

The pursuit of material advancement does not, of course, eliminate ideology or Mustafa Kemal's "illusions and emotions," but it acts as a brake on them. The rediscovery of long-lost Turkish "kinsmen" in the former Soviet Union and to a lesser extent in the Balkans certainly stirred up both illusions and emotions. But material self-interest predominated. Few if any Turks volunteered to fight alongside Bosnian and Kosovar Muslims against the Serbs, or Turkic Azeris against the Armenians. A few went to teach in religiously inspired schools in the formerly communist countries, but even they had at least the inducement of higher salaries. On the other hand, many went to trade or to work for wages. The formerly communist countries are seen above all as a new and promising area for Turkish enterprise.

In his last major speech, the late president Turgut Özal, Turkey's most visionary politician of recent years, declared,

> Together with the new states, which are Muslim and mostly Turkish [Turkic] ... we can make our strength much more effective. If we make good use of this opportunity, if we can promote cooperation in rational, realistic, and fair ways, both we ourselves and these our brethren will emerge as effective individual members of an important world grouping.

In the same speech, delivered at the Third Economic Congress in İzmir, Özal said that "Turkey's principal objective in the next ten years is to become one of the most advanced countries, whose number does not exceed ten or, at most, fifteen. . . . Turkey must join and can join the[se] first-class countries." [34]

This restates Mustafa Kemal's objective of "catching up with contemporary civilization," and although Özal specified Muslim and Turkic countries, his policy had nothing in common with pan-Islamism or pan-Turkism. The key words are "rational," "realistic," and "cooperation." In precisely this respect, Erbakan threatened a break with traditional Kemalist policy. Erbakan's statements during trips to Iran, Libya, and other Muslim countries; his advocacy of "D-8," a putative grouping of developing Muslim countries intended as a counterweight to the wealthy G-8; and his talk of an "Islamic automobile" and an "Islamic aircraft" were all flights from reality that came easily to the lips of a populist politician. His failure to think out his projects doomed them from the start. Eleven months after his accession to power, Turkey's relations with most other Muslim states were worse than before. Populism can never be banished from politics, but the pursuit of self-advancement has spread a spirit of realism that inspires the Turkish Republic's traditional foreign policy.

The emergence of new independent Turkic states produced a glow of satisfaction in Turkey. Ankara has used its limited financial abilities to foster links with newly discovered kinsmen. But "illusions and emotions" have been contained. During the 1919-23 Turkish War of Independence, Mustafa Kemal cooperated rationally and realistically with the first national communist regime in Azerbaijan, while his perennial rival Enver Pasha—who had plunged the Ottoman state into World War I—died in Central Asia in pursuit of the illusion of an Islamic anti-imperialist rising.

The principle that charity begins at home is also applicable to ethnic and immigrant lobbies in Turkey. Many Turks can trace their ancestry to Caucasian (Circassian, Abkhaz, Georgian, Chechen, Lezgi, Azeri, etc.) or Balkan (ethnic Turk, Pomak, Bosnian, or Albanian) origins. Others' ancestors came from the Crimea or Russia. A few are descended from immigrants from further afield—Central Asia or Chinese Turkestan. Partly in response to the U.S. example, and partly as a belated reaction to the nearly 75-year-old ban on looking below the common surface of Turkishness, the search for ethnic roots has become fashionable. There are ethnic societies and at least the beginning of ethnic programming on local private radio stations. Large figures—in the millions for Bosnians and Circassians—are sometimes estimated for these communities, but after generations of assimilation and intermarriage there can be no meaningful statistics. Moreover, attributions and even self-attributions can be imprecise. Presumed Bosnians may be descendants of Slavic speakers from elsewhere in the Balkans. The term "Circassian" often includes Abkhazes, Daghestanis (such as Lezgi), Chechens, and other Caucasians. But however one qualifies them, these immigrant ethnic communities have a certain vestigial identity, which is sometimes expressed in symbolic gestures.

Since the 1930s, there have been instances of immigrants from Bulgaria placing black wreaths outside the Bulgarian embassy or consulate in protest at the maltreatment of Turks there. Bosnian immigrants have promoted demonstrations in support of their kinsmen. Recently, immigrants from Xinjiang burned a Chinese flag to draw attention to the repression of Uighurs. Taking one step further, Turks of Caucasian origin (who were not, it seems, Chechens themselves) seized a Black Sea ferry full of Russian travelers in the so-called "*Avrasya* incident". Less dramatically, a Chechen chained himself to the railing of the Bosporus bridge to protest the heavy-handed intervention of Turkish police trying to disperse a demonstration in Istanbul.

Turks of Chechen and Abkhaz origin are perhaps a special case. Their kinsmen in ancestral lands are few in number. Turks of Abkhaz origin responded with material help and by visiting their country of origin after the Soviet Union collapsed, but few returned permanently. In the case of Chechnya, the traffic appears to have been into rather than out of Turkey, again on a temporary basis as Chechens sent their families to safety during war. In both cases, Turkish citizens took care not to jeopardize their status or prospects in Turkey.

More positively, when the former Soviet frontiers opened, recent immigrants and the children of recent immigrants were active in trade with their countries of origin. Turks of Albanian origin have been active in the "suitcase trade" (also known as "luggage trade") with their kinsmen in Albania, Macedonia, and Kosovo. Turkish citizens of Azeri origin trade with and in Baku. Kazakh immigrants import hides from their original homeland. Tatar immigrants, some of whom have a smattering of Russian, have taken a hand in Turkish enterprise in Russia.

However, as in other countries, immigrants are mindful of their initially probationary status and are keen to identify with their new land. Their main wish is to grow roots, to be accepted, and to prosper in their new surroundings. In most cases, as soon as they arrive in Turkey, they shake from their feet the dust of their country of origin. Participation in ethnic cultural associations and ethnic lobbying are left to small groups, which have had little effect on Turkish foreign policy. In their magazine *Kafkasya Gerçeği* (Caucasian Reality), Turkey's Circassians and Abkhazes have called for a tougher policy toward Georgia. But Turkish diplomacy paid more attention to Georgia's importance as a transit route for Azeri oil.

Turkish diplomats have nevertheless invoked the political clout of domestic ethnic lobbies as they pleaded for a better deal for Bosnian Muslims, for Azeris, and, more circumspectly, for Chechens in the Russian Federation, Tatars in Ukraine, and Gagauz in Romania. No doubt they want better treatment for all of these peoples. They are also aware that maltreatment of these groups fuels anti-Western feeling in Turkey and thus interferes with implementation of traditionally pragmatic Kemalist foreign policy. Of course, Turkish diplomats can also exploit such maltreatment to deflect accusations of human-rights lapses at home.

Turkish diplomacy and mainstream Turkish politicians continue to adapt Kemalist principles to changing circumstances, as preferred by the most dynamic portion of Turkish society. The Islamist RP's attempt to apply ideological criteria to foreign policy proved short-lived, discredited by the Turkish people themselves. The perception of the advantages of Kemalist foreign policy, however, can be altered by domestic mismanagement. Any evaluation of Turkish foreign policy must start from the premise that Turks—including all ethnic communities and probably most Kurds—want to prosper at home by their work at home and abroad and must be allowed to do so.

A caveat should be added. Should Turkey succeed in its domestic endeavors and become a strong regional power, it is extremely unlikely to become expansionary but is nevertheless bound to be more assertive. The West, however, has less to fear from a strong Turkey mindful of the interests of its inhabitants than from an unstable and ill-governed Turkey swayed by "illusions and emotions." Atatürk's linking of domestic and foreign policy is as valid today as when he drew attention to it more than seventy years ago.

Notes

1   John Barham, "Living in the Long Shadow of Atatürk," *Financial Times*, May 26, 1997, p. 9.
2   Barham, "Foreign Policy: Party and Ministry in Competition," *Financial Times*, May 26, 1997, p. 12.
3   Doğu Perinçek (ed.), *Mustafa Kemal: Eskişehir-İzmit Konuşmaları* (Mustafa Kemal: Speeches in Eskisehir and İzmit) (İstanbul: Kaynak Yayınları, 1993), p. 170.
4   Ibid.
5   Ibid.
6   *Atatürk'ün Söylev ve Demeçleri* (Atatürk's speeches and addresses), vol. 2 (Ankara: Atatürk Araştırma Merkezi, 1989), pp. 111, 115.
7   Tülay Alim Baran, "İzmir'de Çiftçi Mübadiller" (Exchangee farmers from Greece in İzmir), *Kebikeç* 2, no. 4 (1996), pp. 176-177.
8   Ibid., pp. 110-111.
9   *Atatürk'ün Söylev*, vol. 1, pp. 214, 216.
10 Sadi Borak, *Atatürk'ün Resmi Yayınlara Girmemiş Söylev, Demeç, Yazışma ve Söyleşileri* (Atatürk's speches, addresses, letters, and interviews not included in official publications) (Ankara: Kaynak Yayınları, 1997), p. 225.
11 Rona Aybar, *Karşılaştırmalı 1961 Anayasası* (A comparative study of the 1961 constitution) (İstanbul: Fakülteler Matbaası, 1963), pp. 199-200; Perinçek, *Mustafa Kemal*, p. l04.
12 Aybar, *Karşılaştırmalı*, p. 12.

13 Doğu Ergil, *Milli Mücadelenin Sosyal Tarihi* (The social history of the national War of Independence) (Ankara: Turhan Kitabevi, 1981), pp. 247-258.

14 Kazım Karabekir, *İstiklâl Harbimiz* (Our War of National Independence) (İstanbul: Türkiye Yayınevi, 1969), p. 28; *İstiklâl Harbinin Esasları* (The fundamentals of the War of National Independence) (İstanbul: Sinan Neşriyat Evi, 1951), p. 51.

15 ATASE, *Atatürk Özel Arşivinden Seçmeler* (Selections from Atatürk's personal archive), vol. 4 (Ankara: Genel Kurmay Basımevi, 1989), p. 19.

16 Perinçek, *Mustafa Kemal*, pp. 96-98.

17 İsmail Soysal, *Türkiye'nin Siyasal Andlaşmaları* (Turkey's political treaties), vol. 1 (Ankara: Türk Tarih Kurumu, 1983), p. 312.

18 Robert Olson, *The Emergence of Kurdish Nationalism and the Sheikh Said Rebellion, 1880-1925* (Austin: University of Texas Press, 1989), p. 141.

19 David MacDowall, *A Modern History of the Kurds* (London: I.B. Tauris, 1996), pp. 203-204.

20 Soysal, *Türkiye'nin Siyasal Andlaşmaları*, p. 420.

21 Ibid., p. 274.

22 Ibid., p. 586.

23 MacDowall, *Modern History*, pp. 240-241, 246.

24 Ibid., p. 343.

25 Ferenc Váli, *Bridge across the Bosphorus* (Baltimore: Johns Hopkins, 1971), p. 305.

26 Ibid., pp. 302-305.

27 Michael Gunter, *The Kurds in Turkey* (Boulder: Westview, 1990), pp. 61, 71.

28 Anat Kurz and Ariel Merari, *ASALA: Irrational Terror or Political Tool* (Boulder: Westview for the Jaffee Center for Strategic Studies, Tel Aviv University, 1985), p. 44.

29 *Newspot*, August 16, 1996, p. 1.

30 Press conference at the Turkish embassy in London on May 29, 1997, at which the author was present.

31 İlhan Tekeli and Selim İlkin, "Kurtuluş Savaşında Talat Paşa ile Mustafa Kemal'in Mektuplaşmaları" (Letters between Talat Pasa and Mustafa Kemal during the War of Independence), *Belleten* (April 1980), p. 321.

32 Saim Özerdim, *Atatürk Devrimi Kronolojisi* (A chronology of Atatürk's reforms) (Ankara: Çankaya Belediyesi, 1995), p. 93.

33 *Milliyet*, May 25, 1997, p. 14.

34 *Cumhurbaşkanı Turgut Özal'ın III. İzmir İktisat Kongresindeki Konuşmaları. 4 Haziran 1992. İzmir* (President Turgut Özal's address at the Third İzmir Economic Congress, June 4, 1992, İzmir), printed pre-released text, pp. 11-12.

William Hale

Economic Issues in Turkish Foreign Policy

Before trying to assess the likely future relationship between Turkey's foreign policy and its economic interests and concerns, one must summarize current positions and trends in the Turkish economy as a guide to future prospects. The task is likely to be baffling, because Turkey breaks most of the conventional economic rules. In spite of this, it maintains a generally high economic growth rate and an apparently healthy external balance of payments. The Gross National Product (GNP) growth rate ran at 8 percent in 1995, 7.1 percent in 1996, and 8.3 percent in 1997, against an annual population growth rate around 1.75 percent.[1] Like democratic regimes all over the world, Turkish governments must maintain a reasonable degree of economic stability and foreign confidence while simultaneously seeking reelection. Conspicuously, successive administrations have ducked the first task to concentrate on the second, but their failures seem to have been less disastrous than might have been expected. The Achilles' heel of the Turkish economy has been huge public-sector deficits, which successive governments covered simply by printing money or borrowing at sky-high interest rates. Consumer price inflation ran at an average annual rate of 85.3 percent from 1993 to 1997, with a high point of 105.2 percent in 1994. Not until 1998 did the coalition led by Mesut Yılmaz act effectively to increase state revenues and bring down the price spiral. The GNP growth rate fell to 3.8 percent in 1998, but in February 1999 the twelve-month rise in the consumer price index fell to 63.9 percent, with a wholesale inflation rate of 48 percent. This was counted as a success for the government, but the rates are still very high by international standards.[2]

Excluding 1994, when the domestic economy was severely squeezed and the government's balance of payments on current account showed a surplus of $2.63 billion, the average deficit on the current account, as officially recorded, was about $2.1 billion per year from 1993 to 1997. In 1998, amid an economic slowdown, the current account moved back into a surplus of $2.7 billion. Given these deficits, Turkey should have experienced an increase in external debt (assuming it could persuade overseas lenders of its creditworthiness), run down its foreign currency reserves, or attracted large volumes of foreign investment. Admittedly, overseas debt had almost doubled from $56.5 billion in 1992 to $100.9 billion by September 1998, but much of the borrowing is explained by the need to meet the internal fiscal deficit rather than the external deficit. Foreign financial institutions appeared to show enough confidence in the country to continue lending. Foreign aid was negligible, and direct foreign investment was also low. However, foreign exchange reserves at the Central Bank (excluding gold and the holdings of private banks) rose rather than fell from $6.2 billion in 1992 to $20.8 billion at the end of 1998, the latter figure equaling about five months of imports at the 1998 rate.[3]

There are two main reasons for Turkey's apparent ability to defy economic laws of gravity. To a large extent, consumers and businessmen appear to have "factored in" inflation when making daily decisions. Industrial workers, civil servants, and farmers expect regular increases in wages or agricultural prices to compensate for increases in consumer prices (though they may not always get them). Businessmen frequently calculate future prices and costs in dollars, then convert back into lira at the current exchange rate at the time of payment. The other reason is that Turkey has a huge black—alternatively, "gray" or "shadow"—economy that fails to show up in most official data, enabling it to ride out crises which could otherwise be expected to be fatal. This shadow economy is largely caused by massive tax evasion and the failure of successive governments to address this problem effectively (although a tax reform law implemented by the Yılmaz government in 1998 should improve matters). In early 1997, a senior treasury official privately estimated the untaxed—hence unrecorded—economy to represent around 40 percent of the "official," or recorded, economy. Others estimate this proportion to be as high as 50 or even 70 percent.[4]

The Turkish Economy and Its External Environment

The unreliability of official data and the consequent difficulty of its analysis need to be stressed when assessing recent macroeconomic trends. The most relevant of these are probably the overall growth and direction of Turkey's foreign trade. Table 1 (next page) indicates the impressive growth of foreign trade since 1980, both absolutely and as a proportion of GNP. As of 1980, Turkey still had a remarkably closed and autarchic economy. These policies were partly reversed during the "Özal era" of the 1980s, when—under Prime Minister (later, President) Turgut Özal's leadership—foreign exchange and trade regimes were liberalized and government controls over the domestic economy were reduced. Liberalization continued during the 1990s, most notably through Turkey's customs union with the European Union (EU) in 1996. A coincidental bonus was the collapse of communism in eastern Europe and the dissolution of the USSR from 1989 to 1991, which opened up the region for exports. By 1997 most of Turkey's exports to the former Soviet Union were accounted for by the then-unrecorded "luggage trade," i.e., purchases by visitors who carried goods back with them. This flow fell after 1997 due to the Russian economic crisis, but it still had a sizable impact on Turkey's overall trade balance.

The result was a dramatic rise in imports and exports, as reflected in the Table 1 figures, which do not even include a concomitant massive rise in service inflows and outflows. (Larger service inflows are attributable mainly to a striking increase in tourism income as well as earnings from other services such as transport and overseas construction contracts.) When the official luggage trade estimate is included, foreign merchandise trade in 1998 rose to around 37 percent of GNP, compared with only about 15 percent in 1980.

Table 1: Turkey's Foreign Trade and GNP

(a) $ billion

	Exports*	"Luggage Trade"	Imports	Total
1980	2.9	-	7.9	10.8
1990	13.0	-	22.6	35.6
1996	32.3	(3.4)	41.9	74.2
1997	32.6	(5.8)	48.0	80.6
1998	31.1	(3.7)	45.5	76.6

(b) As percentage of GNP

	Exports	Imports	Total
1980	4.2	11.4	15.6
1990	8.6	14.9	23.5
1998	14.8*	21.7	36.6

*includes "luggage trade"

Sources: For 1980, *Statistical Indicators, 1923-1990* (Ankara: State Office of Statistics, 1991) pp. 291, 396. For 1990, *Country Report: Turkey*, 4th quarter 1993 (London: Economist Intelligence Unit, 1993) p. 3. For 1996, *Briefing*, June 2, 1997, p. 26; and *Country Report: Turkey*, 2nd quarter 1997 (London: Economist Intelligence Unit, 1997), p. 5. For 1997 and 1998, *Briefing*, March 22, 1999, p. 32; and *Milliyet*, March 27, 1999. Figures for 1998 vary slightly from those shown in Table 2.

Expansion of foreign trade has been accompanied by important changes in its direction (Table 2, next page). The most striking feature is the dominant position of the Organization for Economic Co-operation and Development (OECD) countries, in particular those of the former European Economic Community (EEC, now EU). Were tourism income included in the total, the EU's share would probably be even more impressive. Perhaps significantly, the EEC/EU's share of merchandise trade also increased markedly during the 1980s. Decline in the Middle East's share during the same decade is equally striking, and is largely attributable to fluctuating oil prices. After the 1973-74 oil-price explosion, the value of Turkey's imports from the region rose dramatically.[5] By the 1980s, Turkey was filling the gap in its balance of payments by increasing exports of foodstuffs and manufactured consumer goods to the Middle Eastern oil-producing states. This effect was enhanced in 1979 by a further jump in oil prices after the Iranian revolution. During the 1980-88 Iran-Iraq war, both states depended quite heavily on Turkey as a transit route and a source of imports. By the late 1980s, however, these trends reversed as oil prices fell and normal Persian Gulf trade routes resumed. Economic sanctions after Iraq's occupation of Kuwait in August 1990 further diminished Turkish exports to the Middle East.

The most recent, and perhaps most problematic, feature of Turkey's external trade flows is caused by the "eastern European" (or perhaps, "ex-USSR") factor. As the 1981 figures show, Turkey's trade with the Soviet Union during the Cold War was extraordinarily small, given their geographical closeness and some degree of complementarity in their economies. By 1990, when political tensions had declined and President Mikhail Gorbachev began to restructure the Soviet economy, trade had begun to grow in absolute terms, though less impressively as a proportion of Turkey's total. Between 1990 and 1996, this trade gathered pace, even so far as recorded trade was concerned. The really striking change, however, occurred through the explosion in luggage trade with former communist countries, which was frequently noticed but not accurately measured. Beginning in 1996, the Central Bank estimated the total value of luggage trade exports at $3.4 billion, rising to $5.8 billion in 1997, before falling back to $3.7 billion in 1998. Of this, the figures in Table 2 assume that 90 percent of the total was to the former Soviet Union, and the remaining 10 percent to other Eastern European countries. Assuming that 75 percent of luggage trade exports go to the Russian Federation, it appears that Russia began to rival Germany as Turkey's biggest export market, buying about $4.1 billion in Turkish goods in 1998, compared with $5.4 billion for Germany.[6]

Table 2: Turkey's Foreign Trade by Region

1981	Imports	Exports	Total
Total ($ billion)	8.9	4.7	13.6
Contribution to Total	%	%	%
OECD	47.9	48.1	48.0
(EEC)	(28.1)	(31.9)	(29.4)
Middle East	37.5	36.8	37.3
USSR	1.8	4.1	2.6
Other	12.8	11.0	12.1

1990	Imports	Exports	Total
Total ($ billion)	22.3	13.0	35.3
Contribution to Total	%	%	%
OECD	63.8	68.0	65.3
(EEC)	(41.8)	(53.1)	(45.9)
Middle East	12.0	13.5	12.6
USSR	5.6	4.1	5.0
Other	18.6	14.4	17.1

1998	Imports	Exports*	Exports[†]	Total[††]
Total ($ billion)	45.9	26.9	30.6	76.5
Contribution to Total	%	%	%	%
OECD	72.8	62.9	55.3	65.9
(EU)	(52.6)	(49.8)	(35.6)	(49.1)
Middle East	4.8	8.7	7.6	5.9
CIS	8.1	9.9	19.5[††]	12.7[††]
Other	14.3	18.5	17.6[††]	15.5[††]

* excludes "luggage trade" and transit trade

[†] includes "luggage trade" but excludes transit trade

[††] assumes 90 percent of "luggage trade" is with CIS, and the remainder with other countries in Eastern Europe

Sources: For 1981, *Statistical Yearbook*, 1983 (Ankara: State Institute of Statistics) pp. 356-357. For 1990, ibid., 1991, pp. 492-493. For 1998, *Briefing*, March 8, 1999, p. 36, and March 22, 1999, p. 32.

Apart from the volume and flow of foreign trade, other features of Turkey's external economic relations that might be expected to have a significant effect on foreign policy are foreign investment, overseas debt, aid flows, and energy supplies. Although foreign direct investment in Turkey increased significantly throughout the 1980s, it was still at a remarkably low level given the size and dynamism of the Turkish economy. The actual inflow rose from a trifling $35 million in 1980 to just over $1 billion in 1997.[7] However, the latter figure still represented only about 0.5 percent of Turkey's 1997 GNP. The comparable figure for the United Kingdom in 1995 was 2.9 percent, a proportion that would put Turkey's annual inflow at around $5.8 billion.[8] Portfolio investment has often been much higher than this, but it is highly erratic thanks to periodic booms and slumps in the Istanbul stock market. Moreover, both figures are likely to be dwarfed by other short-term borrowing by the government and private banks. During the first nine months of 1998, the net increase in short-term borrowing stood around $4.6 billion.[9]

OECD countries have by far accounted for most private investment. Nienty percent of total foreign investment—including portfolio investment—approved from January to May 1997 came from these countries (including 70 percent from the EU, 14 percent from the United States, and 1.5 percent from Japan). The Middle East—once expected to be a major source of capital—only accounted for 4.5 percent.[10] Interestingly, Turkish firms and individuals have made quite substantial investments overseas, making Turkey a capital-exporting as well as capital-importing country. Total interest income for 1998 was officially listed just under $2.5 billion, as opposed to outflows of $4.8 billion.[11]

As has been noted, Turkey's total foreign debt has steadily climbed, reaching $100.9 billion in September 1998, equivalent to about 49 percent of recorded GNP for that year. However, this was generally regarded as sustainable, and Turkey usually has not had difficulties servicing its debt since the crisis of the late 1970s. Of the September 1998 total, 73.1 percent consisted of medium- and long-term debt. It is not possible to apportion the debt exactly between different creditor countries, but official figures show that multilateral agencies (such as the International Monetary Fund [IMF], World Bank, and various EU bodies) and other official agencies (such as central governments and other official financial institutions) account for around 16 percent of the total. The distribution of the debt among different currencies is not an accurate guide since many lenders outside the United States may denominate loans in U.S. dollars, but the figures show the proportions as 33.2 percent U.S. dollars, 35.4 percent German marks, and 19.4 percent Japanese yen.[12] It seems quite certain that the vast majority of Turkey's foreign debt is to Western or Japanese financial institutions.

The majority of the capital inflow is provided by commercial borrowing, with only a small proportion by foreign aid, however defined. Only 7.9 percent of the September 1998 debt stock was accounted for by loans from the World Bank, International Development Association

(IDA), International Finance Corporation (IFC), or EU institutions, and a minuscule proportion (0.23 percent) from the Islamic Development Bank.[13] Although foreign aid—mainly from the United States—was an important component in Turkey's economy back in the 1950s,[14] this has long since ceased to be the case. This is partly because of the growing sophistication of the Turkish economy and partly because the end of the Cold War has made the United States and other Western nations less ready to grant military credits. Resolution of difficulties in Turkey's relationship with the EU could increase the foreign aid figure once again. Under the customs union, Turkey was promised budgetary assistance of $495 million over a five-year period, plus access to EU funds under the EU's revised Mediterranean policy (as well as to other loans for improving competitiveness from the European Investment Bank) all totalling $2.3 to $2.4 billion.[15] If realized, this could make a fairly significant difference in Turkey's overall external accounts. A part of these funds are being blocked by Greek objections.[16] Whatever happens on this front, it seems clear that the EU has now overtaken the United States as the major source of concessionary loans and grants.

Lastly, Turkey's energy needs—in particular, the need for natural gas and increased electricity-generating capacity—became an issue that could have important implications for its foreign policy. Between 1990 and 1997, Turkey's total energy demand rose by an average of almost 10 percent per year. In the broader picture of primary energy supplies, Turkey's total energy consumption in 1998 rose to the equivalent of 1.64 million barrels of oil per day (mb/d), of which just over 62 percent was imported. Within the latter figure, petroleum accounted for around 64 percent and natural gas for roughly 20 percent. Although Turkey needs to secure reliable sources of crude oil, this does not normally create serious political problems given the present and likely future state of the world oil market. There are many potential suppliers, and crude oil is a reasonably transportable product.

Natural gas presents a different case. Although gas can be liquefied and transported by tanker, it is far more economical at high volume to pipe it directly from the producer. This creates political dependencies on the supplying country and on the states whose territory the pipeline might have to cross. The importance of this factor for Turkey derives from the fact that it has very limited domestic supplies of gas (only 3 percent of current usage) and that demand is rising fast. So far most of the main western Turkish cities, namely, Istanbul, Bursa, İzmir, and Ankara, have been or are being connected to a national distribution grid, and many others can be expected to follow. Natural gas is also increasingly used as a pollution-free fuel for power stations and other industries. Consumption rose from 1.2 billion cubic meters (bcm) in 1988 to 7.9 bcm in 1996. Within the 1996 total, imports from Russia via a pipeline through Bulgaria accounted for 71 percent, with the remainder imported as liquefied natural gas (LNG) or domestically produced. Consumption is expected to reach as much as 53 bcm by 2010, and the planned pattern of supply is shown in Table 3. Over time, Turkey plans to reduce its dependence on Russian supplies and partially replace it with supplies from Iran, Iraq, and Turkmenistan by pipeline and from others by LNG. The total supply from all these plans, 81.9 bcm per year, well exceeds expected demand, but the authorities presumably allow for the likelihood that their plans will not all be realized and that demand may be well above current predictions.[17]

Table 3: Turkey's Gas Import Plans

Supplier	Planned imports by 2010 (bcm per year)	As percentage of total %
Russia (pipeline)	30.0	36.6
Algeria (LNG)	3.0	3.7
Iran (pipeline)	10.0	12.2
Iraq (pipeline)	10.0	12.2
Turkmenistan (pipeline)	16.0	19.5
Egypt (LNG)	10.0	12.2
Qatar (LNG)	2.0	2.4
Nigeria (LNG)	0.9	1.1
Total	**81.9**	**100.0**

Source: *Country Report: Turkey*, 1st quarter 1997 (London: Economist Intelligence Unit, 1997) pp. 27-28; *Briefing*, May 19, 1997, p. 16, and February 22, 1999, p. 32.

After 1993, when the construction of an oil pipeline between Baku, Azerbaijan, and the Turkish Mediterranean port of Ceyhan was first suggested, the international ramifications of energy supply affected not just Turkey's energy demands but also its potential role as a transit route between producer regions. On this score, there has been seemingly endless international discussion but little physical achievement. Construction of the Baku-Ceyhan line has been delayed—perhaps permanently—by the high cost of the project and the possibility of cheaper alternatives, notably a pipeline across Iran to the Persian Gulf. The last project was ruled out by U.S. sanctions against Iran, although these sanctions will probably not last indefinitely.

Although plans for an oil pipeline between the Caspian basin and the Mediterranean via Turkey are still in the air, proposals for gas pipelines seem far more definite. There is undeniably a substantial market for gas in Turkey itself, and pipelines are by far the most economical method of transporting large quantities of gas. Two prospective gas pipelines, from Russia and Iran respectively, are discussed separately in the following section. A third project—a pipeline from Turkmenistan to Turkey—does, however, have international implications similar to those of the Baku-Ceyhan project (with which it shares much of the same route), since it would also supply central European countries with Turkmenistani gas. Under agreements signed in early 1999, the U.S. consortium PSG, comprising General Electric and Bechtel, was to join the Turkish state pipeline company BOTAŞ in building the 2,000-kilometer (1,250-mile) pipeline under the Caspian Sea and across Azerbaijan and Georgia for around $2.5 billion. Of the eventual total throughput of 30 bcm, 16 bcm would be used in Turkey with the remainder transferred to central Europe. If both this project and the Baku-Ceyhan pipeline were realized (and the first would reportedly reduce the construction costs of the second by around 20 percent), Turkey would become an important transit route for both oil and natural gas.[18]

Economic Links and Foreign Policy Implications

Translating the foregoing analysis into reasonably reliable political predictions is naturally difficult, as it cannot be assumed that economic needs will override other considerations. There is also a severe general methodological problem, summed up by the question as to whether "trade follows the flag" or vice versa. To put it slightly more scientifically, do governments tend to develop close or important economic relations with countries with which they have good political relations or sympathies (the "politically driven" approach) or are political alignments the result of economic links and dependencies ("economically driven")? Are political and economic factors congruent—that is, do they tend toward the same policy outcomes—or are they incongruent?

Turkey's recent history suggests that the politically driven approach may often be more relevant, especially during the Cold War when economic links with the USSR were extremely limited, almost certainly for political reasons. On the other hand, the end of the Cold War, and the overall economic globalization and liberalization starting in the early 1990s, made it likely that future external economic links will depend largely on individual decisions by businessmen and consumers rather than state policies. The last observation is a reminder that, in the current international scene, sovereign states have lost any monopoly they once had as international actors, especially in the economic sphere. Multilateral and international organizations and institutions severely restrict the ability of member states to conduct independent or autarchic economic policies, either internally or externally. Multinational firms, business groups, and even individual businessmen may effectively pursue their own agendas, irrespective of state policies, in addition to having an important effect in determining those policies.

Taking account of these methodological problems, the remainder of this paper will attempt to assess the relationship between Turkey's economic interests and probable future foreign relations in three primary theaters: the OECD countries, in particular the United States and EU, and Western financial institutions; Russia, the Black Sea states, and the Central Asian republics; and the Middle East (including Israel) and other Muslim countries.

OECD Countries, the EU, and Western Financial Institutions

Despite the Cold War's end and an assertion of Islamist values indicated by the rise of the *Refah* (Welfare) Party (RP)—now the *Fazilet* (Virtue) Party (FP)—Turkey still has an overwhelming interest in preserving good relations with Western powers, as well as east Asian states like Japan and South Korea. It still conducts around half if not almost two-thirds of its trade with these countries[19] and depends heavily on them for capital inflows plus debt servicing and repayment (which normally means rolling over existing debts). Even Islamist political leaders had to accept this situation. As the record of the Erbakan-led government of 1996-97 indicates, such leaders may engage in rhetorical flourishes designed primarily to differentiate themselves from the rest of the domestic spectrum, but they cannot abandon Turkey's links with the West except at severe and possibly unacceptable economic cost.[20]

Although Turkey's relationship with the EU is one of its most tangled and conflicted, as well as crucial, it is generally accepted that neither Turkey's links with the EU nor its hope to attain full membership are primarily the result of economic interests. The main motivation is likely the "Kemalist imperative"—the aim of making Turkey a respected member of the Western comity of democratic nations—rather than a desire for Western levels of prosperity or access to financial assistance.

Nevertheless, economic incentives are also important in reinforcing Turkey's drive for full EU membership. Thanks to the customs union, Turkey obtained duty-free and quota-free entry for its industrial products into the EU market and, at least in principle, gained access to economic assistance. With full membership, it would be entitled to access to EU funds for agricultural support and regional development, as well as free entry for agricultural products and free movement of labor. It would also benefit from participation in the bodies that shape these policies. On the other hand, the scale of agricultural price support was almost certain to be reduced in the near future to alleviate the EU's burden if it admitted eastern European applicants. For the EU, the potential financial cost of admitting Turkey, under present conditions, as well as the problems associated with free labor movement, are also among the most powerful incentives for not doing so. Nonetheless, it seems likely that, although Turkey's relations with the EU are essentially politically rather than economically driven, the two factors are congruent and mutually reinforcing.

Attention obviously has to be paid to the Greek and Greek Cypriot factor, since this is clearly a situation in which political factors count far more than economic ones. There can be little doubt that Turkey would not have invaded Cyprus in 1974, and would have settled its differences with the two countries long ago, if economic considerations were the primary determinant of policy. Apart from possibilities of mutual trade, the removal of Greek obstructions would benefit Turkey immensely, both politically and economically, in its relations with the EU and the United States. The importance of tourism to both sides, especially in the disputed Aegean, further underlines the value of securing friendly and stable relations.

Turkey's relations with the United States are broadly similar to those with the EU, given the high degree of congruence between political and economic motivations. However, there are also some points of difference. Most U.S. administrations have attached more importance to Turkey's strategic role, especially in the Middle East, than is common among EU member states. Powerful anti-Turkish ethnic lobbies are a more prominent feature of the political scene in Washington than in Brussels, although the EU does have the Greek government with which to contend. At the same time, U.S. governments have not been faced with the decision to admit Turkey into their economic space. In the 1980s, Prime Minister Özal floated the idea of a U.S.-Turkish free-trade agreement. This proposal seemed to fall by the wayside, but it might be resuscitated, particularly if Turkey were left with no more than a "customs union plus" option for its future relationship with the EU (that is, continuation of present arrangements, with some participation in decision-making where it is important for both sides).

Turkey's relations with its other OECD trade partners—mainly Japan—are far less problematic, if only because the countries are geographically too far apart to have political disputes. In public opinion polls, Turks see Japan very positively and Turkey looks to Japan—often with success—as a source of direct investment as well as debt funding. Japan's share of Turkey's imports stands around 4.5 percent, but its share of exports is far lower, at only 0.4 percent. As in Japan's commercial relations with other countries, the surplus of Japan's exports over its imports is the only serious problem.[21]

Turkey's relations with Western and Japanese financial institutions and private firms are a vital part of the mix of its external economic links and dependencies. However, the link between these relations and interests on one hand and foreign policies on the other is not easy to establish. International funding agencies, as well as commercial banks and potential private investors, are far more likely to be influenced by the government's domestic economic policies and the overall behavior of the economy than by its foreign policy. In other words, no matter how pro-Western a government may be in its foreign political alignments, this will cut very little ice with international bankers and businessmen if its economic policies fail to provide a reasonably stable and healthy business environment. Turkish governments failed signally in this regard in recent years, even though they were to some extent saved by the dynamism and flexibility of the private sector. Similarly, conversations in London with bankers and businessmen interested in the Turkish market suggest that the main disincentives that would-be private investors face are political instability, the high rate of inflation, and uncertainty of economic policies. The government's foreign policy ranks lower as a concern, although such investors would almost certainly be severely discouraged if an avowedly Islamist or anti-Western government assumed overall political control. Considerations of this kind, besides shortcomings in the state bureaucracy and the slow and uncertain pace of privatization, almost certainly explain the low rate of foreign direct investment in Turkey.

Economic interests—in particular, the need to attract more direct investment and to develop new export markets for servicing foreign debt—likely will continue to play a major role in determining Turkish foreign policy. However, economic considerations will not be paramount in all policy theaters, for example, relations with Greece and the Greek Cypriots. Thus, the role of the OECD countries and Western financial institutions will continue to hold vital importance. If a free-trade agreement with the United States were signed, this could be expected to increase the U.S. share in Turkey's trade. This effect would not be dramatic, however, since trade barriers between the two countries, except for farm products, are not too serious.

Russia, the Black Sea States, and the Turkic Republics
Turkey's relations with Russia provide a striking example of the incongruence between political and economic factors, as well as an example of how commercial links may develop in a way quite unplanned by governments. Turkey's political relationship with post-Soviet Russia has not been easy, primarily due to Turkish fears that Moscow is seeking to reestablish something like the old pattern of Soviet control in its

"near abroad." On the other hand, Turkey's growing trade with Russia means that Ankara cannot afford to risk a head-on clash with Moscow, quite apart from the military risks this might entail. Similar calculations seem quite likely on the other side. As has been noted, Turkey has been trying to reduce its dependence on Russian natural gas, but even if the proportion of gas supplies provided by Russia falls, the absolute volume is still set to rise. To increase the supply capacity, and to supplement the present circuitous route via Bulgaria, a "Blue Stream" pipeline under the Black Sea is planned. This is expected to cost approximately $13.5 billion and to deliver up to 16 bcm per year. In the international trade in services, construction contracts by Turkish firms in Russia are reported to have reached a value of $5 billion, putting them in first place among foreign construction firms active in Russia.[22] These links inevitably increase the two countries' mutual dependence. As one Russian observer concludes, Russia and Turkey need to limit their political conflicts wherever possible.[23]

Turkey's relations with the other Commonwealth of Independent States (CIS) members are different, in the sense that it does not have political conflicts with any of them—except Armenia—and is keen to develop influence in Turkic "kin-states" like Azerbaijan and those in Central Asia. On the other hand, it is likely that Russia accounts for 55 to 60 percent of Turkey's total trade with the CIS (including luggage trade), with only about 10 percent accounted for by the Turkic republics.[24] In the 1990s, Turkish governments developed several projects aimed at establishing closer links with the CIS and other Black Sea countries. For instance, the Black Sea Economic Cooperation (BSEC) program was officially launched in Istanbul in 1992. Besides Turkey, it now includes all the Black Sea littoral states (Bulgaria, Romania, Moldova, Ukraine, Russia, and Georgia), plus Albania, Armenia, Azerbaijan, and Greece. Institutionally, the BSEC established a permanent secretariat in Istanbul with a rotating chair and arranged meetings of member states' foreign ministers at least annually. Functionally, its most important institutions are the Black Sea Trade and Development Bank, set up in Thessaloniki, and working groups on trade and industrial cooperation and on transportation. According to the declaration issued by member state leaders in June 1992, the BSEC aims to "reduce or progressively eliminate obstacles [to trade] of all kinds" and to promote joint projects in transportation, energy, mining, and tourism.[25]

The main criticism of the BSEC, as with similar schemes, will probably be that, athough trade among member states has increased, this might well have happened anyway through normal market forces. Cynics may also wonder whether economic cooperation can be much more than a dream when two member states, Azerbaijan and Turkey, operate an economic embargo against a third, Armenia, while Greece and

Turkey are frequently at loggerheads. On the other hand, it can be argued that regular BSEC meetings at the ministerial level at least provide a vehicle through which antagonistic partners can settle their differences. For example, the Istanbul meeting of April 1997 provided a forum for a discussion between Armenian president Levon Ter-Petrossian and Azeri president Haydar Aliyev.[26] Such opportunities suggest that, for Turkey, the BSEC project has as much political as economic purpose.

In the early 1990s, much was written about Turkey's future role in Central Asia and Azerbaijan, suggesting that the Turks could establish a zone of influence stretching to the old Soviet-Chinese border and maybe beyond. Since then, reality has set in as a result of surviving Russian power, Turkey's internal upheavals, and the eagerness of Central Asian states to establish their own sovereignties and identities. As Philip Robins concluded in 1993, there was a shift in Turkey away from "fanciful notions of ethnic solidarity" to one based more on self-interest.[27] However, sentiment and self-interest need not be mutually exclusive.[28] Turkish businessmen and governments would probably not have developed their interest in these relatively small and remote states if they were not aided or inspired by ethnic links, real or imaginary. Although Turkey's economic weaknesses have been alluded to as part of the explanation for the failure of more grandiose projects, Turkish businesses have filled important interstices in Central Asian economies, especially in textiles, telecommunications, and construction. Turkish Eximbank loans to the Turkic republics reached a claimed total of $1.56 billion by 1996, while the value of construction contracts held by Turkish firms in the region was said to have passed $5 billion.[29] On the other hand, Turkey's trade with the Turkic states started from a very low base and has been constrained by the fact that these states have relatively little which they can usefully export to Turkey. The necessity of indirect transport links, which are periodically hampered by difficulties with Iran and the Azeri-Armenian conflict, is another obstacle to trade. As a result, in spite of all efforts by businesses and officialdom, trade with the Turkic republics in 1998 still only accounted for 3.5 percent of Turkey's exports and 1 percent of its imports. Looking at the situation broadly, it could be said that Turkey's economic and political interests in the region are perfectly congruent but that economic links have yet to fulfill the political promise.

Institutionally, Turkey's main multilateral economic link with Central Asia is the Economic Cooperation Organization (ECO). This is the descendant of the Regional Cooperation for Development (RCD) organization, which is itself the nonmilitary descendant of the Central Treaty Organization (CENTO) and, before that, of the Baghdad Pact. When originally established in 1984, the ECO was restricted to former RCD members Turkey, Iran, and Pakistan. In 1992 Afghanistan, Azerbaijan, Kazakhstan, Kyrgyzstan, Tajikistan, Uzbekistan, and Turkmenistan were added to the membership list. As in the case of the BSEC, there are regular ministerial meetings and a secretariat in Tehran with a council of permanent representatives. The ECO emphasizes that it aims to establish a preferential trading system, rather than a free-trade area. To that end, it has established a regional planning council; a trade and development bank; joint organizations for reinsurance, shipping, and air transport; a cultural institute; and a science foundation.[30] From Turkey's viewpoint, however, it may be argued that the ECO does not have much effect on Ankara's economic relations. In 1996 trade with ECO countries accounted for only 4.9 percent of Turkey's total exports and 2.8 percent of its imports, or 3.5 percent of its total trade; of the ECO total, Iran accounted for 40 percent. Iran's pivotal position in ECO is probably the main reason for Turkey's membership. By staying in, Ankara ensures a Turkish input into the ECO's decisions, preventing Tehran from using it to expand Iranian influence in Central Asia, possibly at Turkey's expense.

The Muslim World and the Middle East

As part of an attempt to make his own mark on Turkish foreign policy, Necmettin Erbakan tried to use his 1996-97 tenure in the prime minister's office to develop new links with the Muslim world, both in the Middle East and in South and Southeast Asia. This resulted in the D-8 ("Developing-8") organization, in which Turkey was to be joined by Bangladesh, Egypt, Indonesia, Iran, Malaysia, Nigeria, and Pakistan. Although subsequent governments have not officially abandoned the project, it is hard to see how the D-8 could become a major factor in Turkey's economic relations. Taken together, the seven other members accounted for only 3.9 percent of Turkey's total recorded foreign trade in 1995, including 3.3 percent of exports and 4.2 percent of imports. Only Iran could be called an important trade partner. The conclusion has to be that, regardless of the ideological orientation of its government, Turkey has little to gain from cultivating the "Islamic opening," if only because the Muslim countries as a whole do not have sufficient common interests to bring them together in more than rhetorical terms.

The same does not hold true of Turkey's economic relations with Middle Eastern countries, which are more homogeneous and geographically closer. These factors—plus the fact that they export oil and natural gas—have made them important trade partners. Though their share of Turkey's total foreign trade declined after the early 1980s, it is still substantial. Within the region, Saudi Arabia, Algeria, Egypt, and Iran are all important trading partners, with a total turnover in each case normally around $1 billion per year. These are followed by Israel, Libya, Syria, the

United Arab Emirates, and Jordan.[31] Iraq would also be in the top category were it not for the embargo, as its trade turnover with Turkey in the three years before 1990 ran at an average of $2.2 billion per year, making it Turkey's third biggest trading partner.[32] Turkey's economic and political relations with Iran, Iraq, Libya, Syria, and Israel are of particular significance, and each deserves separate attention.

Iran. Erbakan's visit to Iran in August 1996 provoked a good deal of international attention, primarily because he signed an agreement for the construction of a gas pipeline from Tabriz in northwestern Iran to the eastern Turkish city of Erzurum with a future extension westward to Sivas and Ankara. The line was expected to deliver 3 bcm of gas per year to Turkey, rising to 10 bcm by 2003. Alongside the agreement there was talk of increasing Turkey's overall trade volume with Iran to $2.5 billion per year from the current figure of around $900 million.[33] The proposal ran into some criticism from the United States, but apparently it was eventually accepted in Washington because it did not actually involve investment in Iran by Turkey or other Western countries. The prospect that the line might also be used for gas from Turkmenistan was also discussed.[34] All these schemes underline the point that Iran is economically too important for Turkey to ignore, either as an export market, an energy source, or a transit route to Central Asia. Political considerations reinforce this point since, to put the case negatively, Iran could make itself a substantial nuisance if it gave full-scale support to the Kurdistan Workers Party (PKK, by its Kurdish initials). Turkish governments of all persuasions must try to maintain cooperative links with Tehran, even at the risk of provoking clashes with the United States or other Western powers.

Iraq. The imposition of UN sanctions against Iraq in August 1990 did not mean a complete end to traffic across the Turkish-Iraqi border. Limited deliveries of foodstuffs, medicines, and construction materials continued, with UN compliance, in return for Iraqi deliveries of diesel fuel by truck. Not until December 9, 1996, did Iraq accept a longstanding UN plan allowing it to export $2 billion worth of oil over six months to pay for "humanitarian" supplies under Security Council Resolution 986. Oil began to flow through the Kirkuk (Iraq)-Yumurtalık (Turkey) pipeline on December 11. There did not seem to be a notable increase in exports to Iraq, which are still too small to be recorded as a separate item in available statistics, but a sizable flow of diesel fuel still moved from Iraq to Turkey. The Turkish government and private sector were keen to develop trade with Iraq as quickly as UN rules allowed, since it was claimed that the sanctions had cost Turkey $30 billion (presumably including lost earnings from construction and transit fees, besides exports). These economic incentives are reinforced by political factors, namely, Turkey's commitment to uphold Iraq's territorial integrity and, above all, to prevent the emergence of an independent Kurdish state on Iraqi or any other territory.[35]

Libya. Turkey's political relationship with Libya has gone through a stormy phase in recent years, due to Libyan leader Mu'ammar Qadhafi's declared support for Kurdish nationalism (though whether this goes further than rhetoric is open to question). Turkey still has substantial economic interests in Libya. Bilateral trade has totaled $500 million to $700 million per year. Turkish contractors had around $1.7 billion worth of business in the country, although they had considerable difficulty in recovering their debts. While Turkey and Libya are poles apart in their general international alignments, Turkey has a big enough economic stake that future governments will probably try to keep relations on an even keel, even at the risk of U.S. displeasure or occasional problems caused by the unpredictable Qadhafi.[36]

Syria. The expulsion from Syria of PKK leader Abdullah Öcalan in October 1998 removed a major political obstacle to better relations. On the other hand, old arguments remained unresolved, in particular Syrian fears that Turkey could use the recently constructed Atatürk Dam to cut off or sharply reduce the downstream flow of the Euphrates, on which much of Syria's agriculture depends. The historical dispute over Hatay, or Alexandretta province—annexed by Turkey in 1939—adds to the tension, although Syria does not seem to rank its return as an immediate or realistic objective. Syria insists that a July 1987 agreement between its president Hafiz al-Asad and Turkish prime minister Özal, under which Turkey guaranteed a downstream Euphrates River flow of 500 cubic meters per second, was only a temporary arrangement and demands a long-term flow of 700 cubic meters per second. Politically, Syrian suspicions were exacerbated by Turkey's military and economic agreements with Israel. Given these tensions, it is perhaps surprising that Syrian-Turkish trade turnover, though low for neighboring countries, was still around $600 million per year.[37] Öcalan's expulsion raised the possibility that economic links could be extended—through a much-discussed scheme for connecting electric power grids or even a gas pipeline across Jordan and Syria from Egypt—but the two sides will probably want to test the relationship over a longer time-span before entering any long-term commitments.

Israel. The free-trade agreement between Turkey and Israel—finally passed by the Turkish parliament in April 1997, more than a year after it was signed in March 1996—signaled the possibility of an important strengthening of economic relations. It also reinforced an earlier agreement for limited military cooperation and a $600 million deal for modernization of Turkish F-4 Phantom fighters, signed in December 1996. Almost certainly, Turkey's main motivation was political rather than economic, in that it sought an accord with Israel as a counterweight against Syria as well as a means of maintaining good relations with Washington. The Turks already had Greek and Armenian lobbies to contend with in the U.S. Congress, so the pro-Israel lobby was a useful recruit.

Economically, high hopes were expressed over the free-trade agreement, with predictions that Turkish-Israeli trade volume could increase to $2 billion per year and that Turkish exporters could expand markets in the United States, Canada, and Central America, with which Israel had preferential trade ties. Joint industrial ventures, especially in the garments industry, were also in prospect. Trade volume did rise from around $450 million in 1996 to $730 million in 1998. This figure needs to be put into perspective, however, since the range of products that could be traded profitably was relatively limited. As a result, trade with Israel still represented only about 16 percent of Turkey's total merchandise trade with the Middle East. Other regional countries—notably Egypt, Saudi Arabia, and Algeria—had substantially bigger trade volumes with Turkey.[38] There are also political constraints to the alignment, as Turkey is highly likely to avoid direct or meaningful involvement in Arab-Israeli disputes. Equally, Israel claimed neutrality in the Syrian-Turkish tension over Öcalan. Nonetheless, the fact that even the Erbakan-led administration accepted the Turkish-Israeli agreements—albeit reluctantly—suggests that future governments will try to develop the relationship, if within realistic limits.[39]

Notes

1   Data from State Institute of Statistics, Ankara, as published in *Milliyet*, March 27, 1999.
2   *Briefing*, March 8, 1999, p. 35; *Country Report: Turkey*, 4th quarter 1998 (London: Economist Intelligence Unit, 1998), p. 5.
3   *Country Report: Turkey*, 2nd quarter 1997 (London: Economist Intelligence Unit, 1997) pp. 5, 16; *Country Report: Turkey*, 4th quarter 1998, p. 5; and *Briefing*, March 22, 1999, p. 30.
4   Metin Münir, "Search for a Suitcase Solution," *Euromoney*, April 1997, pp. 153-154.
5   William Hale, *The Political and Economic Development of Modern Turkey* (New York: St. Martin's, 1981), pp. 203-205, 243.
6   *Briefing*, March 8, 1999, p. 37, and March 22, 1999, p. 32.
7   Ibid., March 22, 1999, p. 32.
8   Turkey's 1997 GNP in U.S. dollars is calculated from *Country Report: Turkey*, 4th quarter 1998, p. 5. UK data calculated from National Statistics, *Annual Supplement*, 1996-1997 (London: HMSO, 1996), pp. 10, 142.
9   *Briefing*, March 8, 1999, p. 38.
10   Ibid., June 9, 1997, p. 24.
11   Ibid., March 22, 1999, p. 32.
12   Ibid., March 8, 1999, p. 38.
13   Ibid.
14   See, for example, Hale, *Political and Economic Development*, p. 108.

15 *Briefing,* March 13, 1995, p. 18.

16 *Country Report: Turkey,* 2nd quarter 1996, p. 11; and 3rd quarter, 1996 (London: Economist Intelligence Unit, 1996), p. 6.

17 *Briefing,* June 2, 1997, p. 18; *Country Report: Turkey,* 1st quarter 1997 (London: Economist Intelligence Unit, 1997), p. 27; *Country Profile: Turkey,* 1996-97 (London: Economist Intelligence Unit, 1996), p. 46; and *Country Profile: Turkey,* 1999-2000 (London: Economist Intelligence Unit, 1999), p. 52.

18 *Briefing,* February 22, 1999, p. 32.

19 The proportion obviously depends on whether luggage trade is included or not; see Table 2 (page 24).

20 Philip Robins, "Turkish Foreign Policy under Erbakan," *Survival* 39 (Summer 1997), pp. 82-100.

21 Trade data are for 1998, from *Briefing,* March 8, 1999, p. 37.

22 *Country Report: Turkey,* 2nd quarter 1997 (London: Economist Intelligence Unit, 1997), pp. 24, 26.

23 Vadim Markushin, "Russia-Turkey: Doomed to Be Eternal Neighbours," *Perceptions* 2, no. 1 (March-May 1997), pp. 96-97.

24 This must be regarded as no more than a very rough "guesstimate" since there is no way of knowing how the total luggage trade is distributed between the different states of the CIS (see Table 2, page 24).

25 "Summit Declaration on Black Sea Cooperation," June 1992. Copy kindly supplied by the Turkish Ministry of Foreign Affairs, Ankara.

26 *Briefing,* May 5, 1997, p. 2.

27 Philip Robins, "Between Sentiment and Self-Interest: Turkey's Policy towards Azerbaijan and the Central Asian States," *Middle East Journal* 47 (Autumn 1993), p. 610.

28 Gareth Winrow, *Turkey in Post-Soviet Central Asia* (London: Royal Institute of International Affairs, 1995), p. 22.

29 Tansu Çiller, "Turkish Foreign Policy in Its Dynamic Tradition," *Perceptions* 1, no. 3 (September-November 1996), p. 10.

30 Selim İlkin, "The Economic Cooperation Organisation (ECO): A Short Note," *Journal of Economic Cooperation Among Islamic Countries* 15, nos. 3-4 (1994), pp. 31-43; Önder Özar, "Economic Cooperation Organisation: A Promising Future," *Perceptions* 2 no. 1 (March-May 1997), pp. 15-23.

31 Data are for 1995, from *Direction of Trade Statistics Yearbook* (Washington, DC: International Monetary Fund, 1996), pp. 432-433.

32 *Statistical Yearbook of Turkey,* 1990 (Ankara: State Institute of Statistics, 1992), pp. 393, 395.

33 *Briefing,* August 19, 1996, pp. 4-5.

34 Ibid., June 30, 1997, p. 17, and May 19, 1997, p. 16.

35 Ibid., August 19, 1996, p. 5; March 25, 1997, p. 19; May 19, 1997, p. 16; and June 30, 1997, p. 25; *Country Report: Turkey,* 1st quarter 1997 (London: Economist Intelligence Unit, 1997), p. 26.

36 *Briefing,* October 14, 1996, pp. 1-4; *Briefing,* November 25, 1996, p. 17; *Country Report: Turkey,* 4th quarter 1996 (London: Economist Intelligence Unit, 1996), pp. 13, 27; *Direction of Trade,* pp. 432-433.

37 *Briefing,* March 8, 1999, p. 37.

38 Ibid., pp. 36-37.

39 Robins, "Turkish Foreign Policy," p. 84.

Kemal Kirişçi

Turkey and the Muslim Middle East

During the Cold War, Turkey's foreign and security policies were mainly a function of developments in Europe and relations between the two European blocs. Since the Cold War's end, however, Turkey's national interests have become intimately related to security and stability in all its surrounding regions, from the Balkans to the Black Sea to the Caucasus to Central Asia. At the same time, Turkey is also a Middle Eastern country and its security, stability, and prosperity are closely tied to developments in the Middle East. This is especially so since the 1990-91 Gulf crisis and war. The Arab-Israeli peace process also opened possibilities for regional cooperation.

Pressure for Change after the Cold War

In the 1950s Turkey briefly took an active role in Western efforts to prevent Soviet influence from expanding into the Middle East. It helped establish the pro-Western Baghdad Pact and the Central Treaty Organization.[1] This active policy drew reactions from Soviet-leaning pan-Arabist and Baathist regimes, which viewed Turkey as an agent of the West. The overthrow of the royalist regime in Iraq in July 1958 and its replacement by General Abd al-Karim Qasim's radical pan-Arab regime the following year brought the Baghdad Pact to an end. This short-lived Turkish activism in the Middle East coincided with a domestic political transformation from one-party rule to parliamentary democracy and relative economic liberalization. Turkey's Middle East policy during this period can be attributed partly to this transformation and partly to a new Turkish political elite's efforts to prove its Western credentials by mobilizing against the regional Soviet threat it perceived.[2] Subsequently, Turkish foreign policy became characterized by noninvolvement and noninterference in the region's politics.[3]

Until the early 1970s Turkey maintained balanced relations with Arab countries and Israel. The 1967 Arab-Israeli war, a growing sense of isolation over Cyprus, and a desire to build support among Islamic countries—plus the rise of the pro-Islamist National Salvation Party—brought gradual change in favor of closer relations with Arab countries and greater support for the Palestinian cause.[4] The crisis that the Turkish economy faced as a result of the 1973 oil price hikes led to additional pressures, this time to expand commercial relations with oil-rich Arab countries. The election of the Likud government in Israel in 1977 and its stern policies toward Lebanon and the occupied territories culminated in the downgrading of diplomatic relations with Israel. Turkey developed closer relations with the Palestine Liberation Organization (PLO), despite that organization's intimate relations with Armenian and left-wing terrorist organizations operating against Turkish interests.

The 1980s ushered in more significant change. As prime minister and president, Turgut Özal left an important imprint on the development of Turkey's increasingly activist and internationalist approach to relations with the Middle East.[5] He enhanced bilateral relations with conservative Gulf countries as well as radical countries such as Libya, Iraq, and Iran. He played a critical role in mobilizing Turkish business interests in the Middle East, but also attracted Arab capital to Turkey. During this period, Turkey's economic relations with the Middle East grew significantly.[6] As the dams of the Southeast Anatolian Project (GAP, by its Turkish acronym) increased in number, Özal also tried to allay fears in Damascus by promising that Syria would receive a minimum water flow of five hundred cubic meters per second from the Euphrates River.

In 1986 Özal introduced the idea of a "peace pipeline" to carry water from Turkey across the Middle East. His regionalist approach reached a peak during the Gulf crisis in 1990 when he aligned Turkey with the U.S.'s anti-Iraq effort. He was frustrated by Parliament's reluctance to give him wide war powers, but he did manage to ensure support for United Nations sanctions against Iraq and eventually authorized the anti-Iraq coalition's use of Turkish military facilities. His policy generated considerable criticism and opposition within Turkey and led to the resignation of his military chief of staff, foreign minister, and defense minister. Özal, however, seemed unaffected. In March 1991, in a major departure from established policy, he entered into dialogue with Kurdish leaders in northern Iraq who had rebelled against Saddam Husayn. He also played a critical role in persuading the Western allies to create a safe haven in northern Iraq and launch Operation Provide Comfort to ensure the repatriation of approximately half a million Iraqi Kurdish refugees who, fearing Saddam's wrath, had fled to Turkey in the war's aftermath.[7]

It soon became apparent that Özal's bold approach would not bear fruit. The "peace pipeline" never materialized due to deep regionwide mistrust and Arab fear of becoming dependent on Turkish water.[8] Turkey's role in expelling Iraq from Kuwait did not seem to have been as appreciated by the Arab world as Özal had expected and failed to ensure a place for Turkey in the Arab-Israeli peace process.[9] If anything the increased activism "had one important implicit consequence that had not been foreseen: It increased concerns in Arab capitals about the reemergence of Turkish dominance in the region."[10] Finally, the Soviet collapse and its aftermath diverted Turkey's foreign policy attention elsewhere.[11]

With Özal's death in 1993, policy toward the Middle East seemed to revert to its former cautious and conservative nature. Turkish foreign minister Hikmet Çetin canceled a trip to Israel in July 1993 when that country mounted attacks on southern Lebanon on the eve of his visit. At that point, just weeks before the world was to learn of dramatic progress on the Palestinian-Israeli front achieved through secret negotiations in Oslo, Norway, Turkish policy appeared to be held hostage again to fears of offending the Arab world.

Yet, post-Cold War changes in the Middle East are affecting Turkey and its national interests profoundly. The emerging Middle East creates complex challenges but also opportunities. When economic considerations and growing domestic demand for closer relations with Muslim countries are also considered, it is likely that Turkey will become more engaged in Middle Eastern politics.

Foreign-Policy Decision-Making: The Erbakan Interlude

During the Cold War, the Turkish foreign ministry and the military were the critical shapers of the government's foreign policy. That remains so today, but public opinion and a greater diversity of ideas espoused by political parties have come to play a larger role. The two secular conservative parties, the *Anavatan* (Motherland) Party (ANAP) and the *Doğru Yol* (True Path) Party (DYP), together with the social democratic *Cumhuriyet Halk* (Republican People's) Party (CHP), have advocated pro-Western policies and the continuation of economic integration with western Europe, even in the face of major setbacks to Turkey's quest for European Union membership. The *Demokratik Sol* (Democratic Left) Party (DSP) of Bülent Ecevit traditionally takes a more critical view of relations with the West and advocates closer relations with countries of the region, including the Middle East. The DSP has been part of every government since mid-1997 and has clearly left its mark on recent foreign policy. The *Milliyetçi Hareket* (Nationalist Movement) Party (MHP) generally advocates a nationalist foreign policy. Its platform calls for closer relations with the Turkic world and the establishment of an "East Mediterranean Union" composed of Turkey, Jordan, Egypt, Israel, and Palestine, while taking a critical view of Iran and Syria.[12]

During the 1996-97 coalition government between Necmettin Erbakan's *Refah* (Welfare) Party (RP) and Tansu Çiller's DYP, the traditional methods and tenets of Turkish foreign policy were sorely tested.

Much of this testing focused on the Middle East. As prime minister, Erbakan sometimes departed from established practice by excluding diplomats from his meetings with foreign ambassadors and leaders—those from Syria and Iran, for example.[13]

Erbakan's RP fundamentally opposed traditional Turkish foreign policy. It strongly objected to the 1995 customs union agreement between the EU and Turkey. Instead, Erbakan argued that Turkey should lead the formation of an Islamic United Nations, an Islamic customs union, and an Islamic NATO.[14] On relations with Iran, the RP took a position diametrically opposed to the one shared by other political parties and a large portion of public opinion: It refused to join in allegations of Iranian support for terrorism in Turkey. Iran, in fact, became the first country Erbakan visited as prime minister in 1996. During his visit, he discomfited other Turkish officials by accepting Iranian arguments that forces of the separatist Kurdistan Workers Party (known by its Kurdish initials PKK) were not even present in Iran.[15] He never visited the West officially and in December 1996 turned down an invitation to a dinner at the end of an EU summit meeting in Dublin.[16]

But the RP often seemed to be at cross-purposes with itself. Erbakan emphasized development of closer ties with Arab countries, but most moderate Arab governments were made wary by his Islamist discourse; his visits to Iran and Libya; and his close relations with radical Islamic groups such as Hamas, Lebanese Hizbollah, the Muslim Brotherhood, and Algeria's Islamic Salvation Front (known by its French initials FIS), all of which sent representatives to the RP's fifth party congress in October 1996. The RP position on the peace process was ambiguous, at best. A number of party officials spoke disapprovingly of Yasir Arafat's acceptance of the Oslo accords, arguing that he had betrayed the Palestinian cause by recognizing Israel. Anti-Israeli and anti-Zionist arguments, often with anti-Jewish overtones, were standard in RP discourse. Nevertheless, a number of RP legislators did travel to Israel. And, although he never answered Israeli prime minister Binyamin Netanyahu's letter of congratulations and request for a meeting sent upon Erbakan's assuming the prime ministry, Erbakan did later receive Israeli foreign minister David Levy on an official visit. There were even reports that their private meeting was quite warm.

Notwithstanding Erbakan's iconoclasm, the military and foreign ministry remained the dominant foreign policy influences during his prime ministry. Each played an important role in persuading Erbakan to reconsider his opposition to Operation Provide Comfort (OPC), the U.S.-led military force based in southern Turkey that enforced the "no-fly" zone in northern Iraq. Erbakan eventually was left in the embarrassing position of having to convince members of his own party to accept a U-turn and vote in favor of extending OPC's mandate for another term. He also found himself having to accept continuation of close relations with Israel, as the meeting with Levy suggests.

In January 1998, RP was found guilty of trying to undermine secularism in Turkey and was banned by Turkey's Constitutional Court. The *Fazilet* (Virtue) Party (FP), the *de facto* continuation of the RP, has tried to distance itself from many of its predecessor's more controversial foreign policy ideas.

Important Issues

Among Turkey's new challenges in the post-Cold War Middle East are the Kurdish problem, including violent activities by Kurdish insurgents, and larger military and security concerns. The Iraqi military operation against the Kurdish uprising in northern Iraq in late March 1991 precipitated one of the largest refugee crises in recent history. More than a million and half mostly Kurdish refugees fled toward Iran and Turkey. The crisis drew the world's attention to the Kurds and intensified scrutiny of Turkey's own Kurdish problem. It also led to establishment of a Kurdish-controlled area in northern Iraq, increasing the ability of the PKK to launch operations into Turkey. This conflict has cost more than thirty thousand lives and strained the Turkish treasury.[17] The PKK's ability to operate from Iraq led the Turkish military to mount numerous cross-border operations. And Turkish accusations that Iran and Syria encourage and support the PKK severely affected relations with these two countries. Furthermore, the human cost of security operations and Turkey's inability to find a democratic solution have strained its relations with the U.S. and the West.

The sophisticated military capabilities of neighboring Middle Eastern countries with war-making pasts also constitute an important threat to Turkish national security. Iran and Syria possess ballistic missiles capable of delivering weapons of mass destruction, and there are reports of Iranian efforts to acquire a nuclear capability.[18] Turkey's important population centers, dams, power stations, air bases, and military headquarters are within range of these missile systems. The threat became quite real during the October 1998 crisis over Syria's harboring of PKK leader Abdullah Öcalan.

Loss of trade and commerce with the Middle East after the Gulf War also adversely affected Turkish security. Sanctions on Iraq not only closed a lucrative market but also undermined Turkey's comparative advantage in supplying the Gulf countries with agricultural products. Turkish exports to the Middle East dropped from 23 per cent of its overall exports just before the war to 14 per cent in 1996.[19] A fleet of more than forty thousand trucks fell idle.[20] Most of these trucks were based in Kurdish-populated southeastern Turkey and had provided considerable employment possibilities. Turkey also lost revenues from the Kirkuk (Iraq)-Yumurtalık (Turkey) oil pipeline, which was closed after Iraq invaded Kuwait in August 1990. In 1998, the foreign ministry put the revenue and trade costs of the sanctions at more than $35 billion.[21] These economic consequences of the Gulf crisis and war aggravated the Kurdish problem and the violence surrounding it.

Energy needs of Turkey's expanding economy are increasingly a matter of national security. Turkey purchases most of its crude oil from Middle Eastern countries. This dependence makes the economy vulnerable to regional developments and creates unbalanced trade structures. While Turkey imported $1.382 billion worth of goods from Saudi Arabia—mostly oil—in 1995, it could sell only $470 million worth in return. Turkey's natural gas consumption is increasing, too. It traditionally has depended mostly on Russian supplies. Yet projected demand for natural gas is expected to reach forty to fifty billion cubic meters by 2010 and sixty-three billion by 2025. Current supplies meet only one-fifth of this projected demand. Turkey's most likely future supplies are either in the Middle East or in the Caspian Basin.

Finally, Turkey needs electricity. It buys electricity from Iran and has also finalized negotiations to build an electricity grid between Turkey, Syria, Jordan, Egypt, and Iraq. Such a grid might indeed increase interdependence, and the Turkish government has been pursuing the idea for some time.[22]

Turkey's need for electricity and energy raises another major issue related to the Middle East, namely water and the sharing of the Euphrates-Tigris river system. Water is crucial not only in agriculture but in hydroelectric power generation. With twenty-two dams and nineteen hydropower plants, GAP is one the world's most ambitious water-resources development and electricity-production programs. But while the Turkish side insists on the "Turkishness" of the Euphrates and Tigris, Iraq and Syria see GAP as a clear infringement of their riparian rights and as a systematic attempt to dominate the region. Both Syria and Iraq have tried to mobilize the support of the Arab League in support of their position, straining Turkey's relations with the larger Arab world and engendering additional instability in the region.

Assessing Turkish–Arab and Turkish–Iranian Relations

Turkey's post-Cold War relations with Arab countries reflect a mixed record of cooperation and conflict. Conflict continues to characterize the relationship between Turkey and its immediate Arab neighbors,

Iraq and Syria. In the case of Egypt, Jordan, and the Palestinian Authority, relations are clearly positive, though conflicts do arise now and then over relations with Israel and over Turkey's problems with Iraq and Syria. Turkey's relations with the Gulf countries are marginal and basically limited to trade, although the Saudis, too, have expressed their displeasure over Turkish-Israeli relations.

Iraq

Turkish policy toward Iraq might best be described as ambiguous. Iraq presently does not constitute a major or immediate military threat to Turkey, but, if armed again with sophisticated weaponry, it could. Although there have been numerous official Turkish visits to Iraq to express "friendship," it would be wrong to assume that future relations will be smooth. Saddam has accused Turkey on a number of occasions of acting treacherously by assisting in the "thirty-state aggression against Iraq," as the Iraqis call the 1991 Gulf War. He has also criticized Turkey's policy of permitting use of İncirlik air base by U.S. and British planes striking Iraqi targets. In February 1999, Baghdad actually threatened to attack Turkey if it continued to allow the U.S. and Britain to use its territory to bomb Iraq. Saddam's belligerence has not always been limited to words. He has not hesitated to support the PKK and actually helped PKK supporters settle into villages near the Turkish border after his offensive against Kurdish groups in 1988.[23] In 1998, Saddam reportedly allowed the PKK to open an office in Baghdad and has been extending growing support to it.[24]

Turkish policy toward Iraq since the end of the Gulf War has primarily focused on efforts to prevent the PKK from establishing itself in northern Iraq. This has led to an uneasy cooperation with the two major Iraqi Kurdish groups, Massoud Barzani's Kurdistan Democratic Party (KDP) and Jalal Talabani's Patriotic Union of Kurdistan (PUK) in northern Iraq. Turkey has permitted continuation of Operation Provide Comfort (renamed Northern Watch in 1997) in return for tacit U.S. agreement not to criticize Turkey's many anti-PKK incursions into northern Iraq. At the same time, Turkey has been a persistent supporter of Iraq's territorial and political integrity, even while calling on Iraq to comply with U.N. resolutions. Turkish decision-makers have viewed U.S. policies in the area with great suspicion and fear a U.S. intention to assist in the emergence of a Kurdish state. This fear has led Turkey to adopt policies often independent from those of the U.S., if not in conflict with them.

Turkey's commitment to Iraqi territorial integrity is genuine. Iraq's disintegration into chaos would leave Turkey in a very difficult situation. Iran and Syria share Turkey's outlook. Though these two historically have had even worse relations with Iraq than has Turkey, they also remain committed to Iraq's territorial integrity. Furthermore, all three countries are concerned about the threat that a Kurdish state could pose to their own territorial integrity.

Even if the regime in Baghdad were to change, the memory of Turkey's Gulf War role and disputes over the Euphrates and Tigris are likely to sour future Turkish-Iraqi relations. Yet, there would also be room for economic cooperation. Iraq has all the necessary inputs for a successful economy: vast oil reserves, well-educated people, and potentially one of the richest land areas in the region. The existing oil pipelines between Iraq and Turkey are still an important source of cooperation, and Turkey is likely to be a major consumer of both Iraqi oil and gas. In the 1980s Turkish exports to Iraq boomed, and business contacts developed then could be rejuvenated in a post-Saddam Iraq. Close economic relations with Iraq would also benefit the Kurdish-populated areas of the two countries. However, it is intrinsically important for both states that they effectively address their respective Kurdish problems.

Syria

For years, relations with Syria were dominated by concern about Damascus's support for the PKK and sheltering of Öcalan, a dispute over water resources, and Syria's territorial claims to Turkey's Hatay province. Syrian ballistic missile capabilities and possession of weapons of mass destruction have also been a major worry for Turkey. Concern over rumored Greek-Syrian defense cooperation led a prominent retired diplomat, Şükrü Elekdağ, to argue that Turkey should base its national defense strategy on an ability simultaneously to fight two and a half wars: against Greece, Syria, and the PKK.[25]

Although the PKK issue is in abeyance, at least for the time being, the water dispute over the Euphrates is likely to continue. Syria fears that the GAP dams along the Euphrates will allow Turkey to use water for political blackmail. Access to cheap and abundant water is critical for Syria's Baath Party regime, which would like to keep food prices as low as possible, particularly in urban centers, whence it derives most of its political support.[26] The Syrian leadership is also likely to use traditional claims on Hatay as a tool to build domestic support for the regime.

All these concerns played a critical role in Turkey's decision to develop close military cooperation with Israel. However, this cooperation engendered a sense of encirclement in Damascus,[27] leading Syria to mobilize the Muslim world against Turkey and to increase efforts at greater cooperation with longtime rival Iraq, which is also hostile toward Turkey. Furthermore, this trend also seems to be accompanied more generally by dangerous efforts at establishing alliance networks throughout the region, characterized by an Israel-Turkey-Jordan-Azerbaijan axis, on one hand, and an Armenia-Greece-Syria-Russia axis, on the other.[28]

Furthermore, it is quite possible that, after a settlement with Israel, Syria may actually use conflict with Turkey as an excuse to maintain a large army and security apparatus. If greater liberalism and pluralism can be achieved in Syria, better relations might develop between the two countries. This will also depend on the emergence of commercial and other Syrian interest groups with a stake in better relations with Turkey. Traditionally, there have been close ties between families and business people on both sides of the Syrian-Turkish border, especially in Gaziantep and Aleppo. During a Muslim festival at the end of March 1998, border controls were relaxed by both sides for the first time in ten years, and families and old friends were able to greet each other at the frontier crossing of Nusaybin.[29] A meeting between Syrian and Turkish officials, also in March 1998, seemed to suggest that the relaxation might be followed by increased commerce and revived border trade. The expulsion of Öcalan from Syria in October 1998 also boosted prospects for improved bilateral ties. However, reconciling the deep societal and governmental divisions between the two countries will be a difficult task.

Egypt

Egyptian-Turkish relations have come a long way since the end of the Cold War. The "Free Officers" coup in 1952 and the ascent of Gamal Abd al-Nasser to power in 1954 very quickly led to a marked deterioration in relations. In 1955, soon after Syria and Egypt signed an accord critical of the Baghdad Pact, Turkey amassed troops on the Syrian border.[30] The tension escalated in 1957 to a point where Turkish and Egyptian troops faced each other across the Syrian border.[31]

During the height of the Cold War relations remained cool. However, with the Egyptian decision in the early 1970s to rupture its strategic relations with the Soviet Union and develop closer ties with the U.S., prospects emerged for better Turkish-Egyptian relations. Yet, not until the early 1990s did real improvement become visible. Since then there has been regular contact between top-level officials, and the presidents of both countries have visited each other on a number of occasions. Egyptian president Hosni Mubarak personally shuttled between Turkey and Syria in a successful effort to ease the 1998 crisis.

Nevertheless, bilateral ties are not without strains. For example, Cairo has regularly criticized Turkish military incursions into northern Iraq as violations of Arab territory. Also, as a downstream country whose economy depends on the Nile River, Egypt would support the

Syrian position on transboundary rivers even were there no "Arab soli-darity" factor. Lastly, although Cairo has said it considers Turkey to have an important role in the search for peace in the Middle East and that it has no objections to close Israeli-Turkish relations, it has warned that Turkish-Israeli military relations could develop into a strategic threat to the Arabs.

These differences are nothing like the tense rivalry of the 1950s. Today both countries support the peace process, maintain close strategic relations with the U.S., and perceive similar threats to their national security from radical Islamic groups. Arab solidarity and Egypt's natural role as leader of the Arab world sometimes seem to cause friction. It would be unrealistic to expect Egypt to support Turkey or even to remain silent when Turkey's conflicts with its Arab neighbors reach crisis levels.

Jordan

Relations between Jordan and Turkey have traditionally been good. Jordan's pro-Western position during the Cold War and frequent conflicts with radical Arab countries with which Turkey also had cool relations were important binding factors. Like Turkey, Jordan has had problematic ties with Syria, though for different reasons. Jordanians still remember Syria's brief invasion in September 1970 to support radical Palestinian groups against the king. Even in the late 1990s, King Hussein accused Syria of supporting radical groups and terrorism in his country.

Turkish-Jordanian relations began to expand significantly in the late 1990s. High-level visits took place in both directions, along with frequent lower-level meetings. The late King Hussein attracted considerable praise in Turkey for his moderate and balanced approach to issues such as the water problem, northern Iraq, and Turkish-Israeli military cooperation. Jordan participated as an observer in the unprecedented search-and-rescue naval exercise conducted by Israel, Turkey, and the U.S. in January 1998.[32] In April 1998, Jordan and Turkey agreed on an exchange of troop visits, and Turkish military deputy chief of staff General Çevik Bir received a medal of merit from the king.[33] This trend toward closer ties appears to be continuing under Hussein's son and successor, King Abdullah II.

The Palestinians

Turkey has had an up-and-down relationship with the Palestinian cause. In 1947 Turkey voted in the United Nations with the Arab states against partitioning Palestine. However, in 1949 Turkey became the first Muslim country to recognize Israel and remained essentially aloof from the

Palestinian cause until the late 1960s. From then on Turkey regularly voted in favor of UN resolutions supporting Palestinian rights. The development of relations and the opening of a PLO office in Ankara had to wait until 1979 because of the PLO's support for radical groups involved in terrorism against Turkey.[34] Since then, however, Turkish-Palestinian relations have been very positive. Turkey was one of the first non-Arab countries to recognize Palestinian "statehood" when the PLO's Palestine National Council declared independence in 1988. Arafat visited Turkey soon after setting up the Palestinian Authority in 1994, and, later that year, prime minister Tansu Çiller became the first head of government in the world to visit Arafat in Gaza when she made a side trip from an official visit to Israel.

Arafat has visited Turkey on numerous occasions, stressing the importance of Turkey's involvement in the peace process and seeking Turkish support for Palestinian economic development. Arafat, like King Hussein, has been much more balanced in his reactions to Turkish-Israeli relations and Turkish cross-border operations into northern Iraq. In June 1997 the PLO envoy in Ankara, Fuad Yaseen, noted that "Turkey has the right to protect its borders against terrorist attacks," while adding that Palestinians expected Turkey to be more sensitive toward issues of importance to them.[35]

In the late 1990s, persistent deadlock in the peace process seemingly made the Palestinians less relaxed about Turkish-Israeli relations. During Turkish foreign minister İsmail Cem's visit to Israel and the Palestinian Authority in July 1998, Arafat said Turkey's close ties with Israel increasingly were hurting the Palestinians. One Palestinian legislator complained to Cem that the more Turkey strengthens relations with Israel, "the more Israel takes advantage ... to impose a new status quo in Jerusalem."[36] Turkish president Süleyman Demirel tried to respond to these complaints when he met with Arafat in Ankara in April 1999. Demirel pointedly criticized Israel for "policies on the West Bank and Jerusalem, which we do not approve of ... [and which] play a significant role" in causing "deadlock" in the Middle East peace process. He assured Arafat of Turkey's continued support for the Palestinian cause and pledged to use Turkey's influence with Israel to get the peace process moving.[37]

In spite of apparently warm bilateral relations, Turkish foreign policy has several times disappointed Palestinians and even fallen short of its own commitments. In January 1996 Turkey sent only four of the sixty Turkish monitors that Arafat had personally requested from Demirel to participate in international observation of the Palestinian elections; many other countries did send large numbers of monitors, including members of parliament and important politicians. As of early 2000, Turkey still had not released $50 million in credits that it pledged the

Palestinian Authority in 1993, and a foreign ministry project to train Palestinian refugees had not materialized because the necessary $4 million could not be found.

Turkey is falling well short of fulfilling its potential in supporting the peace process and the Palestinians. This is particularly disappointing because Turkey is one of the few countries with a reservoir of goodwill among both Israelis and Palestinians. Turkey ought to make more effective use of this goodwill, if only because negative developments in the peace process and the suffering of Palestinians directly affect Turkish domestic politics and benefit radical groups and Turkey's Middle Eastern rivals.

The Gulf Countries

Until the Gulf crisis of 1990-91, Turkey had extensive economic relations with the Gulf states. Turkey imported oil from Saudi Arabia and Kuwait; they, in turn, imported Turkish agricultural products. Many Turkish companies were involved in large construction projects in the Gulf region, particularly in Saudi Arabia. However, Turkey had no meaningful political or security ties with the Gulf.

Iraq's invasion of Kuwait brought a completely new dimension to Turkey's relations with the Gulf states, while undermining trade. Turkey's role in the crisis—massing some one hundred thousand troops on its Iraqi border and allowing the U.S. to stage bombing raids from its territory—was critical to the defeat of Iraq.[38] Both Kuwait and Saudi Arabia expressed their gratitude for Turkey's role and promised to extend financial assistance to help Turkey recover some of its losses resulting from the trade embargo imposed on Iraq.[39] Turkey received some of this assistance in the form of grants as well as oil,[40] but short of the levels expected, leaving Turks with a sense of betrayal and under-compensation for their sacrifices.[41] Since the Gulf crisis, exports to the area have fallen because of the loss of direct routes through Iraq, and Turkish construction companies have moved to Central Asia, Russia, and Europe. Turkey's oil imports from Saudi Arabia did rise significantly to compensate for loss of Iraqi oil. For future oil and natural gas imports, however, Turkey is increasingly inclined to look to Iran, Central Asia, and Azerbaijan, rather than the Gulf. Unless sanctions on Iraq are lifted, and there is a governmental effort to rebuild economic relations, it is difficult to see how Turkey could regain its economic position in the Gulf, especially since business contacts and networks have been lost.

It is doubtful that Ankara would take a major initiative toward the Gulf states. When foreign minister Cem surveyed Turkey's foreign policy plans in a late 1998 interview, he emphasized that Turkey was as much a Middle Eastern as a Balkan country, but nowhere in the interview did he make a direct reference to the Gulf countries.[42]

Iran

Turkey and Iran have been rivals in the region for many centuries. Yet, as many scholars have pointed out, they have not fought each other in wars since the seventeenth century and do not have any territorial disputes.[43] This long period of relative peace appears to have helped them develop a pragmatic relationship.

Since the 1979 Islamic revolution in Iran, relations have experienced many low points. Often these were the product of each country's accusing the other of intervening in its domestic affairs. Turkey has frequently accused Iran of supporting Islamic fundamentalist groups and the PKK. Iran has accused Turkey of harboring Iranian opposition groups, such as the Mujahedin-e Khalq, and encouraging separatism among its large Azeri minority.[44]

Over the last few years, there were a number of occasions when crises even came to the brink of military confrontation, as PKK and Turkish military operations near the Iranian border intensified. In 1994 and again in 1999, Turkish fighter planes damaged Iranian border villages in their pursuit of the PKK. A frustrated Turkish government reportedly considered a military attack on PKK bases in Iran as early as May 1995.[45] In July 1996 the PKK attacked a Turkish military post on the Iranian border. Demirel visited the border and criticized Iran bitterly.[46] Relations got even worse in February 1997 when the Iranian ambassador to Turkey spoke provocatively at an Islamic fundamentalist gathering in a suburb of Ankara.

In summer 1999, relations deteriorated once again. Prime minister Ecevit called antigovernment demonstrations racking Iran's cities a "natural" reaction against an "outdated regime of oppression." Four days later, Tehran claimed that Turkish jet fighters pursuing the PKK had hit an Iranian border town, killing five civilians. Turkey initially denied the charge but later implicitly acknowledged its accuracy. Just days after the bombing, Iran captured two Turkish soldiers in the border area, threatened to put them on trial, and held them two weeks before releasing them. With the return of the soldiers to Turkey, tension abated and conflict was averted.[47]

Aside from Turkish allegations about Iranian support of the PKK and Islamic fundamentalism, there are a number of other areas of bilateral conflict. Intense Turkish-Iranian competition exists over which country offers the best model for the former Soviet republics in Central Asia. This competition has diminished, however, as it has become clear that neither country has the resources to exert decisive influence and that Central Asian governments seemed much keener to diversify their relations rather than simply choose the Turkish or Iranian model. Iranian fears of pan-Turkism and its effect on its own Azeri minority were assuaged by the fall of Azerbaijan's pan-Turkist president Ebulfez Elchibey in 1993.[48] Other areas of conflict include Iranian efforts to develop long-range missiles and weapons of mass destruction. Tehran, in turn, has sought a strategic relationship with countries such as Armenia, Greece, Syria, and, to a lesser degree, Russia.[49]

Whatever the bilateral problems and regime differences, pragmatism and nonconfrontation usually prevail in Turkish-Iranian ties. Turkey needs natural gas and plans to diversify its supplies. It has agreed to purchase Iranian gas starting in mid-2001. Turkey sees Iran as an important market, as well as a transit country to Central Asia. Similarly, Iran sees Turkey as an important transit country for trade with the West.

Turkey takes hope from the emergence of some moderate leaders in Iran, highlighted by the 1997 election of Mohammad Khatami as president. In 1998, Khatami's government contributed to mediation of Turkey's crisis with Syria. His foreign minister, Kamal Kharrazi, reportedly brought initial word to Ankara that Syria was ready to cease its support for the PKK and expel Öcalan.[50] Nevertheless, Ankara shares the view of most observers that hardline clerics, rather than Khatami, continue to hold most sway in Tehran. Still, if the trend toward liberalization of the political system in Iran continues, it is highly likely that Turkish-Iranian relations will increasingly be characterized by pragmatism, fewer problems, and a recognition that the two neighbors share common interests.[51]

Turkey and the U.S. in the Middle East

Turkey and the U.S. have been allies since the U.S. battleship *Missouri* sailed into Istanbul's harbor in response to Stalin's threats in 1946. However, relations have not been uniformly smooth. The two countries have often disagreed about the Middle East, although more over nuances than fundamentals. In the 1950s and most of the 1960s, Ankara and Washington usually shared a common outlook on the Middle East. Both countries viewed the Middle East through Cold War lenses, and there were no major differences over Israel.

The break in this harmony came with the 1967 Arab-Israeli war. Israeli occupation of Arab territory, particularly that of east Jerusalem, played an important role in Turkey's joining the Islamic Conference Organization. Turkish diplomats also began to court Arab and Muslim support for the Turkish position on Cyprus, though, to their dismay, with little success. Thanks to the influence and prestige derived from their membership in the nonaligned movement, Greek Cypriots maintained the upper hand among Arabs and Muslims. The rise of an Islamist party in Turkey in the early 1970s and Turkey's growing need to gain access to Arab markets after the 1973 oil crisis also took Turkey in a direction different from that of U.S. policy. However, Turkey did not sever its relations with Israel. It supported the Palestinian cause and opened diplomatic relations with the PLO, but with the clear understanding that Israel was here to stay and that only its boundaries were being contested.

During the course of the Iran-Iraq war, Turkey remained neutral, as opposed to the U.S., which tilted toward Iraq. Turkey also refrained from supporting Washington's increasingly confrontational approach toward Iran. Instead, under Özal's leadership Turkey developed a foreign policy toward the Middle East that blended commercial interests with appeals to Islamic and cultural solidarity.

Iraq's increasingly threatening posture toward Turkey after the end of the Iran-Iraq war in 1988, followed by its 1990 invasion of Kuwait, helped bring convergence to U.S. and Turkish policies toward the Middle East. Özal's government lent critical support to U.S. efforts to dislodge Iraq from Kuwait and, in return, received U.S. support to ensure repatriation of the half-million Iraqi Kurdish refugees that had poured into Turkey after the Gulf War.

Following the Iraq crisis, Özal seemed very enthusiastic about prospects for creating a new Middle East through the multilateral Middle East peace process launched in 1992. The thinking behind this process—with its multilateral workshops that included Israelis and representatives from nearly a dozen Arab states and its comprehensive approach to regional peace and security—seemed to coincide with Özal's vision of an interdependent Middle East. However, Turkey's contribution to the multilateral process remained modest and its impact limited. After the process stalled, considerable frustration surfaced, especially among the Turkish public, over a perception of U.S. reluctance to induce Israel to compromise.

Turkey's influence in the Middle East is far too limited to enable it to restart a stalled peace process or, for that matter, even significantly to affect events in the region. Nevertheless, the U.S. came to see a democratic, pro-Western Turkey as an important asset in the post-Cold War Middle East, particularly as the Clinton administration tried to apply a "dual containment" policy against Iran and Iraq.[52]

Pursuit of dual containment—intended to isolate or even precipitate regime changes in Iran and Iraq—would have been impossible without Turkey's cooperation. Turkey's support in maintaining effective UN economic sanctions against Iraq is critical. Turkish authorization for continuation of Operation Provide Comfort/Northern Watch (OPC/

ONW) is vital to protecting northern Iraq. OPC/ONW enabled the U.S. to organize the opposition Iraqi National Congress (INC) in northern Iraq—at least until Iraqi troops essentially destroyed it in August 1996—and keeps the major Kurdish groups there beyond the control of Baghdad. In the case of Iran, U.S. policy has been based on unilaterally declared sanctions requiring the goodwill and cooperation of its allies. Turkish restraint in developing close economic relations with Iran has been crucial, including its seeming delay in implementing its natural gas deal with Iran from January 2000 to July 2001. (Given Turkey's energy needs, this restraint may not be endless.) Displeasure with Iranian support for the PKK and Islamic fundamentalist groups also inclined Turkey to facilitate U.S. efforts to contain Iran.

There is full convergence between the stable, economically interdependent Middle East that the West would like to see emerge and the Middle East that would best serve Turkey's interests. In terms of day-to-day policy, however, Ankara and Washington continue to differ on a number of issues.

OPC/ONW and U.S. involvement in northern Iraq have led to a widely shared belief in Turkey that the U.S. supports the establishment of a Kurdish state at the expense of Turkey's territorial integrity.[53] As a result, many in the Turkish military regard the U.S. with suspicion, despite of decades of alliance.[54] The U.S. does indeed seem to favor a federal arrangement for northern Iraq that would possibly give Kurdish-populated areas a status well beyond the autonomy granted in Iraqi law. Turkey objects to this, as was most conspicuously demonstrated during the crisis in relations of fall 1998 after the U.S. persuaded the PUK and KDP to cooperate in reviving their shared federated administration, originally established in 1992.

While Turkey supports the idea that Iraq must comply with UN resolutions, its immediate interests favor a relaxation or lifting of U.S.-supported trade sanctions. Turkish decision-makers are increasingly wary of Iraq's weapons-of-mass-destruction capability, but they generally oppose use of force to undermine it. In this regard public opinion plays a very important role, and Turkish leaders are very reluctant to be seen as a tool of U.S. policy in the region. In February 1998, during a crisis over Iraq's interference with UN arms inspections, Ankara refused to allow the U.S. to use Turkish territory to attack Iraq. This decision was in line with public opinion. According to a poll taken during the February 1998 crisis, some 80 percent opposed the use of Turkish military bases for attacks against Iraq.[55] But when a similar crisis broke out again at the end of the year, the Turkish government was quite willing to cooperate. This significant turnaround was no doubt a result of the support the U.S. extended Turkey on the Öcalan issue.[56]

Turkish decision-makers also are concerned that the U.S. prefers not to pressure Syria on a number of issues related to Syrian support of terrorism. Many believe that Washington is more concerned with gaining Syria's good will for the sake of the Middle East peace process than with taking Turkish antiterrorism interests into account. Similarly, they worry that the U.S. might pressure Turkey to give in to Syria on the Euphrates-Tigris water dispute in order to ensure that Syria will cede the water resources of the Golan Heights to Israel.

Conclusion

Middle Eastern developments are likely to continue to affect Turkey's relations with the United States. Statements by two diplomats in the mid-1990s that Turkey does not always see "eye to eye" with the U.S. and that it does not intend to be America's "subcontractor" are very revealing, suggesting that U.S.-Turkish divergence regarding the region may be enduring.[57] However, this does not mean that Turkey and the U.S. are on a collision course—far from it. The two countries share interests and, to a large extent, a common strategic vision for the future of the Middle East. Liberalization efforts in Iran also might reduce U.S.-Turkish differences. Moreover, for now, these differences are largely mitigated by the good will Washington generated in Turkey with its support for Ankara regarding Öcalan and the PKK.

Turkey's resources and capabilities are too limited for it to exert significant influence over political developments in the Middle East. However, Turkey can make its presence felt. Turkish decision-makers assign growing importance to the Middle East and have demonstrated the will to behave assertively in the region, as was the case in the 1998 crisis with Syria. Problems over northern Iraq and the regional water dispute cannot be resolved without Turkey. Also, growing economic development may boost Turkey's regional influence. Egypt, Iran, Israel, and more recently, Syria, have sought to expand trade and commercial relations with Turkey. If Turkey can get its democracy to function better and further open up its society, this might encourage more trans-societal interactions in the Middle East. That, in turn, could contribute to creation of a regional framework for cooperation and integration that would include Israel as well as the Arabs.[58]

Notes

1   George McGhee, *The U.S.-Turkish-NATO Middle East Connection: How the Truman Doctrine and Turkey's NATO Entry Contained the Soviets* (New York: St. Martin's Press, 1990).

2   Hüseyin Bağcı, "Demokrat Parti'nin Ortadoğu Politikası" (Democrat Party's Middle East policy), in Faruk Sönmezoğlu (ed.), *Türk Dış Politikasının Analizi* (Analysis of Turkish foreign policy) (İstanbul: Der Yayınları, 1994), pp. 89-90; Hakan Yavuz, "Turkish-Israeli Relations and the Turkish Identity Debate," *Journal of Palestine Studies* 27, No. 1 (Autumn 1997).

3   Philip Robins, *Turkey and the Middle East* (London: Pinter, 1991), pp. 65-66.

4   Mahmut Bali Aykan, "The Palestinian Question in Turkish Foreign Policy from the 1950s to the 1980s," *International Journal of Middle East Studies* 25, no. 1 (1993); Yavuz, "Turkish-Israeli Relations."

5   Soli Özel, "Of Not Being a Lone Wolf: Geography, Domestic Plays, and Turkish Foreign Policy in the Middle East," in Geoffrey Kemp and Janice Gross Stein (eds.), *Powder Keg in the Middle East: The Struggle for Gulf Security* (Lanham, Md.: Rowan & Littlefield, 1995).

6   Halis Akder, "Turkey's Export Expansion in the Middle East, 1980-1985," *Middle East Journal* 41, no. 4 (Autumn 1987); Robins, *Turkey and the Middle East.*

7   Kemal Kirişçi, "Provide Comfort and Turkey: Decision Making for Refugee Assistance," *Low Intensity Conflict and Law Enforcement* 2, no. 2 (Autumn 1993), p. 240.

8   Robins, *Turkey and the Middle East.*

9   George E. Gruen, "Turkey's Potential Contribution to Arab-Israeli Peace," *Turkish Review of Middle East Studies* 1, no. 1 (March-April 1993), p. 189.

10 Sabri Sayarı, "Turkey and the Middle East in the 1990s," *Journal of Palestine Studies* 26, no. 3 (Spring 1997), p. 41.

11 Kemal Kirişçi, "New Patterns of Turkish Foreign Policy Behaviour," in Çiğdem Balım et al. (ed.), *Turkey: Political, Social and Economic Challenges in the 1990s* (Leiden: Brill, 1995).

12 Sami Kohen, commentary in *Milliyet*, April 22, 1999.

13 Gencer Özcan, "Yalan Dünyaya Sanal Politikalar" (Virtual politics for a temporary world), in Gencer Özcan (ed.), *Onbir Aylık Saltanat: Siyaset, Ekonomi ve Dış Politikada Refahyol Dönemi* (The eleven-month-long splendour: politics, economics, and foreign policy during the *Refahyol* government) (İstanbul: Boyut Yayınları, 1998), pp. 183-184.

14 Necmettin Erbakan, "Türk Dış Politikası Nasıl Olmalı" (What kind of foreign policy should Turkey have?" *Yeni Türkiye* 1, no. 3 (March-April 1995); İhsan D. Dağı, *Kimlik, Söylem ve Siyaset: Doğu-Batı Ayrımında Refah Partisi Geleneği* (Identity, discourse, and politics: the Welfare Party's tradition at an East-West crossroads) (Ankara: Imge, 1998).

15 Özcan, "Yalan Dünyaya Sanal Politikalar," p. 184.

16 *Turkish Daily News (TDN)*, December 4, 1996.

17 *TDN*, April 13, 1998; *Yeni Yüzyıl*, June 8, 1997.

18 S. Egeli, *Taktik Balistik Füzeler ve Türkiye* (Tactical ballistic missiles and Turkey) (Ankara: TC, MSB, Savunma Sanayii Müsteşarlığı, 1993).

19 Ali Çarkoğlu, Mine Eder, and Kemal Kirişçi, *Türkiye ve Ortadoğu'da Bölgesel İşbirliği: Türkiye'nin Bölgesel Orta ve Uzun Dönem Politika Analizi* (Regional cooperation in Turkey and the Middle East: An analysis of Turkey's middle- and long-range policies) (İstanbul: TESEV, 1998), p. 190, calculated from Table 7.1.

20 Şerif Egeli, chairman of the Turkish-Jordanian and Turkish-Pakistan Business Councils and former chairman of the Foreign Trade Association of Turkey, interview with author, October 11, 1996.

21 Oğuz Çelikkol, "Turkey and the Middle East: Policy and Prospects," opening address at the conference on "Turkish Foreign Policy toward the Middle East," The Washington Institute for Near East Policy, April 6-7, 1998.

22 Philip Robins, "Avoiding the Question" in Henri J. Barkey (ed.), *Reluctant Neighbor: Turkey's Role in the Middle East* (Washington, D.C.: United States Institute of Peace, 1996).

23 Ümit Özdağ, "Kuzey Irak ve PKK" (Northern Iraq and the PKK), *Avrasya Dosyası* 3, no. 1 (Spring 1996).

24 *TDN*, June 30, 1998; *Milliyet*, November 11, 1998.

25 Şükrü Elekdağ, "2-1/2 War Strategy," *Perceptions* 1, no. 1 (March-May 1996).

26 Ali Çarkoğlu and Mine Eder, "Domestic Concerns and the Water Conflict over the Euphrates-Tigris Basin," *Middle Eastern Studies*, forthcoming.

27 Alain Gresh, "Turkish-Israeli-Syrian Relations and Their Impact on the Middle East," *Middle East Journal* 52, no. 2 (Spring 1998), p. 203; Muhammad Muslih, "Syria and Turkey: Uneasy Relations" in Barkey, *Reluctant Neighbor*, p. 129.

28 Malik Mufti, "Daring and Caution in Turkey's Foreign Policy," *Middle East Journal* 52, no. 2 (Spring 1998), pp. 40, 41; Gresh, "Turkish-Israeli-Syrian Relations," pp. 193, 196.

29 CNN, March 29, 1999; *Milliyet,* March 30, 1999.

30 Malik Mufti, *Sovereign Creations: Pan-Arabism and Political Order in Syria and Iraq* (Ithaca and London: Cornell University Press, 1996), p. 72.

31 Don Peretz, *The Middle East Today* (Westport: Praeger, 1994), p. 419.

32 *TDN*, March 19, 1998.

33 *TDN*, April 22, 1998.

34 Aykan, "The Palestinian Question," p. 98.

35 "'Wait and See' Policy from Arab World," *TDN*, June 18, 1997, internet edition.

36 As quoted in *TDN*, July 9, 1998.

37 "Demirel Criticizes Israel during Arafat Visit," *TDN*, April 6, 1999, internet edition.

38 William Hale, "Turkey, the Middle East and the Gulf Crisis," *International Affairs* 68, no. 4 (October 1992).

39 Sabri Sayarı, "Turkey: The Changing European Security Environment and the Gulf Crisis," *Middle East Journal* 46, no. 1 (Winter 1992), p. 19.

40 William Hale, "Turkey (Türkiye Cumhuriyeti)," in Ami Ayalon (ed.), *Middle East Contemporary Survey 1991*, vol. 15 (Boulder: Westview, 1993), p. 713; William Hale, "Turkey (Türkiye Cumhuriyeti)," in Ami Ayalon (ed.), *Middle East Contemporary Survey 1992*, vol. 16 (Boulder: Westview, 1995), p. 773.

41 Özel, "Of Not Being," p.173.

42 *Sabah*, September 2, 1998.

43 Tschanguiz Pahlavan, "Turkish-Iranian Relations: An Iranian View," and Atila Eralp, "Facing the Challenge: Post-Revolutionary Relations with Iran," in Barkey, *Reluctant Neighbor*; Shahram Chubin, "Iran's National Security: Threats and Interests," in Kemp and Stein, *Powder Keg in the Middle East*; Süha Bölükbaşı, "Turkey Copes with Revolutionary Iran," *Journal of South Asian and Middle Eastern Studies* 13, nos. 1-2 (Fall-Winter 1989).

44 Bülent Aras, "Turkish-Iranian Relations," paper presented at the Conference on "Turkish Foreign Policy Towards the Middle East," The Washington Institute for Near East Policy, April 6-7, 1998.

45 *Tempo*, no. 18 (May 1, 1996).

46 *TDN*, July 18, 1996.

47 Alan Makovsky, "Turkish-Iranian Tension: A New Regional Flashpoint?" *Policywatch* no. 404 (August 9, 1999), The Washington Institute for Near East Policy.

48 Eralp, "Facing the Challenge," pp. 105-107.

49 Gresh, "Turkish-Israeli-Syrian Relations," p. 196; Mufti, "Daring and Caution," pp. 36-40.

50 *Milliyet*, October 10, 1998.

51 Aras, "Turkish-Iranian Relations"; Eralp, "Facing the Challenge"; Mufti, "Daring and Caution."

52 Zbigniew Brzezinski, Brent Scowcroft, and Richard Murphy, "Differentiated Containment," *Foreign Affairs* 76, no. 3 (May-June 1997); Harvey Sicherman, "The Strange Death of Dual Containment," *Orbis* 41, no. 2 (Spring 1997).

53 Baskın Oran, *'Kalkık Horoz': Çekiç Güç ve Kürt Devleti* ('Poised Hammer': The Hammer Force and the Kurdish state) (Ankara: Bilgi, Yayınevi, 1996).

54 Kemal Kirişçi, "Turkey and the United States: Ambivalent Allies," in Thomas Keaney and Barry Rubin (eds.), *Friends of America: U.S. Allies in a Changing World* (London: Frank Cass, forthcoming 2000).

55 Private survey conducted by Strategy/Mori, February 1998.

56 *Milliyet*, February 20, 1999.

57 Mufti, "Daring and Caution," p. 48.

58 Ali Çarkoğlu, Mine Eder, and Kemal Kirişçi, *The Political Economy of Regional Cooperation in the Middle East* (London: Routledge, 1998).

Meliha Benli Altunışık

Turkish Policy toward Israel

Alignment with Israel constitutes one of the most important aspects of post-Cold War Turkish foreign policy. Close relations with Israel largely resulted from a redefinition of Turkish regional security concerns, as Turkey's political and military elite came to view its Middle East policy as directly tied to Turkish regime maintenance, secularism, and territorial integrity.

Turkish-Israeli alignment created shock waves in the region, and Turkey became the focus of criticism from several regional states, especially Syria and Iran. However, in contrast to earlier times when it pursued a strict balance between Israel and the Arab states, Ankara this time did not pay much attention to problems in the Arab-Israeli peace process and largely disregarded the criticism.

Normalization of Relations

The Middle East was at a critical juncture at the beginning of the 1990s. Repercussions of the end of the Cold War were just beginning to be felt. The Gulf War further changed the politico-strategic environment. Turkish leaders, like their counterparts in many countries, tried to make sense of these developments. Turkey had indirectly but actively participated in the U.S.-led coalition against Iraq. This policy and the bold leadership style of President Turgut Özal were hotly debated domestically. But Turkish foreign policy in the Middle East soon reverted to its traditionally cautious style. The widely shared view that Turkey did not receive the expected benefits from the Gulf War, as anticipated by Özal, strengthened the hands of those who criticized what they saw as adventurist tendencies. Özal's death in 1993 seemingly put a definitive end to the era of risk-taking in foreign policy.

Normalization in Turkish-Israeli relations was largely a reaction to new international and regional developments. The impetus was the Arab-Israeli peace process that started in 1991 with the Madrid peace conference. This process freed Turkey from its policy of uneasy balancing between Arab countries and Israel, which it had pursued especially since the 1960s. But even at the height of its "pro-Arab" policy and despite pressure from Arab governments, Ankara had never considered breaking relations with Israel completely. As a North Atlantic Treaty Organization (NATO) member and U.S. ally, Turkey traditionally looked favorably upon Israel. The political elite was particularly interested in enlisting the help of the pro-Israel lobby and Jewish-American organizations in the U.S.

In some ways, normalization with Israel after the Gulf War was the culmination of increasing contact between the two countries in the late 1980s. From 1985 on, Turkey and Israel assigned high-ranking diplomats to one another even though formal diplomatic relations remained at the level of *charge d'affaires*. Diplomatic ties returned to their pre-1980 level, when Turkey downgraded them to second-secretary level. Paralleling this were signs of increased political links. In September 1987 Turkish and Israeli foreign ministers met at the United Nations (UN) during a General Assembly meeting. Then-Prime Minister Özal openly argued for improving relations with Israel. He justified this on the grounds that relations with Israel, in addition to those with Arab countries, were a practical necessity if Turkey were to play a role in solving Middle Eastern problems. There were also rumors of increased intelligence cooperation in the 1980s.[1] Therefore, initiation of the peace process removed the last barrier to the betterment of relations. More importantly, the process made such relations publicly acceptable, since Arab states, too, were normalizing relations with Israel.

Two other factors further facilitated improvement of relations in this early period. First, the U.S. considered both countries strategically important during the Cold War, and it was concerned with their role in the emerging "new world order."[2] It thus welcomed and supported closer ties between its two allies.

Second, Ankara was disappointed with the results of its pro-Arab policy. This disappointment began to be voiced privately by policymakers but openly by many journalists and academics.[3] One of the original reasons for a pro-Arab tilt in Turkish foreign policy, dating back to the mid-1960s, was an expectation of support from the Arab states for Ankara's foreign policy interests, primarily regarding the Cyprus dispute.[4] But no support on that issue or others was forthcoming.

In the end, what remained from the pro-Arab policy of the mid-1960s to the 1980s was improved economic ties with the Arab world. However, under close scrutiny one could easily see that these ties depended on special circumstances. In the 1970s, the emergence of a regionwide oil economy facilitated increasing commercial ties.[5] Even then, relations remained limited to oil-producing states. In the 1980s, the eight-year Iran-Iraq war gave impetus to the boom in trade relations. But declining oil revenues starting in the mid-1980s decreased the attractiveness of the region for Turkish businesses. Turkey's exports to the Middle East dropped from 27 percent of total exports in 1987 to 14 percent in 1993. In the same period, imports from the region decreased from 19 percent to 11 percent.

Furthermore, the Kurdish problem and the water issue had already strained Turkey's relations with its Middle Eastern neighbors in the 1980s. In 1977 Turkey launched the Southeast Anatolia Project (GAP, by its Turkish acronym) to meet its hydroelectric and irrigation needs by constructing more than twenty dams on the Tigris and Euphrates rivers. This massive project caused problems in Ankara's relations with Damascus and Baghdad.[6] Syria's decision to give sanctuary to Abdullah Öcalan, leader of the Kurdistan Workers' Party (PKK, by its Kurdish initials), after the 1980 military coup in Turkey also created tensions.[7]

With these considerations in mind, the Turkish political elite decided to normalize relations with Israel. In December 1991 Ankara upgraded its relations with Israel, as well as with the Palestine Liberation Organization (PLO), to ambassadorial level. The 1993 Oslo accords gave a further push to normalization. At this early stage, improvement in bilateral relations made its most visible impact on trade. Volume of trade increased 62 percent between 1992 and 1994 (see table). To prepare a legal framework for improving economic relations, the two nations began negotiations on the prevention of double taxation, encouraging investment, and a free trade agreement. A dramatic increase in the number of Israeli tourists visiting Turkey, up to 300,000 per year, was another strong sign of normalization.

Turkish–Israeli Bilateral Trade (in US $million)

Year	Export	Import	Balance*	Volume
1989	30.799	60.567	-29.768	91.366
1990	46.505	62.516	-16.011	109.021
1991	78.669	78.047	0.622	156.716
1992	90.089	97.075	-6.986	187.164
1993	80.238	121.794	-41.556	202.032
1994	178.079	125.890	52.189	303.969
1995	239.769	166.635	73.134	406.404
1996	254.569	192.038	61.928	446.004
1997	391.457	229.282	162.175	620.739
1998	478.631	282.749	195.882	761.380
1999	585.045	298.268	286.777	883.313

* In this column, positive values indicate a trade balance in Turkey's favor; negative values indicate a balance in Israel's favor.

Sources: For 1989-98 figures, Undersecretariat for Foreign Trade; for 1999 figures, State Institute of Statistics website: http://www.die.gov.tr/TURKISH/SONIST/DISTICIST/10030008.gif

However, there were still limitations on Turkey's improvement of ties with Israel, as Ankara denied any possibility of political and security cooperation. In October 1992 the general secretariat's office at the joint chiefs of staff declared that Turkish-Israeli relations did not involve anything of a military nature. The declaration further stated, "In the light of the realities of the Middle East, Turkey, which is an Islamic country, is careful to balance its relations with Israel and the Arab world."[8] Turkey canceled Foreign Minister Hikmet Çetin's visit to Israel in July 1993 after Israel mounted attacks in southern Lebanon. Therefore, in the immediate aftermath of the Gulf crisis, Turkey seemed to retreat from active involvement in the Middle East to its earlier position of balance and caution. Ankara carefully linked the improvement of its ties with Israel to the Arab-Israeli peace process.

Furthermore, during this period Turkey sought to solve its problems with Syria, and Turkish-Syrian relations did improve in the early 1990s. In April 1992 a delegation consisting of top Turkish officials, including Foreign Minister Hikmet Çetin and Interior Minister İsmet Sezgin, went to Damascus and negotiated a new security protocol. Turkey and Syria agreed "to cooperate against terrorism and to prevent terrorists from crossing from one country to the other."[9] Upon his return, Sezgin publicly announced that Syria would not support the PKK nor let it launch attacks against Turkey and that the PKK base in the Syrian-controlled Bekaa Valley in Lebanon would be closed.[10] In 1994 Interior Minister Nahit Menteşe visited Syria and declared that relations were very good. Starting in November 1992, Turkey initiated regular tripartite meetings with Syria and Iran to discuss major regional issues, mainly the situation in northern Iraq. The immediate reason for these meetings was the election of a Kurdish national assembly in May 1992, which Iraq's three neighbors perceived as a potentially serious step toward Kurdish statehood. Syria and Turkey called for the reestablishment of the territorial integrity of Iraq. Both countries voiced their criticisms when, in January 1993, U.S. warplanes from İncirlik Air Base in Turkey fired on Iraqi installations. Prime Minister Süleyman Demirel flew to Damascus to discuss the developments with President Hafiz al-Asad. After the meeting Demirel said, "We are against any event that might harm [the] civilian population in Iraq."[11]

Trilateral meetings including Iran also provided an opportunity for Turkey and Syria to sort out bilateral problems. Before a 1994 trilateral meeting in Istanbul, the Syrian and Turkish foreign ministers met for an hour. Afterward, Syrian foreign minister Faruq al-Sharaa announced that he was satisfied with the talks, and his Turkish counterpart Çetin said the two sides agreed "to do our best to further improve Turkish-Syrian relations in all areas."[12] This was followed by reports in the Turkish press that Syria had arrested 400 PKK militants.[13] When Israeli president Ezer Weizman visited Turkey in January 1994, he stated that Israel needed to develop better relations with Syria and asked Turkey to play the role of intermediary.[14]

Turkey's Changing Perceptions of the Middle East

Tansu Çiller's visit to Israel in November 1994 was the first-ever by a Turkish prime minister. Despite a mini-crisis created by her unscheduled visit to the Palestinians' Orient House offices in Jerusalem,[15] in disregard of known Israeli objections, Çiller's trip was the first sign of the changing nature of relations between Turkey and Israel. Çiller pushed for increasing security cooperation, and during her visit several agreements were signed. The most important allowed Israeli Aviation Industries to modernize Turkey's F-4 Phantom aircraft.[16]

By late 1994, the Turkish political and military elite had reevaluated the regional and domestic environment, and Ankara had become more willing to strengthen its strategic and political ties with Israel. The elite saw Turkey as facing widespread threats to its territorial integrity, mostly from the south. The Kurdish issue and the perceived threat of Islamic radicalism became dominant elements in Turkey's relations with the Middle East. Within this context, Turkey's decision-makers emphasized its neighbors' increasing support for the PKK, while linking the domestic Islamic fundamentalist threat to Iran. More importantly, the Turkish leadership considered these issues directly tied to the territorial integrity and survival of the regime.

Postwar developments in Iraq especially exacerbated Turkey's security concerns. The internationalization of the Kurdish issue was particularly problematic from Ankara's perspective. Turkish officials argued that the power vacuum in northern Iraq constituted a safe haven for the PKK to launch cross-border raids into Turkey.[17] At the same time Turkey viewed the disintegration of Iraq and the establishment of a Kurdish state there as unacceptable, since such developments would give new momentum to the PKK. Consequently, reestablishment of Iraqi territorial integrity became the cornerstone of Turkish policy regarding Iraq.

Ankara actually was apprehensive that the U.S. and Israel supported Kurdish nationalism in Iraq. In the case of Israel, its support for Kurdish nationalists in Iraq in the 1960s and 1970s and its interest in weakening Iraq formed the basis of this suspicion, Nevertheless, this concern did not prove to be an impediment to Turkey's pursuit of close ties with Israel.

Meanwhile, relations with Syria deteriorated steadily. Ankara was convinced that Damascus was supporting the PKK in order to gain leverage regarding Euphrates water use. In the summer of 1995 Ankara was also alarmed by increasing reports of PKK incursions into Hatay, a southern Turkish province on the Mediterranean coast.[18] This was a sensitive province as its 1939 annexation by Turkey was never accepted as legitimate by Damascus, which at least in rhetoric continued to claim it. In December 1995 there was again tension when Syria protested the construction of Birecik Dam, which was part of GAP. Turkish foreign minister Deniz Baykal accused Syrian officials of "wanting to wash the blood on their hands with more water." In response, Syria hastened efforts to internationalize its water problem with Turkey. Damascus was especially interested in bringing the issue to the attention of the Arab world. In the same month, the so-called "Damascus Declaration" countries (Syria, Egypt, and the six states of the Gulf Cooperation Council) met in Syria and issued a declaration that criticized Turkey's water policies.[19] The final blow in 1995, however, came when it was reported that Syria had agreed to allow Greek aircraft to use its air bases in a conflict with Turkey.[20] Although Syria denied this,[21] its rapprochement with Greece was enough to increase the sense of encirclement that many in Turkey felt. In June 1996 tensions grew on the Turkish-Syrian border. Responding to news that up to 40,000 Syrian troops were moving toward the border, State Minister and Deputy Prime Minister Nahit Menteşe told the press, "If [the Syrians] go too far they will get a slap."[22] It was a harbinger of future crises.

As was the case with Iraq, Turkish policy vis-à-vis Syria differed from that of its allies. From Turkey's perspective, the United States— eager to achieve progress in Israeli-Syrian negotiations—was too accommodating toward Syria. Three issues were of particular concern to Ankara regarding these negotiations. First, if Damascus were relieved of its overriding preoccupation with Israel, Turkey might face a more aggressive Syria on its border, with Syria free to redeploy troops now concentrated on the cease-fire line with Israel.[23] Second, the Euphrates water issue could become a bargaining chip in Israeli-Syrian talks, leading to U.S. pressure on Turkey to meet Syria's demands.[24] Finally, the talks might not include the PKK among the terrorist organizations whose futures were to be addressed, and therefore the Syrian regime might continue supporting the PKK even as it jettisoned Palestinian terrorist groups. In sum, Israeli-Syrian talks created an uneasy feeling among the Turkish elite that Turkey's problems in the region might be ignored.

Problems also intensified in Turkey's relations with Iran.[25] Turkish authorities accused Iran of providing shelter for the PKK and permitting it to set up training camps in Iranian territory, accusations rejected by Tehran. In May 1996, newspapers reported that "Iranian PKK members" were caught during military operations. Islamic fundamentalism became a source of bilateral dispute in February 1997, as the infamous "Sincan affair" put relations at their lowest point. At "Jerusalem Day" celebrations organized by the *Refah* (Welfare) Party (RP) mayor of

Sincan, a suburb of Ankara, the Iranian ambassador called for adoption of *sharia* (Islamic law) in Turkey. The Turkish government declared him *persona non grata*, and Iran responded by expelling the Turkish ambassador. This development revived Turkish claims that Iran was supporting Islamic fundamentalism in Turkey. Close Iranian-Syrian ties also disturbed the Turkish government. [26]

As a result of these considerations, Ankara decided to engage more actively in protecting its interests against Middle Eastern threats. This new activism would differ from that of the Özal period. Whereas Özal saw opportunities in the Middle East and advocated an "activist foreign policy" to exploit them, the Turkish political and military elite in the mid-1990s considered the Middle East a source of threats and the activism arose from a desire to offset them. Foreign policy intertwined with domestic issues. Specifically, defense of Turkey's territorial integrity was seen as linked to defense of the regime and its secular nature. This had implications for the policy-making process. The security-defense establishment became more prominent in the formulation of Turkey's policies vis-à-vis the Middle East, exercising its influence through the National Security Council, which increasingly became the central organ for policy-making.

In 1997 the Turkish military became unusually open about how it saw relations with Middle Eastern neighbors Syria and Iran. The chiefs of staff gave several "briefings" to different segments of the Turkish elite, including academicians, journalists, and representatives of several civil society organizations. In those briefings the military announced a change in the "national military strategic concept." The new concept identified two internal threats, separatism and Islamic fundamentalism, mainly fed by two external actors, Syria and Iran.[27]

Paralleling the change in Ankara's perception of the Middle East, emphasis fell on building security aspects of Turkish-Israeli relations. Policy-makers, especially the military, seemed to believe that strategic cooperation with Israel might solve many of their problems by posing a deterrent to Syria and Iran. The October 1998 crisis with Syria partly demonstrated what Ankara had in mind. The long-running dispute between Turkey and Syria flared up when Turkish officials publicly stated that Syria had been waging an "undeclared war" against Turkey and that Ankara had the "right to respond." Tension quickly escalated, and Turkey reinforced its Syrian border. The crisis was finally resolved when Öcalan left Damascus, and representatives of the two countries met in Adana, Turkey, to sign "minutes" in which Damascus agreed to end its support of the PKK. Turkish-Israeli alignment was a key factor in this crisis because it increased Syria's sense of encirclement. Despite Israeli attempts to dissociate itself from the crisis, Damascus and the Arab League accused Israel of fomenting the row.

A related consideration in Turkish-Israeli relations was the desire of the Turkish military to obtain high-quality hardware and technology. Turkey had announced a very ambitious $150 billion, twenty-five-year defense modernization program.[28] However, it had become difficult to obtain arms from Western allies because of their concern about Turkey's human-rights situation and poor relations with Greece. In 1995 Ankara applied to several European states for modernization of its F-4 fighter jets but was turned down. Israel, on the other hand, had the technology and the arms and did not tie their availability to political or human-rights issues.

Finally, one could also argue that internal developments in Israel—the May 1996 victory of Binyamin Netanyahu and the freezing of the peace process between Syria and Israel—also facilitated closer ties with Turkey. Netanyahu had clear views about Syria and the PKK. A Turkish journalist who had interviewed Yitzhak Rabin and Shimon Peres in the past wrote that while they both skirted questions regarding the PKK and the Kurdish issue, Netanyahu openly and clearly called the PKK a "terrorist" organization and said Israel did not support the establishment of an independent Kurdish state.[29]

The framework for Turkish-Israeli security cooperation was provided by two agreements. First was the Military Training and Cooperation Agreement (MTCA), signed on February 23, 1996, between Turkish deputy chief of staff General Çevik Bir and Israeli defense ministry director-general David Ivry. The agreement was publicized two months after it was signed and sparked severe criticism in Turkey and in the Middle East. In Turkey the RP and some Islamist media led the way, but other circles also criticized the government's secretive approach.

The published parts of the MTCA[30] listed areas of cooperation such as joint training, sharing of training information, observation of one another's training exercises, and port visits. Its most controversial aspect was the provision allowing air force training missions in each other's airspace. The Turkish chiefs of staff and the government argued that the agreement would be very beneficial for Turkish security. One of the benefits, they said, was that Turkish pilots would be trained in electronic warfare technology in Israel. Officials also complained that critics and the media had distorted the agreement and that there was, in fact, no difference between the agreement signed with Israel and many MTCAs signed with other countries. But critics and others were convinced this agreement was different and that it would have far-reaching consequences for Turkey, Israel, and the region as a whole.

The second key agreement was signed on August 26, 1996. A framework agreement, it provided for technology transfer; training of technicians and researchers[31]; intelligence sharing; and regular biannual "strategic dialogue" meetings of the two countries' security and foreign policy officials.[32]

There was also an agreement on joint military exercises. The first of these, Operation Reliant Mermaid, was a trilateral search-and-rescue exercise held with U.S. participation off the coast of Israel in January 1998.[33] To much of the world, this exercise became a symbol of deepening strategic alignment between Turkey and Israel. Although merely a search-and-rescue exercise and thus not directed against any third party, it nevertheless drew angry protests from Iran and some Arab countries. Jordan took part as an observer, but Egypt rejected a similar invitation.[34] Operation Reliant Mermaid II, again with U.S. participation, was held in December 1999, this time off the Turkish coast. Again, Jordan attended as observer, and Egypt rejected an invitation to do so.

A second important aspect of security cooperation has been military sales. As mentioned above, Turkey believed it could get U.S. hardware and technical knowledge via Israel, without political conditions, and this prospect was one of the major incentives motivating Ankara to build security ties with Israel. On December 5, 1996, Israel agreed to modernize fifty-four Turkish F-4s for $650 million.[35] In late 1997 a second upgrade contract was awarded to Israel for Turkey's forty-eight F-5 aircraft. Israel and Turkey also agreed to co-produce the sophisticated Popeye II air-to-ground missile. Turkey had already bought fifty Popeye I missiles for its F-4s. The Popeye II deal involved a consortium with two Turkish firms to produce a smaller version of the Popeye I with more advanced technology.[36] There was also ongoing discussion regarding co-production of Israeli-developed Arrow II anti-missile missiles[37] and Merkava III tanks, upgrades to Turkey's M60 main battle tanks,[38] and manufacture of an assault rifle to replace the G-3 currently used by Turkey.[39]

Other Areas of Cooperation

Despite the heavy emphasis on security ties, Turkish-Israeli relations also developed in other areas, primarily economic, in the 1990s. During Prime Minister Çiller's 1994 visit to Israel, she and Rabin agreed to pursue a free-trade agreement that would cover all sectors. Failure to reach agreement quickly was largely due to opposition from the small, influential, and crisis-ridden Israeli textile industry. After Turkey had accepted Israel's demands for a transition period for this industry, the agreement was signed in March 1996 and became effective May 1, 1997. Turkish businessmen saw this agreement as important, not only because it provided access to the Israeli market, but also as a stepping-stone to other markets, such as those in the U.S., Palestinian areas, and Jordan. A second agreement on the prevention of double taxation was signed in March 1996 and entered into force May 27, 1998. Finally, an agreement for mutual encouragement and protection of investments was signed in March 1996 and entered into force August 27, 1998. A Turkish-Israeli Business Council, established March 1, 1993, actively contributed to the flourishing of bilateral economic relations.

Trade grew rapidly. Trade volume increased approximately 600 percent between 1990 and 1998. More significantly from Ankara's perspective, Turkey has enjoyed a trade surplus with Israel every year since 1994. In 1997 exports to Israel increased 54 percent over the previous year, while imports increased 19 percent. Inexpensive imports from Turkey have led to some complaints in Israel regarding Turkish "dumping."[40]

Israeli tourists visited Turkey in increasing numbers in the early and mid-1990s, following a cooperation agreement on tourism signed in June 1992. A slight decline in Israeli tourism to Turkey was registered after Turkey banned casinos in early 1998.[41] There has been relatively little bilateral commercial investment, partly due to lack of an institutional base and a legal framework until August 1998.[42] Turkish investment opportunities in Israel are limited due to high production costs, especially in land and labor. The lure of lower production costs is likely to attract some Israeli businesses to Turkey, however. For example, in the summer of 1998 Rav-Car Industries, a manufacturer of air-conditioning units for cars and trucks, said it would close down its business in Israel and establish a joint venture plant in Turkey.[43] The Israeli government seemed especially interested in launching Turkish-Israeli joint ventures in agriculture and other sectors in the newly independent Transcaucasian and Central Asian republics. Israel's advanced agricultural technology also creates possibilities for cooperation in Turkey itself, especially in the southeast. In general, economic relations have been beneficial for Turkey. There are limits to how much these ties can improve, however. Both economies are mainly directed toward European markets, and they are not very complementary.

Domestic Implications

Turkish-Israeli alignment in the 1990s was an important factor in Turkish domestic politics. The military was the real architect of this alignment, a reflection of the increasingly prominent role the military played in foreign policy in the 1990s. But alignment with Israel created an unusual coalition in Turkey and drew support from a broad segment of the body politic. All political parties except the RP supported the growing Turkish-Israeli relationship. The support of two parties was especially significant. One was the *Demokratik Sol* (Democratic Left) Party (DSP), since its leader, Bülent Ecevit, was influential in the pro-Arab tilt of the 1970s and for years had been critical of Israel and the role the

U.S. played in the Middle East.[44] Another was the ultra-right *Milliyetçi Hareket* (Nationalist Movement) Party (MHP) of the late Alparslan Türkeş, since the ideology and discourse of this party historically contained anti-Zionist elements.[45] Finally, another possibly tacit supporter was the Fethullahçı movement, led by Islamist-nationalist religious leader Fethullah Gülen. The Fethullahçıs did not openly support Turkish-Israeli relations, but the lack of criticism in their daily newspaper and on their TV station suggested acquiescence. This broad coalition came about because many Turks felt relations with Israel were tied to issues at the very core of Turkish national survival.

Another domestic political development that had a bearing on Turkish-Israeli relations was the coming to power of the RP in June 1996 in coalition with Çiller's *Doğru Yol* (True Path) Party—the so-called "*Refahyol*" coalition that governed Turkey until June 1997. *Refahyol*'s one-year tenure was characterized by increased tensions between the government and secular groups in Turkey, especially the military. The military used Turkey's ties with Israel to remind the Islamists that their power was in fact limited. Before coming to power, the party was openly and harshly critical of Israel in general and of Turkish-Israeli ties in particular. RP officials had declared on various occasions that they would tear up the 1996 military cooperation agreement when they came to power. But the military had different plans. When asked about the issue, General Bir made it clear that the military viewed relations with Israel as a matter of state policy. "Governments are like hats; they come and go. What is permanent is the state," he said.[46]

Soon after formation of the *Refahyol* government, RP leader Necmettin Erbakan found himself in a position to test his room to maneuver with respect to Turkish-Israeli relations. The military was prepared to sign another agreement with Israel which was put on the new government's agenda. Erbakan delayed the authorization to sign until he could get more information on the reasons for the agreement. In the meantime, Israeli official David Ivry's visit was postponed. In the end, the agreement was signed after Erbakan was briefed by defense ministry officials.[47]

This style of sending a message to *Refah's* supporters by appearing reluctant to endorse official polices, yet giving in at the end, seemed to characterize the RP's approach to relations with Israel throughout its term in office. In April 1997, Erbakan delayed until the last moment before agreeing to receive visiting Israeli foreign minister David Levy and, in the presence of Levy and the media, criticized Israel for building new settlements in the occupied territories. Yet, according to Levy, the two had a friendly meeting behind closed doors.[48] The free-trade agreement with Israel was brought to parliament by the *Refahyol* government and ratified on December 23, 1996, by an overwhelming majority that included the RP's votes. RP officials declared that "mutual interests direct bilateral relations."[49] Perhaps more significantly, as signs of acceptance of Israel, RP officials visited Israel on several occasions and attended Independence Day celebrations at the Israeli embassy in Ankara.[50] Thus, the RP's coming to power did not alter the pace of relations between Turkey and Israel. This was partly because the military allowed the government little room to maneuver. But it is also safe to argue that, when in power, *Refah* began to approach the issue of Turkish-Israeli relations with pragmatism and a sense of national interest.

The experience of the government formed after the *Refahyol* coalition further reinforced the view that Turkey's Middle East policy had become a "state policy" and that change would not be allowed. The coalition headed by Mesut Yılmaz that came to power in mid-1997 aimed to introduce some flexibility into Ankara's Middle East policies. The reasons partly lay in the nature of the coalition government itself. One of the junior partners, the DSP, to which Foreign Minister İsmail Cem belonged, had long been an advocate of a "regionally focused foreign policy." Such a policy considered good relations with Turkey's immediate neighbors crucial to building a strong Turkey.

In the coalition's early months there were indeed some signs of an effort to build bridges with Turkey's Arab neighbors and with Iran. For its part, the Turkish military apparently was displeased with the government's permitting even a slight change in Ankara's regional policy, especially so the perception of a slowdown in Turkish-Israeli relations. As if to defer such criticisms, Cem visited Israel in July 1998 and told the press, "You know that certain circles in Turkey say that our relations with Israel are hindered by our efforts in searching for better relations with neighboring countries, but quite the contrary, this was declared untrue by the Israeli prime minister himself."[51] In Turkey, the locution "certain circles" is normally used to refer indirectly to the military. Meanwhile, the government's efforts to establish better relations with Syria failed, and Yılmaz's visit to Israel in October 1998 signaled the abandonment of the "good-neighbor" policy, such as it was. Asked about Syrian criticism of his visit, Yılmaz said, "Frankly, I do not care how Syria comments [on] my visit. Everyone is aware of Syria's hostile intentions toward Turkey."[52] Soon after, a crisis over Öcalan erupted with Syria.

Conclusion

Turkish-Israeli alignment not only was one of the region's most important developments in the 1990s, but also marked a significant shift in Turkish foreign policy in the Middle East. Ankara's decision to initiate and to advertise this relationship, together with the autumn

1998 Syrian crisis, signaled a departure from an earlier policy of disinterest and caution. This policy even differed from Turkey's relatively active regional involvement in the 1950s, since it seemed no longer to be only an extension of ties with the West.

In the 1990s Turkey's interests, as defined by the political and military elite, at times differed from those of its allies. Turkey's boldness was mainly a response to a fluid and unstable internal and external environment. Turkish-Israeli alignment became one of the main pillars of a new regional policy.

Although both Turkey and Israel expected considerable benefits from bilateral relations, areas of tension emerged soon enough. Israel fretted over the constant possibility of being dragged into Turkey's problems and seemed particularly wary of being seen as a party to the Greek-Turkish dispute. Greece openly declared its discontent with Turkish-Israeli ties. Another such problem was the Kurdish issue. Again Israel did not want to be seen as a party to the dispute or to become a PKK target. However, as long as its alignment with Turkey continues, it is almost impossible for Israel to dissociate itself fully from this issue. After Öcalan's capture, there were attacks on Israeli embassies in Europe for Israel's alleged role in the operation, despite Israeli denials of involvement. These difficulties from time to time spark discussion in Israel, in government and the public, about the limits of Turkish-Israeli relations.[53]

Relations with Syria are a mixed bag for both Israel and Turkey. On the one hand, both countries welcomed Damascus's perception of encirclement. For Turkey, the 1998 crisis with Syria demonstrated the benefits of this perception. However, neither Turkey nor Israel wants its relations with the other to obstruct peace prospects with Syria. In Israel the Labor Party especially seemed apprehensive about possible negative effects of Turkish-Israeli ties on the stalled Israeli-Syrian peace process. On the other hand, Israeli-Syrian peace might actually facilitate Turkish-Syrian relations, which have been gradually improving since Damascus expelled Öcalan.

From Ankara's perspective, Turkey and Israel have divergent interests in Iraq. Israel continues to prefer the status quo and would not be terribly disturbed by the division of that country. Turkey continues to call for reintegration of Iraq into the international community and sees the status quo itself as a problem.

Another potential limitation for Turkey is the Arab-Israeli peace process. Total breakdown of this process would create problems for Ankara in its ties with Israel, despite the fact that Turkish-Israeli alignment developed largely independently. Breakdown would strengthen the hand of Turkish critics of relations with Israel and make Ankara's relations with some other countries in the region more problematic.

Despite these embedded tensions, Turkish-Israeli alignment seems solidly based. The real challenge for both parties is not to turn this relationship into one that could prevent more cooperative relationships with other parties and to avoid provoking counter-alignments that would further destabilize the region.

Notes

1   Mahmut Bali Aykan, "The Palestinian Question in Turkish Foreign Policy from the 1950s to the 1990s," *International Journal of Middle Eastern Studies* 25, no. 1 (1993), p. 103; George E. Gruen, "Turkey and the Middle East after Oslo I," Robert Owen Freedman (ed.), *The Middle East and the Peace Process: The Impact of Oslo Accords* (Gainesville: University Press of Florida, 1998), p. 173; Hakan Yavuz, "Turkey's Relations with Israel," *Dış Politika* 5, nos. 3-4 (1990), pp. 48-50; Amikam Nachmani, *Israel, Turkey, and Greece: Uneasy Relations in the East Mediterranean* (London: Frank Cass, 1987); Samuel Segev, *The Iranian Triangle* (New York: Free Press 1988).

2   Duygu Bazoğlu Sezer, "Turkey's Grand Strategy Facing a Dilemma," *International Spectator* 27, no. 1 (January-March 1992); Adam Garfinkle, "U.S.-Israeli Relations after the Cold War," *Orbis* 40, no. 4 (Fall 1996).

3   Hasan Cemal, "Ortadoğu'da Türkiye . . . " (Turkey in the Middle East . . .), *Sabah*, December 5, 1997.

4   Ömer E. Kürkçüoğlu, *Türkiye'nin Arap Orta Doğusuna Karşı Politikası* (Turkey's policies toward the Arab Middle East) (Ankara, 1973).

5   Erol Manisalı, *Foreign Economic Relations of Turkey: A General Appraisal of Turkey's Economic Relations with the EEC and Other Economic Regions* (İstanbul: Güney Matbaası, 1979), pp. 7-8.

6   Ali İhsan Bağış, "Turkey's Hydropolitics of the Euphrates-Tigris Basin," *Water Resources Development* 13, no. 4 (1997), pp. 567-581; Süha Bölükbaşı, "Turkey Challenges Iraq and Syria: The Euphrates Dispute," *Journal of South Asian and Middle Eastern Studies* 16, no. 4 (1993), pp. 9-32; John F. Kolars and William Mitchell, *The Euphrates River and the Southeast Anatolia Development Project* (Carbondale: Southern Illinois University Press, 1991).

7   Robert Olson, "Turkey-Syria Relations Since the Gulf War: Kurds and Water," *Middle East Policy* 5, no. 2 (1997), pp. 169-70.

8   *Middle East International*, October 23, 1992, p. 3.

9   Olson, "Turkey-Syria Relations," pp. 170-171.

10   *Milliyet*, April 19, 1992, and May 14, 1992, cited in William Hale, "Turkey, the Middle East, and the Gulf Crisis," *International Affairs* 68, no. 4 (1994), p. 682, fn 7.

11   *Middle East Monitor* 23, no. 1 (1993), p. 3.

12   *Milliyet*, February 7, 1994.

13   *Sabah*, February 7, 1994.

14   *Hürriyet*, January 27, 1994.

15   "Çiller Meets Delegation at Orient House," *Qol Yisra'el* (Jerusalem), November 5, 1994; and "Rabin on Regret over Orient House Visit," *Qol Yisra'el*, November 6, 1994, both in Foreign Broadcast Information Service Daily Report, Near East and South Asia (FBIS-NES), November 7, 1994, p. 36.

16   Alan Makovsky, "Israeli-Turkish Relations: A Turkish 'Periphery Strategy'?" in Henri J. Barkey (ed.), *Reluctant Neighbor: Turkey's Role in the Middle East* (Washington, D.C.: United States Institute of Peace, 1996), pp. 151-152.

17 *Milliyet* and *Cumhuriyet*, September 5, 1996.
18 *Hürriyet*, September 17, 1995.
19 *Turkish Daily News (TDN)*, January 1, 1996.
20 *Hürriyet*, August 1, 1996.
21 "Turkey: Syrian Foreign Minister on Accord with Israel, PKK," SHOW TV (Istanbul), July 2, 1996, in Foreign Broadcast Information Service Daily Report, Western Europe (FBIS-WEU), 96-129, July 3, 1996, p. 38.
22 "Turkey: Menteşe Warns Syria on Massing Troops," *Yeni Günaydın*, June 19, 1996, in FBIS-WEU, 96-222, June 24, 1996.
23 Ibid.
24 Itamar Rabinovich, *The Brink of Peace: The Israeli-Syrian Negotiations* (Princeton: Princeton University Press, 1998) p. 219.
25 Atila Eralp, "Facing the Challenge: Post-Revolutionary Relations with Iran," in Barkey, *Reluctant Neighbor*, pp. 93-150; Süha Bölükbaşı, "Turkey Copes with Revolutionary Iran," *Journal of South Asian and Middle Eastern Studies* 13, nos. 1-2 (1989).
26 Anoushiravan Ehteshami and Raymond A. Hinnebusch, *Syria and Iran: Middle Powers in a Penetrated Regional System* (London: Routledge, 1997).
27 Şükrü Elekdağ, "Is the Internal Threat More Important than the External One?" *Milliyet*, May 12, 1997, p. 19.
28 *Yeni Yüzyıl*, January 6, 1998.
29 Mehmet Ali Birand, "The Turkish-Israeli Agreement from Netanyahu's Perspective," *Sabah*, May 26, 1997.
30 The unofficial text of this agreement was first published in *Aksiyon*, no. 76 (May 18-24, 1996) and in *Hürriyet* (July 14, 1996).
31 *Yeni Yüzyıl*, August 29, 1996.
32 *Yeni Yüzyıl*, May 2, 1997.
33 *Washington Post*, January 7, 1988.
34 *Washington Post*, January 5, 1998.
35 *Jane's Defense Review*, no. 2 (1998), p. 71.
36 *Middle East Dispatch*, Daily News From Israel, no. 358, May 18, 1997.
37 Metehan Demir, "Training to Destroy S-300s in Israel," *Hürriyet*, July 13, 1998.
38 *Yeni Yüzyıl*, January 28, 1997.
39 *Middle East Security Report* 1, nos. 15-16 (April 1997).
40 *Hürriyet*, March 23, 1998.
41 Information aquired from the Turkish Undersecretariat of Foreign Trade, Ankara.
42 Ibid.
43 *Ha'aretz* (English edition), June 12, 1998.
44 Gruen, "Turkey and the Middle East," p. 179.
45 *TDN*, April 13, 1996.
46 *ATV Television*, evening news, May 5, 1997.
47 *Yeni Yüzyıl*, August 1 and August 9, 1996; *Milliyet*, August 6, 1996.
48 *Yeni Yüzyıl*, April 10, 1997.
49 *Cumhuriyet*, July 2, 1996.
50 *Yeni Yüzyıl*, January 21, 1997.
51 Alparslan Esmer, "Caught in the Middle East Quandary," *Turkish Probe*, July 11, 1998.
52 *Ha'aretz* (English edition), October 14, 1998.
53 *Ha'aretz* (English edition), July 14, 1998; *Jerusalem Post* (English edition), October 22, 1998.

Şule Kut

Turkish Policy toward the Balkans

The end of the Cold War, coupled with the dissolution of the Soviet Union and the violent breakup of Yugoslavia, opened a brand new chapter in Turkey's foreign relations. Between 1989 and 1992, Turkey found itself in a totally altered, and volatile, geopolitical environment. The reliable North Atlantic Treaty Organization (NATO) ally at the margin of several regions almost instantly came to be seen as a rising regional power in Eurasia. Turkey's new position required it to face new neighbors, risks, and opportunities, and to formulate a new foreign policy.

The Balkans is one region where the change and continuity in Turkish foreign policy may be depicted with relative ease. This essay concentrates on Turkey's bilateral relations with the post-communist Balkan states after 1990 and discusses regional issues and concerns as viewed from Ankara. Although Greece is a Balkan state, this essay does not discuss Greek-Turkish relations, except in the context of Turkey's policy toward the rest of the Balkans. Greek-Turkish relations, in their fullest sense, involve a separate set of issues and are covered elsewhere in this volume.

Albania: A Natural Ally in the Balkans

When Albania, once the world's most isolated communist country, entered the ranks of the newly democratizing countries of Europe in 1990, it attached special importance to relations with Turkey. With close historical, cultural, and humanitarian ties to Albania and no outstanding bilateral disputes, Turkey also considered Albania a natural regional ally. Albanian president Ramiz Alia, who had held power since 1985, approached Turkey in 1990 for urgent political, diplomatic, and economic assistance, and Turkey did not hesitate to extend its hand. Ankara gave grants, extended credits, and provided humanitarian aid to Tirana in this difficult transition period. During the early 1990s Turkey supported Albania's bid to join European institutions; provided diplomatic, military, police, and judicial training; and hosted Albanian students at Turkish universities. Turkey thus became Albania's major ally in the region.[1]

Sali Berisha's election as Albania's first noncommunist and freely elected president in 1992 further deepened relations as bilateral cooperation became more institutionalized. Turkey and Albania continued to exchange official visits, signed agreements in virtually all fields— including a Treaty of Friendship, Good Neighborliness, and Cooperation, and a Military Training and Cooperation Agreement—and further cultivated their historical-cultural ties. Already in 1992, Greek foreign minister Andonis Samaras described Albania as part of a "Muslim belt" in the Balkans supposedly created under Turkish leadership.

However, Turkish-Albanian relations soon lost their momentum. In 1995 Greece started to alter its mistrustful, even hostile, attitude toward Tirana and to move toward a policy of rapprochement. Greek-Albanian relations improved considerably in 1996 as the two states sought to ease their bilateral problems, which ranged from concerns about Albanian illegal workers to the territory-related northern Epirus (southern Albania) question. Although Albania's strained relations with Greece were not the major determinant in Tirana's initial approach to Turkey, their improvement comforted Albania a great deal, giving ties with Turkey less urgency. This improvement took place at a time when governments in Turkey under Tansu Çiller and Necmettin Erbakan were paying less attention to the Balkans, including Albania.

Ankara-Tirana relations entered a new phase in 1997. The collapse of so-called "pyramid schemes" in Albania in early 1997 and a subsequent economic crisis threw the country into unprecedented chaos, leading to a change of government.[2] Based on the record since the fall of Albanian communism, it was expected that Turkey would rush to help the Albanians. However, during the early days of the crisis, Turkey acted as if it were a distant neighbor rather than Albania's closest ally in the region. Busy with the evacuation of Turkish citizens from Albania, Ankara was satisfied to declare its wish that law and order be restored there. It lagged behind Italy and Greece in humanitarian and financial assistance, diplomatic support, and high-level official visits. Turkey later took part in all international efforts, participated in the international force deployed to restore law and order, and continued to provide aid. Still, it was clear that Tirana was not receiving as much attention from Turkey as in the first half of the 1990s.

At the peak of the 1997 crisis, the Erbakan-Çiller coalition was busy with internal power struggles and on the verge of collapse. Furthermore, close relations established with Athens by the new socialist government in Tirana seemed to have made Ankara cautious. Although Albanian prime minister Fatos Nano continued to refer to Turkey as its most important regional ally, the Albanian leadership had already started to diversify the country's foreign relations. The Yılmaz-Ecevit government, which came to power in June 1997, gave priority to changing the Albanian misperception that Turkey was "pro-Berisha." Foreign Minister İsmail Cem's visit to Tirana in October 1997 was intended to reassure Albanian leaders that Ankara's support was directed toward Albania as a whole, not toward a particular government or leader. In this respect, Albanian prime minister Pandeli Maiko's visit to Ankara in February 1999, right after the unsuccessful Rambouillet conference between Yugoslav and Kosovo Albanian delegations, was a reassurance that Turkey's importance in the region was acknowledged by the new Albanian leaders.

The Yılmaz-Ecevit coalition (1997-99) and the Ecevit-led governments (1999-) reenergized Turkey's regional relations in a manner reminiscent of the 1990-94 period. Cem, foreign minister in the Yılmaz and Ecevit governments, repeatedly stressed that he would make the Balkans again a "top-priority area" for Turkey and asserted that Turkey attached special importance to its relations with Albania.[3] Turkish-Albanian military cooperation, the most developed dimension of bilateral relations, again picked up pace. Although the Turkish military contingent in the international force was withdrawn from Albania after a few months,[4] a smaller force remained as part of a bilateral agreement. Apart from the military training and assistance that Turkey has provided Albania, Turkish-Albanian military cooperation has also been visible in Partnership for Peace maneuvers within NATO. One potentially noteworthy example of military cooperation is that Turkey reportedly will gain access to an Albanian naval base in return for rebuilding it. The base, located at Pasa Limani on the Adriatic Sea coast, was completed in mid-2000.[5]

Three points need to be stressed here. First, Turkish-Albanian relations are fundamentally solid, despite ups and downs. This is not due only to historical and cultural affinities between these two Balkan nations. Rather, both countries' strategic concerns will likely keep them allied for a long time to come, as the 1999 Kosovo crisis suggested. Second, a new period has opened in Turkey's relations with Albania in which Ankara now has to compete with Athens for Tirana's favor. Finally, the broader "Albanian question" in the Balkans, involving Albanians living in Kosovo and Macedonia, could disturb bilateral relations in the future. The ethnic Albanian lobby in Turkey, which pays more attention to Albanians in former Yugoslav territories than to those in Albania proper, has already accused Ankara of pursuing an overly cautious policy toward the Kosovo issue. However, Turkey's stance has not so far disturbed Turkish-Albanian relations. Albanian governments themselves have been quite careful not to try to exploit diaspora Albanians. Moreover, Turkey has made it clear to its partners in the region, and to all others, that the central pillar of its foreign policy is respect for territorial integrity.

Bulgaria: A New Beginning

The regime change in Bulgaria at the end of 1989 had more significant implications for Turkey than for any other neighboring country, since it occurred during the most tense period in Bulgarian-Turkish relations for decades. Between 1984 and 1989, the Turks of Bulgaria—about 10 percent of Bulgaria's population—were subjected to a vigorous assimilation campaign by the communist regime of Todor Zhivkov. The exodus of Turks from Bulgaria reached its peak in 1989, amounting to more than 300,000 people within weeks. It is possible to argue that the "Bulgarification" campaign, which provoked a substantial international reaction against Bulgaria, in fact paved the way for the demise of the Zhivkov regime. Democratization efforts in Bulgaria radically improved Ankara's relations with Sofia, both by ameliorating relations between ethnic Bulgarians and ethnic Turks in Bulgaria and by putting in place a Bulgarian regime more amenable to good ties with Turkey.

Bulgaria is particularly important to Turkey for two reasons. It is one of Turkey's two bordering neighbors in the Balkans—Greece is the other—and the most numerous Turkish minority in the Balkans (about 800,000) lives there. Relieved by the end of the Bulgarian Turks' forced assimilation, Turkey publicly welcomed the regime change as well as the Bulgarian Socialist Party's denunciation of the "Bulgarification" campaign in 1990. In so doing, the Turkish government was literally choosing not to hold a whole nation responsible for "Zhivkov's sin."[6] Ankara readily joined Bulgarian citizens in putting all the blame on Zhivkov and his corrupt regime and declared it was ready to open a new chapter in bilateral relations. In the early 1990s the dominant bilateral issues were repatriation of refugees and their property rights. Most of the problems, including social security arrangements for the expatriates, were resolved during the course of the 1990s.

Other factors also contributed to the improvement of relations. The remarkable success, especially in the 1991 elections, of the Rights and Freedoms Movement—a Bulgarian political party composed mainly of ethnic Turks—and its role in the formation of the new government had a positive impact.[7] The sympathetic stance of president Zhelu Zhelev, Bulgaria's first post-communist president, and the relatively unbiased approach of his Union of Democratic Forces party toward Turkey also helped. The most significant step in this "honeymoon period" was the 1992 Treaty of Friendship, Good Neighborliness, Cooperation, and Security. A more-than-symbolic gesture, of course, was the withdrawal of Turkish and Bulgarian troops from their common border the same year. Ankara quickly emerged as a strong supporter of NATO membership for Bulgaria. Throughout the 1990s, Turkish businessmen showed increasing interest in investing in Bulgaria, and bilateral trade increased steadily.

Aside from the crisis over Bulgarification, Turkey and Bulgaria traditionally have had very few bilateral problems. In fact, their ties have been much smoother than either nation's relations with neighboring Greece. One of the few lingering issues of Turkish-Bulgarian contention—a longstanding border demarcation problem at the mouth of the Rezve River on the Black Sea—also was resolved in the 1990s. During Prime Minister Mesut Yılmaz's December 4, 1997, visit to Sofia, agreements were signed concerning maritime borders and delimitation of the Black Sea continental shelf.

However, Turkish-Bulgarian relations are not trouble-free. Obviously, the status and welfare of the Turkish minority will continue to be an important concern for Ankara. Turkish officials usually describe relations as "excellent," but they never forget that, only a decade ago, extreme anti-Turkish attitudes prevailed in Bulgaria. Moreover, economic relations remain underdeveloped, and certain Bulgarian political groups, most notably former communists, remain deeply suspicious of Turkey and reticent about friendship with it.

The "Ottoman legacy" itself is a major obstacle to improvement of Turkey's bilateral relations with its Balkan neighbors, including Bulgaria.[8] Drawing largely on that legacy, a large part of the Bulgarian political elite perceives Turkey as a serious threat. Despite numerous problems in their own bilateral relations, nationalists in Athens and Sofia may yet find a basis for cooperation in warding off a perceived common Turkish enemy. Since 1995, Greece has made a strong effort to build close ties with Bulgaria. Rivalry with Greece in the Balkans and the need to overcome the negative residue of the "Ottoman legacy" are always matters for consideration by Ankara when formulating longer-term policy toward Bulgaria.

Following the honeymoon of the early 1990s, Turkish-Bulgarian political and economic relations entered a relative cooling-off period from 1994 to 1997, when former communists were in power in Sofia and Turkey was enduring a series of shaky coalitions. But new governments in both countries gave mutual signals of readiness to enhance relations in 1997. Prime Minister Ivan Kostov in Sofia, who came to power following a prolonged economic and political crisis in 1996, and Yılmaz, who assumed power the following year, played an important role in giving new impetus to Turkish-Bulgarian ties. Yılmaz's two-day visit to Sofia in December 1997 produced four historic agreements and marked another turning point. The first official visit to Bulgaria by a Turkish prime minister in nineteen years, Yılmaz's visit also signaled that Turkey was once again ready to pay due attention to Bulgaria and the Balkans. Thereafter, Turkey and Bulgaria also exhibited a closer working relationship within multilateral frameworks, including the Black Sea Economic Cooperation (BSEC) project and various meetings of southeast European states, including regular trilateral summits among Turkey, Bulgaria, and Romania.

Romania: Warm Relations with a Distant Neighbor

Turkish-Romanian relations showed steady positive development after the fall of Romanian communism in 1990. The fact that Turkey and its most distant Balkan neighbor had no bilateral problems in the past was a facilitating factor. Despite lingering problems in democratization, Romania made significant efforts to move toward a market economy, and the complementarity of the Turkish and Romanian economies contributed to improved relations. Ankara viewed Romania as a significant economic partner from the very beginning of the post-Cold War era. Turkish businessmen and investors quickly grasped the market opportunities there. A steady increase in bilateral trade volume ensued after 1990, and Turkey has more enterprises in Romania than does any other foreign country.

Although Turkey and Romania were in different camps during the dissolution of Yugoslavia and the Bosnian war, Turkish-Romanian relations remained relatively problem-free. Romania is one of the four Balkan countries with which Turkey signed a Treaty of Friendship, Good Neighborliness, and Cooperation in the post-1990 period, and one of the six countries in the world from whose citizens Turkey does not require an entry visa. The "Ottoman legacy" has relatively less negative impact in Romania than elsewhere in the region, and Romania's small Turkish minority is one of the better-treated and most integrated minorities in the Balkans. Rather than causing tension, Turkey's attention to the needs of the Turkish, Gagauz (Orthodox Christian Turk), and Tatar communities in Romania is known to be welcomed by Romanian leaders. One sign of good Turkish-Romanian ties is the frequency of senior-level bilateral contacts. Presidents Süleyman Demirel and Emil Constantinescu held regular biannual meetings alternately in Bucharest and Ankara. Overall, Turkey and Romania have established a close working relationship free from the shadow of regional conflicts.

Duality in Relations with Serbia

In 1990, when its last federal parliament announced the end of socialism and called for multiparty elections, Yugoslavia had already entered into a process of dissolution. International recognition of Slovenia and Croatia on January 15, 1992, six months after these former Yugoslav republics declared independence, sealed Yugoslavia's fate. In less than three months, the bloodiest war in Europe since World War II was under way in Bosnia. Turkey had close ethnic ties and traditionally good bilateral relations with the former Yugoslavia, and its breakup had major implications. It gave birth to four new regional neighbors, and Turkey would develop close relations with three of them. The breakup also helped shape the contours of a new post-Cold War Turkish foreign policy, especially as a result of the war in Bosnia,[9] and strained Ankara's bilateral relations with Belgrade.

At first Ankara hoped that Yugoslavia would be able to maintain its territorial integrity,[10] but, once it failed to do so, Turkey had to face the new Balkan reality. On January 17, 1992, the Turkish government announced plans to recognize the four former federal republics: Croatia, Macedonia, Slovenia, and Bosnia. Five days later, Serbian president Slobodan Milosevic flew to Ankara to try to dissuade the Turkish government. However, Ankara considered the dissolution process irreversible by this time, and the government went through with its plan on February 6, 1992. Formal diplomatic relations were established on August 26. For its part, the Yugoslav government withdrew its ambassador, an ethnic Macedonian, from Ankara on January 31.

Since the breakup, Turkey's relations with the new "rump" Yugoslavia (widely identified simply as "Serbia") have followed a dual course. Ties were deeply strained by Serbia's role in the war against the Bosniacs (Bosnian Muslims) and the anti-Turkish rhetoric of its nationalist leaders, loaded with negative historical references to Turks, as in Milosevic's historic 1989 speech in Kosovo. But despite Turkey's firm and vocal stance in all international fora against Serbian aggression in Bosnia, Turkish-Yugoslav relations were not totally severed. The fact that most of Turkey's exports to Europe are transported via Yugoslav territory was an important factor. In any case, it fell mainly on Turkey to keep tension at a manageable level.

Turkey was careful not to provoke a wider division in the Balkans or to draw itself into a broader conflict. To their credit, Turkish foreign-policy-makers avoided the trap of contributing to an Orthodox-Muslim split in the Balkans. In fact, Ankara pursued a policy specifically designed not to turn Serbia, Greece's main ally in the Balkans, into Turkey's enemy.[11] Furthermore, despite anti-Serb sentiment in Turkish public opinion due to Serbian actions in Bosnia, official communiqués of the Turkish Foreign Ministry consistently tried to distinguish the Serbian people from the pro-war Serbian government, even when this proved rather difficult.

Turkey's Kosovo policy, too, contributed to preventing a total collapse of Ankara-Belgrade relations. Turkey adopted a cautious and moderate stance toward the Kosovo problem after its outbreak in 1989, and Serbian authorities were well aware of this. Although the Kosovo issue received widespread publicity in Turkey, creating strong sympathy for the Kosovo Albanians, Ankara refrained from provoking or supporting separatist tendencies in the region. Turkish governments at all international fora presented the Kosovo issue strictly as a human-rights matter and stressed the need to find a just and sustainable solution without further compromising the territorial integrity of Yugoslavia. In this context, Turkey's Kosovo policy could be seen as testimony against "neo-Ottomanism" arguments often advanced to discredit Turkey's new Balkan initiatives.

Two main considerations were behind Turkey's cautious Kosovo policy. First, territorial integrity is a sacred principle in Turkish foreign policy. Tampering with the territorial integrity of any state is, in Ankara's view, ultimately dangerous. Second, difficult relations between ethnic Albanians and ethnic Turks in Kosovo disturbed Ankara. The tiny Turkish minority was known to have concerns about the prospect of Albanian hegemony.[12]

Ankara-Belgrade diplomatic relations were kept at a low level for almost four years after the Yugoslav breakup. Both governments were ready to start normalizing relations following the Dayton Peace Accords on November 21, 1995. Six months later, Turkey and Yugoslavia upgraded relations to ambassadorial level, and official contacts were actively resumed.[13] Belgrade was aware that Turkey had joined the international reaction in response to Serbian aggression, not because of anti-Serb sentiment or because Ankara had secret designs on the Balkans.

Ankara's soft approach and speedy rapprochement with Serbia provoked some negative reaction in Turkey. Domestic critics accused Ankara of opportunism, naïveté, and betrayal. However, Ankara's decision-making regarding Serbia should be viewed in the light of the pragmatic approach that traditionally dominates Turkish foreign policy.[14] Turkey's willingness to invite the Federal Republic of Yugoslavia (FRY), along with its former republics, to join the BSEC and Yılmaz's willingness to meet with Milosevic in Crete during the November 1997 Balkan Summit demonstrated that Ankara was preparing for further normalization of bilateral relations.

Hence, the outbreak of fighting and ethnic cleansing in Kosovo in March 1998 was a blow to Ankara-Belgrade relations, which were just about to stabilize. Turkey once again found itself firmly positioned against Belgrade, this time as an active NATO member. Turkey also was among the strong supporters of the 1999 peace plan put forward by the Contact Group in Rambouillet and Paris. Yugoslavia rejected the plan, which called for Kosovar autonomy within Yugoslavia, the stationing of NATO troops in the province, and a referendum to determine its future status in three years.

Turkish officials saw the Kosovo crisis, like the Bosnian crisis, as a fatal mistake of the Serbian leadership, requiring a collective response from the international community. However, Turkey was not one of the most vocal international advocates of the Kosovar cause, as it had been for the Bosnian cause. Although Turkey took part in all the NATO operations, it did not take the lead in formulating action plans or pushing for tougher military action, as it had on behalf of the Bosnians. If one reason was Turkey's relatively cautious stance on the Kosovo issue, another was that the international community was more inclined to take tougher measures than it had been in the early stages of the Bosnian crisis.

NATO air operations against Yugoslavia started on March 24, 1999. Turkey contributed eighteen F-16s to the NATO command and a limited number of military personnel to the extraction force and the verification mission. On the humanitarian front, Ankara opened its borders to twenty thousand refugees, and the Turkish Red Crescent extended help to a like number who reached Albania and Macedonia.

Bosnia–Herzegovina: Springboard for a New Balkan Policy

The new, more assertive Turkish foreign policy of the late 1990s owes many of its characteristics—such as active involvement in international problems, a pro-interventionist stance against aggression, and extensive use of multilateral diplomacy—to the Bosnian crisis.[15] From the very beginning, the Bosnian war became the top foreign issue in Turkey and dominated Turkey's Balkan foreign policy agenda. Between 1992 and 1995, the Balkans were perceived as "Bosnia and the others" in the minds of most Turkish politicians, diplomats, bureaucrats, military officials, and ordinary citizens. Public reaction to the Bosnian crisis outstripped even the response to Bulgaria's expulsion of Turks in 1989. The Bulgarian crisis created a strong response in Turkey, but it was of a different nature and fell along more predictable lines. Its context was both Cold War and kinship, as a communist government abused ethnic Turks. Bosnia was not primarily about communism or Turkishness. Instead, it touched Turkish hearts on behalf of a non-Turkish Muslim people, reminding Turks of their Balkan past and cultivating in them a deepened Balkan identity. And, as a result of Bosnia, the vast majority of secular, democratic, and pro-Western Turks experienced a sense of betrayal by the West and began to question the concept of a lofty "Europe."

Since the Yugoslav breakup, Ankara's relations with the Bosnian government have been carried out through both bilateral and multilateral channels. Ankara recognized Bosnia-Herzegovina on February 6, 1992, just after the Bosnian parliament declared independence and three weeks before Bosnians voted by referendum in favor of independence. Once full-scale war broke out, Ankara actively involved itself in almost all diplomatic and military efforts aimed at ending it. It was simply out of the question for Ankara to turn a deaf ear to the pleas of Bosniacs who turned to Turkey for help.

Turkish policy was based on three premises. First, once Bosnia-Herzegovina became a *de facto* and then a *de jure* reality, its independence and territorial integrity had to be protected. Second, the war against Bosnia was one of aggression and, as such, had to be deterred by a resolute effort of the international community. From the beginning, Turkey maintained that an early and credible threat of force was necessary. Later, it strongly argued for the necessity of international military action. Third, the United Nations (UN) arms embargo—imposed under the pretext of impartiality—punished the victim by denying Bosnia its legitimate right of self-defense and, as such, violated the UN charter itself. In line with these premises, Turkey launched efforts to alert the international community to Bosniac suffering; advocated a credible threat of force against the Serbs and the lifting of the arms embargo on Bosnia; led the Islamic Conference Organization in its efforts to aid Bosniacs; and mediated in a low-profile manner between Bosniacs and Croats for a cease-fire in 1993 and for the creation of a Bosniac-Croat Federation in 1994.[16]

Turkey did not consider unilateral military action in Bosnia but did participate actively in every international military operation there. Turkish frigates and submarines took part in the joint NATO-Western European Union (WEU) Operation Sharp Guard (July 1992 to October 1996) staged in the Adriatic to enforce the UN arms embargo, and eighteen Turkish F-16s joined Operation Deny Flight, which has monitored and enforced a "no-fly-zone" over Bosnia-Herzegovina since 1993. In 1994 Turkey contributed a brigade to the UN Protection Forces (UNPROFOR) and later maintained its presence in the Implementation Force (IFOR) and Stabilization Force (SFOR). Turkish governmental and nongovernmental humanitarian aid to Bosnia was more than $50 million during the war.[17] An estimated 100,000 people fled from Bosnia to Turkey from 1992 to 1995, including refugees and those officially accepted as "tourists" but allowed to stay indefinitely. After the Dayton accords were signed, Turkey, in cooperation with the U.S., assumed responsibility for training the Bosniac-Croat federation army within the framework of the Train-and-Equip Program and pledged $80 million for the nation's reconstruction.[18]

Turkey played a significant role in the Bosnian crisis. Though Turkish actions did not end the war, the fighting ended only when the measures proposed much earlier by Turkey were actually taken up by the international community and, in particular, by NATO under U.S. leadership. Turkish policy ultimately was proven to be morally correct and politically justified. Yet, it was criticized at the time in various circles for various reasons. Turkey's far right claimed that Ankara did too little, while regional rivals like Greece claimed it did too much. The majority of Turks endorsed their government's approach, however. Contrary to the wish of some Turkish Islamists (and some nationalists), Ankara was in no position to intervene unilaterally.[19] The possibility of a "new Balkan war" was and still is simply a nightmare for Ankara.[20] And, notwithstanding claims that Ankara's relations with the Bosniacs demonstrated Turkey's neo-Ottoman aspirations (which were, in fact, held by some Turkish nationalists), Ankara simply never harbored such aspirations.

If Bosnia-Herzegovina had gained its independence without warfare, if its Muslims had not been subjected to ethnic cleansing and genocide, if the international community had not committed fatal mistakes,[21] and if Bosnia's legitimate government not looked upon Turkey so desperately, then Turkish-Bosnian relations would still have developed in a very friendly manner but would not necessarily have acquired the properties of a close alliance. It is important to underline that these relations developed under the shadow of war, which Turkey did not provoke, fight, or prolong. Nor did Turkey exploit the crisis in order to establish its influence over the Bosniacs. In the eyes of Turks, it was a war of aggression against the independence and territorial integrity—indeed, against the physical existence—of a whole nation.

Turkey continues to support Bosnia and remains its only reliable ally in the region. The Dayton settlement was welcomed by Ankara mainly because it ended the war, but officials in Ankara are deeply aware that it is prone to violation and that peace in Bosnia is very fragile. Hence, Turkey not only continues its financial, economic, and humanitarian assistance, trains the Federation's army, and provides institutional assistance in education, reconstruction, and the judiciary, but it also tries to strengthen the Bosniac-Croat alliance, to which it attaches great importance. Turkey views Bosniac-Croat cooperation as the only viable means to preserve Bosnian territorial integrity. Given the uneasy situation in Bosnia, Ankara strongly favors continuing the international military presence there.

Bosnia lost most of its political and diplomatic urgency for Turkey after Dayton, though Turkish officials continue to keep a close eye on the situation, which could again become volatile. The time has not yet come for developing normal bilateral relations, that is, free of the shadow of Serbian aggression. In fact, it is quite possible that a stable peace would diminish somewhat Sarajevo's enthusiasm for close coordination with Ankara.

Croatia: Test Case for Turkey's Potential as an Honest Broker

Croat leaders approached Turkey in 1991 seeking support for their prospective independence. After Turkey recognized Croatia in 1992, the two nations established a close working relationship.[22] In 1993, regular consultative meetings started between Turkey, Bosnia-Herzegovina, and Croatia upon the initiative of Turkish foreign minister Hikmet Çetin. Although Turkey was determined to establish good relations with each of the new states, ties with Zagreb and with Croats in general became critically important, mainly because of the Bosnian crisis. Turkey's potential role in the Balkans as an "honest broker" was tested and sustained by its successful mediation between Bosniacs and Croats during the Bosnian war. Ankara was instrumental both in the November 1993 Bosniac-Croat cease-fire and in the realization of the U.S.-led Washington Agreement of March 1994, which established the Bosniac-Croat federation. Between 1992 and 1997, there were thirteen high-level official visits between Ankara and Zagreb, and eighteen bilateral agreements were signed.

Zagreb remains relevant to Turkish interests in the post-Dayton period. For example, Turkey advocates NATO expansion toward the Balkans. In that context, Demirel announced during his visit to Zagreb in September 1997 that Ankara supports Croatian membership in NATO. Turkey took a neutral position when the Zagreb administration was criticized for human rights violations and for not cooperating with the International War Crimes Tribunal at the Hague. But Turkey's relations with Croatia will remain largely tied to Bosniac-Croat and Sarajevo-Zagreb relations. If the fragile peace gives way to renewed hostilities, it is very likely that Turkey again will assume the role of honest broker between these parties.

Macedonia: The Logic of Close Ties

Turkish-Macedonian relations in the 1990s became a curious matter for many. Macedonia was the most hesitant of the former Yugoslav republics regarding independence. Once it declared independence in September 1991, it developed its closest bilateral relationship in the region with Turkey. To Greece's displeasure, Turkey recognized Macedonia in February 1992 under its constitutional name, the "Macedonian Republic." In August 1992 Turkey became the first state to open an embassy in Skopje at a time when three of the new country's four bordering neighbors had not recognized it. At that point, only Bulgaria had recognized Macedonia—in fact, it was first state in the world to do so, but Sofia refused to accept the existence of a "Macedonian nation." Greece rejected the name, flag, and constitution of Macedonia—all of which it saw, for various reasons, as an implied aggression against its own territory—and made an issue of these matters through a frenzied international campaign.[23] Albania followed in Greece's footsteps for a time, albeit for different reasons. And, although Serbia withdrew the Yugoslav National Army from Macedonian territory in 1992, it did not recognize its southern neighbor until 1996.

Turkey built ties with Macedonia during that country's most troubled period. It provided financial, economic, and humanitarian assistance while Macedonia was struggling under a double embargo imposed by the UN and unilaterally by Greece. It also supported Macedonian independence in international fora. Turkey was motivated mainly by a sense that Balkan stability requires a stable Macedonia.

Ankara's unequivocal support created question marks in many minds. Athens saw it as a step toward encirclement. Albanians were irritated by Turkish support for the "Orthodox" Macedonians, who ruled an Albanian minority. However, Ankara was firm in its support and its reasoning. Ankara's policy was to establish good relations with each of the new Balkan states from the very beginning. The presence and welfare of the 77,000 Turks in Macedonia was another important consideration. Finally, it was out of the question for Turkey to turn its back on this vulnerable, distant neighbor, especially as it saw the recognition and strengthening of Macedonia as critical to regional peace and stability. Greek hostility toward Macedonia also contributed to Turkey's decision to establish close relations.

By 1995 Turkish-Macedonian relations had acquired the properties of an alliance. About thirty bilateral agreements had been signed, including a Military Training and Cooperation Agreement and a Treaty of Friendship, Good Neighborliness, and Cooperation on July 14, 1995. Turkey continued to provide financial and humanitarian assistance. Macedonia was politically and geographically central to the West-East Motorway (WEM) project—a major highway envisioned to connect Durres (Albania) with Skopje, Sofia, and Istanbul—which Ankara promoted with high expectations. However, economic relations failed to match the level of political relations. Turks remained behind others in investment in and trade with Macedonia. Small and poor, Macedonia was not very attractive for Turkish businessmen, and Ankara apparently did not care to offer them incentives.[24]

After 1995, Macedonia's relations with its neighbors improved, but Turkish interest had already ebbed—not because of Greek-Macedonian rapprochement but because of an overall loss of interest in the Balkan region by Turkish governments. Greece recognized Macedonia as the "Former Yugoslav Republic of Macedonia" (FYROM) and lifted a sixteen-month embargo in September 1995. Yugoslavia recognized Macedonia under its constitutional name on April 8, 1996. Albania had already recognized it as "FYROM" in 1994 and was trying to normalize relations with Skopje despite the Albanian minority problem in Macedonia. Meanwhile, Ankara took no new initiatives and left the WEM project unimplemented, and overall Turkish-Macedonian relations entered a relatively low-key period.

After the fall of the pro-Islamist Erbakan government in 1997, Ankara's relations with Skopje were reenergized. The first of a series of official visits to Balkan countries from October to December was Cem's visit to Skopje on October 27, also the first high-level Turkish visit to Macedonia in more than two-and-a-half years. Yılmaz and Demirel followed suit, each visiting Macedonia twice thereafter.

The exodus of nearly 200,000 Kosovars into Macedonia in April 1999 deepened Turkey's interest in Skopje. When the human flood seemingly threatened Macedonian stability, Turkey offered to take as many as 20,000 refugees from Macedonia and Albania. It did so not only for humanitarian reasons but also to relieve some of the pressure on these two fragile states.

Turkish-Macedonian relations are not free of concerns. Both the charismatic Macedonian president Kiro Gligorov and the Social Democratic Alliance (SDA) that ruled the country in different coalitions from 1992 to 1998 were eager to develop close relations with Turkey. There was some doubt in Ankara whether a new Skopje government would follow the SDA's path. However, the Macedonian nationalists who took power in 1998 formed a coalition government with the nationalist Albanian party, proving they were more pragmatic than had been expected. Thus, bilateral relations continued without significant change.

Another bilateral issue that causes concern in Turkey is the Turkish minority in Macedonia. Although they are much better off than their kin in some neighboring countries, they still face problems, and their situation could worsen if Macedonia is destabilized. Finally, if an Albanian-Macedonian conflict erupts, Turkey will find itself in a very difficult position. Turkey's only option would be to act as an honest broker. Mediation would benefit both sides, but it would be a more difficult task for Turkey than the one it accomplished in Bosnia, because, in this case, Albania and Macedonia each consider Turkey its most reliable ally.

Slovenia: Distant Neighbor, Distant Relations

Turkey established diplomatic relations with Slovenia in August 1992 and opened an embassy in Ljubljana in 1993. Ankara's relations with Slovenia have been its least developed among all the Balkan states. Slovenia adopted a calculated policy of shedding its Yugoslav past and Balkan heritage. Slovenia and Turkey are also competitors for EU membership. Nevertheless, as demonstrated during reciprocal presidential visits in 1997 and 1998, the two parties attach importance to their relations. Slovenia also seeks Turkey's support for its bid to join NATO. For Turkey, Slovenia's significance is that it is a transit point for most of Turkey's exports to Europe.

Conclusion

All of Turkey's Balkan neighbors except Greece were communist states for about half a century. The end of the Cold War was a genuine turning point in Turkey's bilateral relations with each of these states and resulted in general upgrading of the Balkans in Turkish foreign policy priorities. This was true even before the breakup of Yugoslavia. That development, however, created an unprecedented Balkan reality for Turkey. With the onset of the Bosnian war, the Balkans became not only a top priority but also one of the regions—others were the Caucasus and Central Asia—where the contours of a new, more activist Turkish foreign policy took shape. Turkey chose to act in concert with the international community during the various Balkan crises. It also initiated and became active in various regional multilateral cooperation efforts.

During the Bosnian war, some Balkan leaders claimed that Turkey, "the heir of the Ottoman Empire," should stay out of Balkan affairs. But Turkey, too, is a Balkan country with strategic interests in the Balkans. National interests require it to be active in the region to contain elements of instability in the land mass that connects Anatolia with Western Europe. In any case, Turkey could not be expected to act as if it had no interests in or ties with the region. While pursuing its own interests, Turkey played the role of a mature, rational, and unbiased regional power. It deserves credit for what it has not done as well as for what it has. Given its foreign policy traditions and its performance in the 1990s, it may safely be argued that Turkey will continue to avoid any tempting, irresponsible moves that would undermine regional stability.

Ankara was careful not to follow an ethno-religious policy in the Balkans. However, the fact that its people have close historical, cultural, and religious affinities with Bosniacs, Albanians, and of course Balkan Turkish minorities, is a reality one cannot change. It stems from a common history of nearly six centuries. Turks settled in the Balkans in the early fourteenth century, and, to a great extent, Turkey is still a Balkan country; by far, the largest city in the Balkan peninsula is Istanbul. The notion that Turkey is creating a "Muslim belt" is clearly false in view of its close relations with Orthodox-majority countries—Bulgaria, Romania, and Macedonia—and with Catholic-majority Croatia. Often overlooked are Turkey's respectful relations with Serbia, its cautious policy toward Kosovo, its avoidance of playing one Balkan state against another, and its abstention from encouraging Turkish minorities to cause problems for their governments. It is also significant, in this context, that Turkey had no major disputes with any of the formerly communist Balkan states once they shed communism and that each one initiated contact with Turkey.

Turkey's Balkan policy is a regional policy, consistent in concept, rather than a simple sum of bilateral relations. The overall concept remained in place throughout all of Turkey's government changes in the 1990s. Despite a generalized diminishing of interest in the Balkans as Ankara focused on its own political instability between 1995 and 1997, no Turkish government sought to change basic policy toward any single state in the region. However, it is often forgotten in Ankara that relations with Balkan neighbors are subject to the effects of changes in government and political leadership in those states. Hence, there is a real need for a long-term policy that considers possible power alterations. Bilateral relations must be cultivated at the leadership level whenever possible but should transcend personalities.

A major problem in Turkish-Balkan ties is over-cautiousness on the part of Turkish policy-makers. Turkish diplomats, influenced by others' concerns about the Ottoman legacy, often are so careful not to irritate their Balkan neighbors that they shy away from bold projects. When calibrating its policies and actions, Turkey must consider the sentiments and responsiveness of the other side; however, this cannot justify inaction at critical times, usually explained as "bureaucratic problems," when Turkey delays a credit or fails to follow through on an announced project.

Turkey's Balkan policy cannot be considered successful unless the WEM is completed, economic relations flourish, and Ankara keeps all its promises to its neighbors. To achieve these objectives, Ankara needs support. It is certainly to the benefit of the U.S. and others in the West that Ankara further develop relations with the Balkan states for the sake of regional stability. The U.S., Turkey's main ally, should support Turkish initiatives and pay attention to Ankara's concerns, as it has with the newly established Balkan Multinational Peace Force.

Turkey is a factor for stability in the often troubled Balkans. As manifested in the 1990s, Turkey has the political will and capability to contribute greatly to regional security. At the beginning of the twenty-first century, it seems likely that Turkey will continue contributing to the security, welfare, and stability of the Balkans, not only through its role in peacekeeping operations and regional cooperation schemes, but also through responsible and mature regional policies.

Notes

1   Misha Glenny, "Heading Off War in Southern Balkans," *Foreign Affairs* 74, no. 3 (May-June 1995).
2   Paul Kubicek, "Albania's Collapse and Reconstruction," *Perceptions* 3, no. 1 (March-May 1998), pp. 117-133.
3   Turkish foreign minister İsmail Cem, interview by the author in Ankara, October 17, 1997.

4   Turkish chief of general staff Hüseyin Kıvrıkoğlu, interview, *Defence and Aerospace*, June 1998, p. 16.

5   "Turkey Set to Rebuild Albanian Naval Base," *Jane's Defence Weekly*, September 2, 1998; "Turkish Base in Adriatic," *Hürriyet*, May 13, 2000. In 1995 Bülent Ecevit suggested that Turkey should have a military base in Albania. See Serhat Güvenç, "TSK'nın Sınırötesi Girişim Yetenekleri: Ulusal Güvenlik Politikasında Yeni Boyut" (The TAF's [Turkish Armed Forces's] capacity for cross-border initiative: a new dimension in national security policy) in Gencer Özcan and Şule Kut (eds.), *En Uzun Onyıl: Türkiye'nin Ulusal Güvenlik ve Dış Politika Gündeminde Doksanlı Yıllar* (The longest decade: the 1990s on Turkey's national security and foreign policy agenda), (İstanbul: Boyut Kitapları, 1998), p. 166.

6   Ahmet Kurtcebe Alptemoçin, Budget Speech of the Minister of Foreign Affairs, Ankara, November 10, 1990, pp. 20-21.

7   D. Bates, " The Ethnic Turks and the Bulgarian Elections of 1991," *Turkish Review of Balkan Studies Annual* 1 (1993), pp. 193-203; Nurcan Özgür, *Etnik Sorunların Çözümünde Etnik Paktı: Hak ve Özgürlükler* (The ethnic pact in the solution of ethnic problems: rights and freedoms) (Istanbul: Der Yayınları, 1999).

8   Maria N. Todorova, "The Ottoman Legacy in the Balkans," in Kemal Saybaşılı and Güney Özdoğan (eds.), *Balkans: A Mirror of the International Order* (İstanbul: Eren, 1995), pp. 55-74.

9   Şule Kut, "Turkish Diplomatic Initiatives for Bosnia-Herzegovina," in Saybaşılı and Özdoğan (eds.), *Balkans*, pp. 295-315; Duygu Bazoğlu Sezer, "Implications for Turkey's Relations with Western Europe," in *The Implications of the Yugoslav Crisis for Western Europe's Foreign Relations*, WEU Chaillot Papers no. 17 (Paris: Institute for Security Studies, October 1994), pp. 65-81; İsmail Soysal and Şule Kut, *Dağılan Yugoslavya ve Bosna-Hersek Sorunu: Olaylar-Belgeler 1990-1996* (Fragmentation of Yugoslavia and the problem of Bosnia-Herzegovina: developments and documents, 1990-1996) (İstanbul: ISIS, 1997).

10   "Turkey and the New World Order," transcript of news conference given by Prime Minister Süleyman Demirel, Ankara, December 11, 1991, p. 12.

11   Şule Kut, "Yeni Balkan Savaşı ve Makedonya'nin Sonu Senaryoları" (The new Balkan war and scenarios about Macedonia's end), *Türkiye Günlüğü*, no. 34 (1995), pp. 5-10.

12   Arslan Tekin, *Balkan Volkanı* (The Balkan volcano) (İstanbul: Ötüken, 1993).

13   It is important to note that Turkey continued to recognize the rump Yugoslavia as "the Federal Republic of Yugoslavia (FRY)." However, in a peculiar manner, it also presently considers FRY as "one of the successor states" of former Yugoslavia and not as the continuing state itself. Hence, the status of bilateral agreements between Turkey and the former Yugoslavia is ambiguous.

14   Sezer, "Implications," pp. 73-74.

15   Kut, "Turkish Diplomatic Initiatives," pp. 295-315.

16   Ibid.

17   Dış Ekonomik İlişkiler Genel Müdürlüğü (Foreign Economic Relations General Directorate), *Türkiye'nin İkili Dış Yardımları (1992-1996)* (Turkey's bilateral aid [1992-1996]), March 1998.

18   Soysal and Kut, *Dağılan Yugoslavya*.

19   Sezer, "Implications," pp. 75-77.

20 Kut, "Yeni Balkan," pp. 5-10.

21 *Unfinished Peace: Report of the International Commission on the Balkans* (Washington, D.C.: Carnegie Endowment for Peace, 1996), pp. 68-74.

22 Yüksel Söylemez, "An Overview of Turkish-Croat Relations," *Turkish Review of Balkan Studies Annual* 3 (1996-1997), pp. 99-113; Miomir Zuzul, "Croatia and Turkey: Toward a Durable Peace in Southeastern Europe," *Perceptions* 3, no. 3 (September-November 1998), pp. 82-88.

23 Şule Kut, "Makedonya-Yunanistan Anlaşmazlığının Boyutları" (The dimensions of the disagreement between Macedonia and Greece) in Gencer Özcan and Kemâli Saybaşılı (eds.), *Yeni Balkanlar, Eski Sorunlar* (New Balkans, old problems) (İstanbul: Bağlam, 1997), pp. 287-311.

24 Şule Kut, "Turkey in the Post-Communist Balkans: Between Activism and Self-Restraint," *Turkish Review of Balkan Studies Annual* 3 (1996-1997), pp. 39-45.

Duygu Bazoğlu Sezer

Turkish–Russian Relations: From Adversity to 'Virtual Rapprochement'

Turkish-Russian relations in the post-Soviet era are marked by a fundamental contradiction. While competition for regional influence in the new Eurasia defines the essence of the two countries' political relations—creating a powerful force for discord and mistrust—extensive economic relations lock Turkey and Russia into one of the most impressive bilateral partnerships in this vast region.

Thus a paradoxical new dynamic has arisen in post-Soviet Eurasia. On one hand, rivalry and mistrust between Turkey and Russia constitute a potential source of instability. On the other, unprecedented growth in economic ties has created considerable Turkish-Russian interdependence, and the determination of both sides to expand those ties offers an enormous opportunity for achieving mutual trust. Turkish-Russian relations at the beginning of the twenty-first century thus should be defined as "virtual rapprochement": neither adversity nor friendship, but a mixture of the two that both sides find challenging to manage.

The circumstances of the still emerging post–Cold War world order have had adverse reverberations on Turkish-Russian relations. The striking feature of this new order is the fact that the United States, Turkey's core ally, remains the sole superpower. Even when Washington's "Russia first" policy seemed in full swing and U.S.-Russian cooperation essentially remained on course in the early 1990s, Russians felt uncomfortable about the strategic implications of Turkey's alliance, within the North Atlantic Treaty Organization (NATO), with the U.S. superpower. NATO's eastward enlargement and its initiation of Partnership for Peace (PfP)—a program to increase security cooperation between NATO and non-NATO European states, particularly former Warsaw Pact and Soviet states—added a greater sense of urgency to Moscow's desire to secure its southern borders. As U.S. interest in Central Asia and the southern Caucasus became more explicit in the mid-1990s, Russia watched U.S.-Turkish cooperation grow in regions it considered to be part of its own backyard.

Regional conflicts and instabilities are another prominent feature of the new order, and some of the most acute are in the Balkans, the southern

Caucasus, and the Middle East, where both Russia and Turkey perceive important and often clashing political, economic, and cultural interests.

In the two major post–Cold War crises in the former Yugoslavia, in Bosnia from 1992 to 1995 and in Kosovo from 1998 to 1999, Russia sided with Belgrade and Turkey sided with Bosnian Muslims and Kosovars, actively supporting NATO's punitive actions against the Serbs.

Friendship between Greeks, Greek Cypriots, and Russians also blossomed in the 1990s, creating in Ankara the impression of an evolving anti-Turkish entente. One of the more ominous manifestations of Russia's revived strategic interest in the eastern Mediterranean was the sale to Greek Cyprus of S-300 air-defense systems, deployment of which was eventually canceled as a result of Western pressure. Greece and Russia coordinated their pro-Serbian positions during the Bosnian war, and their respective attitudes toward the Kosovo crisis and the NATO operation in Kosovo had much in common, even though Greece is a NATO member.

In the southern Caucasus, Russia sides with Armenia, Turkey with Azerbaijan. In the Middle East, Russian-Israeli relations remain underdeveloped while Turkish-Israeli relations have acquired unprecedented intimacy. On the question of Iraq, both Ankara and Moscow support preservation of Iraqi territorial integrity and are skeptical about long-term U.S. intentions concerning northern Iraq. At the same time, the Turkish military's large-scale operations in northern Iraq against the Kurdistan Workers Party (known by its Kurdish initials, PKK) have irked the Russians.[1]

In short, bilateral tensions and those emanating from regional dynamics have merged, driving each country toward opposing regional groupings of states. A virtual political axis seems to be growing between Moscow, Athens, Nicosia, Yerevan, and Tehran, on one hand, and between Ankara, Baku, and Tel Aviv, on the other.[2] The Greek-Turkish rapprochement that flowered in late 1999, if it proves durable, may stymie this trend. Meanwhile, historical perceptions and memories of past conflict further poison Turkish-Russian relations.

Setting the Stage: Prudence in the Shadow of Mistrust

Turkish-Russian relations in the 1990s survived numerous crises and sources of tension, including:

- The 1992-93 Armenian-Azerbaijani war over Nagorno-Karabakh, which resulted in Armenia's occupation of about 20 percent of Azerbaijani territory.
- Turkey's unilateral imposition of new traffic regulations in 1994 concerning the transit of foreign vessels through the Turkish Straits.

- The 1994-96 Russo-Chechen war, which provoked Russian allegations of Turkish complicity in support of Grozny.
- Deployment of Russian military equipment in the northern Caucasus in excess of limits set by the 1990 treaty on Conventional Armed Forces in Europe (CFE).
- Violations of Iraqi sovereignty by the Turkish armed forces during incursions into northern Iraq designed to deprive the PKK of sanctuary.
- The Russian Duma's appeal to President Boris Yeltsin in November 1998 to grant political asylum to Abdullah Öcalan, the PKK leader who had fled to Russia following his expulsion from Syria the previous month. Tensions over the Öcalan affair resumed when he again briefly hid in Russia in January 1999.
- The hijacking of the Black Sea ferry *Avrasya* in January 1996.[3]
- Russia's sale of S-300 air-defense systems to the Greek Cypriot government in Nicosia, deployment of which would have radically changed the eastern Mediterranean military balance.

As this list suggests, causes of tension went beyond the strict confines of bilateral relations, interacting with regional and international developments. In fact, only one major area of disagreement could truly be considered strictly bilateral: mutual allegations of support to separatist movements in one another's country.

Some areas of tension were managed diplomatically through regular consultations between the two foreign ministries; others were allowed to bide their time. Even so, underlying causes of tension persisted. During the Öcalan crisis, Moscow and Ankara kept lines of communication open and acted with restraint despite strong domestic pressures to take a hard line. Diplomacy helped defuse the tension, but neither side emerged confident that the other was firmly committed to its neighbor's territorial integrity. A similar dynamic prevailed with regard to the entire range of tensions throughout the 1990s.

Another important factor was Turkish reticence. Although seemingly poised to assume wide regional responsibilities in the early 1990s, Ankara was aware it lacked the means to confront Russia alone in a regional conflict. As one Russian analyst wrote about those early post-Soviet years, "Ankara's understanding that Russia, even when immersed in crisis and deprived of the former union republics' resources and support, is still a great power makes the Turkish government behave extremely circumspectly."[4]

The Turkish-Russian Friendship Treaty, 1992

Despite rough sailing, the two countries engaged in diplomacy carefully steered to set bilateral relations on a generally steady course. As

early as March 1992 they endorsed an elaborate set of principles intended to anchor those relations in friendship, mutual confidence, and
cooperation. A treaty embodying those principles was signed May 25,
1992, by Yeltsin and Prime Minister Süleyman Demirel during the
latter's visit to Moscow, the last leg of a journey that had taken Demirel
also to Azerbaijan and the four Turkic republics in Central Asia.

Just before Demirel's visit, the outlook for Turkish-Russian relations seemed gloomy as a result of spring 1992 developments in the
southern Caucasus. An Armenian offensive in April against
Nakhichevan, an Azerbaijani enclave on the border with Turkey and
Iran, led to speculation that Turkey would intervene on Azerbaijan's
behalf. Turkish president Turgut Özal, political opponents of the
Demirel government, and Azerbaijani leaders called attention to the
1921 Treaty of Kars, which designates Turkey a guarantor of
Nakhichevan's territorial integrity. In response came a stern warning
from Marshal Yevgenii Shaposhnikov, commander of the Commonwealth of Independent States (CIS) forces: "We may find ourselves on
the verge of a third world war."[5]

In Moscow, Demirel assured Yeltsin that Turkey would not intervene in the Armenian-Azerbaijani war. In return he sought assurances
that Moscow would not recognize the land corridor established by Armenian troops between Armenia and Nagorno-Karabakh. Reportedly,
Demirel also tried to assure Yeltsin that Turkey's diplomatic and trade
push into the southern Caucasus and Central Asian states was not aimed
at undermining Russian influence.[6]

The treaty of friendship, the visit's crowning achievement, covered
cooperation in all spheres, including political-military issues. Each side
pledged to eschew force or the threat of force in bilateral relations and
to prevent its territory from being used for aggression, subversion, or
separatist actions against the other.[7]

The 1992 agreement forms the fundamental basis of Turkish-
Russian relations in the post-Soviet era. Adherence to its principles are
of critical importance if Ankara and Moscow are to achieve mutual trust
and cooperation.

Chernomyrdin Visits Turkey, 1997

The next high point in Turkish-Russian relations was reached when
Prime Minister Viktor Chernomyrdin paid an official visit to Turkey
on December 16 and 17, 1997, the first in twenty-five years by a Russian
or Soviet head of government. The major focus of the trip was economic.
Chernomyrdin came to Turkey primarily, if not exclusively, to put
Russia's signature on a natural gas deal, known as "Blue Stream," which
would bring Russian gas to Turkey through an underwater pipeline in
the Black Sea. He was accompanied by a powerful delegation that in-

cluded five ministers, three deputy ministers, and general managers of Russia's major state and private industries and banks.[8]

Both sides attached great importance to the visit. Chernomyrdin said Russia and Turkey would be "strategic partners in the economic field in the twenty-first century."[9] He asserted that "the closeness of both our approaches to a number of practical issues . . . gives one confidence that relations between our countries will acquire a new, solid impetus."[10]

Prime Minister Mesut Yılmaz of Turkey also struck an optimistic note. Arguing that it is natural for the two countries to differ on certain issues, he said he believed that

> it is possible . . . to find rational solutions to all these issues through mutual respect, trust, and dialogue. . . . The historical dimension of our bilateral relations, our countries' loyalty to democracy, and the importance they attach to regional and international peace will create a further rapprochement between Turkey and Russia, which are already geographically united.[11]

The Chernomyrdin visit created much excitement in Turkey. It came in the throes of the European Union's (EU) Luxembourg summit decision on December 12, which had seemingly closed the door to Turkey's prospects for full EU membership. Frustrated, the Turks began to consider new foreign policy directions. Russia, some Turks claimed, could be one such alternative. Yet, as it turned out, the visit was not the harbinger of a genuine spring thaw. Its enormous commercial significance was insufficient to surmount mutual suspicions or to forge a feeling of shared strategic interests, especially regarding the southern Caucasus and Central Asia.

Defining Dynamics in Turkish–Russian Relations

Mutual trust thus has been an elusive element in Turkish-Russian relations in the 1990s. Three fundamental obstacles have stood in the way: the negative influence of collective historical memory, clashing worldviews and national interests in Eurasia, and change in the relative "correlation of forces" between Russia and Turkey.

The Negative Role of Collective Memory

Present generations in Turkey and Russia have not quite forgotten the course of their shared history. When suddenly faced with dramatic changes and challenges, decision-makers and publics in each country have found it convenient to recall historical images and national stereotypes to give meaning to each other's behavior. History reminds present Turkish and Russian generations that their respective imperial ancestors were bitter enemies for centuries[12] and that the two nations then faced each other as Cold War adversaries for more than forty years.

This history generally has conditioned Turks reflexively to think of Russia as the country most dangerous to their national security. In the eyes of generations of Turks, czarist Russia—by waging war and championing Christian Orthodoxy and Slavic nationalism in the Balkans—was the most important external cause of Ottoman territorial loss in nineteenth-century and early twentieth-century eastern Europe. Most Turks are familiar with Nicholas I's admonition to England to carve up "the sick man of Europe" so that Russia could occupy the Straits.[13] Some historians have even suggested that Russia undertook its advance into Central Asia only in order to weaken the Ottoman Empire, a detour on the planned czarist road to the coveted Constantinople and Turkish Straits.[14]

Turkey's image of Russia as enemy was moderated to an important degree during the early years of the Soviet Union and the Turkish Republic. Lenin was the first Russian leader in centuries who firmly agreed to respect the Russian-Turkish territorial status quo. He also extended generous support to the Turkish war of independence. However, bilateral relations could not withstand pressures generated by World War II. Stalin's demands in 1945 and 1946 for joint control of the Straits and territorial concessions in eastern Turkey ended the rapprochement. Having regained power and prestige, Soviet Russia once again set out on an expansionist course in the direction of "warm waters." In response, Ankara found security in a full-fledged alliance with the West.

Moscow perceived the very presence of a Turkish-Muslim state directly to the south as a potential threat to the integrity of a multinational empire whose Turkic-Muslim population was its second largest ethnic element (after Slavs). Russia has viewed pan-Turkism—broadly defined as the advocacy of unifying all Turkic peoples under one state—as a clear and present danger since the early twentieth century.[15] The exertions of Enver Pasha (war minister in the Ottoman cabinet that declared war on the Allies in World War I) on behalf of Turkistan's Basmachi anti-Soviet liberation movement in 1921-22 perhaps defined in Russian eyes Turks' commitment to pan-Turkism.

Moscow in 1991-92 feared that religious and ethnic nationalist "contagion" from the former Soviet republics might spread into the Russian Federation's own multi-ethnic and multi-religious population, threatening its political and territorial integrity.[16] Tatarstan was already seeking to negotiate terms of independence. Chechnya unilaterally declared independence in 1991. It is not difficult to understand how the assertive rhetoric of Turkish leaders in Ankara at that time could conjure up the image of a pan-Turkist Turkey pointing its arrows north toward

Russia's Tatars, Bashkirs, Balkars, and everybody else with Turkic or Muslim identity. At the time Turkey was feeling strongest, Russia felt its weakest.

The problematic legacy of Turkish-Russian history has at least two important implications. It has the potential to prejudge and stifle Turkish-Russian relations on issues of strictly contemporary concern. It also has the potential to push the two countries apart in their approach to regional issues. Current Russian policies of sympathy for Serbia and Armenia and Turkish policies of sympathy for Bosnian Muslims, Kosovo Albanians, and Azerbaijan are partly driven by the strength of historical ties.

Clashing Worldviews and National Interests in Eurasia

Turkish and Russian approaches to maximizing their respective interests, particularly in Central Asia and the southern Caucasus, basically conflict. From Moscow's perspective, Central Asia and the southern Caucasus historically formed part of what it calls its "near abroad." In 1993 Russia proposed that it be recognized by the international community as the sole guarantor of security in the former Soviet Union, a policy one analyst dubbed "the Russian Monrovsky Doctrine."[17] Without granting such a mandate, the international community nevertheless has not objected to the near monopoly Russia enjoys as a peacekeeper in the former Soviet space.

The Turkish perspective is entirely different. Turks start with the premise that the former Soviet Union's newly independent states (NIS) joined the international community as sovereign and equal members. They reason that, as independent states, Turkey and the NIS have every right to cultivate a broad range of relations so long as they are peaceful. The Turkish policy response to the new Eurasian geopolitical map was brisk. President Özal and Prime Minister Demirel, who fiercely disagreed on almost everything else, quickly moved to embrace Azerbaijan and the new Turkic states with the aim of weaving an extensive network of political, cultural, and economic relations. This fundamental incongruence of perspectives has shaped Turkish-Russian relations since 1991.

Synergy between two profoundly important assessments lay at the foundation of the Turkish decision to embark on a policy of turning "to the East" in the early 1990s. First, Turkey had achieved a substantial sense of security with regard to Russia for the first time in roughly three centuries. Serious reservations persisted in the early 1990s among Turkish security officials concerning Russia's residual military muscle and long-term intentions, but Turks in general felt that, for the time being, Russia no longer posed an existential threat to Turkey. Second, Turks concluded that the disintegration of the Russian/Soviet empire released them from the political and security inhibitions that had long separated them from their land of origin of a millennium ago: Central Asia. Turkey was encouraged in its new eastward drive by the West in general and the United States in particular. The United States generally viewed Turkey as its favorite in the late-twentieth-century "great game" with Russia and Iran.[18]

Russian suspicions of Turkish intentions. It is important to note that Turkish leaders did not entirely overlook Moscow's sensitivities, as George Harris, a seasoned Turkey analyst, explains:

> As the transition accelerated . . . in the latter half of 1991, the Turks focused their attention more and more on the individual Turkic components of the USSR. Yet to the end, the Ankara government took extreme care not to appear to be working around Moscow, but rather appealed for understanding by the Soviet leadership that popular pressure in Turkey gave no option but to emphasize direct ties. Ankara thus reacted cautiously to the initial declarations of independence. . . . As late as November 5, 1991, the Turkish government said 'it would do everything possible to boost relations with the Soviet Union, but called on Moscow to show understanding for Ankara's decision to recognize the recently declared independence of Azerbaijan.'[19]

In this spirit, Demirel used his May 1992 visit to Moscow to reassure Yeltsin that Turkish engagement in the former Soviet south was not intended to damage Russian interests.[20] Tansu Çiller—who chose Moscow as the destination of her first foreign visit as prime minister—stated on September 23, 1993, that Russia and Turkey viewed the world from "practically the same" position. According to her, Russian-Turkish relations were entering a new stage based on mutually beneficial cooperation rather than competition.[21]

Russians nevertheless remained suspicious of Turkish intentions, especially in the Caucasus, which, according to presidential adviser Sergei A. Karaganov, is "Russia's backyard. Nobody can play in this field without Russia's consent."[22] Many Russians believe Turkey, seeking disintegration of the Russian Federation itself, promotes Chechen-style separatism and pan-Caucasian projects throughout the region.

There are some objective reasons for Russian apprehension. While Turkey's relations with the Central Asian Turkic republics generally traced a lackluster path after an initial, but short-lived, burst of activity, relations with Azerbaijan and Georgia progressively blossomed in the late 1990s. Presidents Haydar Aliyev of Azerbaijan and Eduard Shevardnadze of Georgia publicly professed friendship for Turkey and sought intensified cooperation almost across the board. At the opening of a Turkish television channel in Baku on September 29, 1998, Aliyev praised Turkey as Azerbaijan's closest friend and supporter.[23]

The choice of pipeline routes for transporting Caspian Sea oil to Western markets is the basis of one important interest shared by Azerbaijan, Georgia, and Turkey. The three countries agreed in principle that a pipeline between Baku (Azerbaijan) and Ceyhan on Turkey's Mediterranean coast, and traversing Georgia, should become the main export pipeline for Azerbaijani Caspian oil. But more significantly, perhaps, Baku and Tbilisi have come to view Turkey as their main security partner in the region. At a trilateral meeting on April 27, 1998, at the opening of the Deriner Dam near the Turkish-Georgian border, Demirel, Shevardnadze, and Aliyev not only endorsed the Baku-Ceyhan pipeline but expressed a common desire to develop a "strategic partnership" for the security of the Caucasus.[24]

In 1998 Vafa Guluzade, foreign policy adviser to Aliyev, and General Safar Abiyev, the Azerbaijani minister of defense, advocated the hosting of Turkish, U.S., or NATO military bases in Azerbaijan to counter Russia's reinforcement of its bases in Armenia.[25] Arguing that the main target of Russian-Armenian strategic relations is not Azerbaijan but Turkey, Guluzade maintained that the Armenian-Azerbaijani conflict is "the latest action in the old Russian-Turkish confrontation."[26] Abiyev paid an official visit to Ankara in February 1999 "to look into the possibility of concluding a military alliance ... similar to the Russian-Armenian treaty."[27]

Georgia signed its first defense cooperation agreement with Turkey in June 1997, whereby Ankara provides training for Georgian officers. More agreements were signed in Tbilisi in early March 1999 during a visit by several senior Turkish military officials. One provided for Turkish financial and technical aid to the Georgian armed forces over a five-year period, including training for Georgian military personnel in Turkey.[28] In 1998 Ankara allocated $5.5 million to Tbilisi for defense purposes. Meanwhile, Turkey now outranks Russia as Georgia's major trade partner.

Turkish perceptions: A mirror image. The initial Turkish reading of Russian attitudes and policies toward the southern NIS roughly mirrored Russian thinking about Turkey. The Turks believed that Russia's heart was not reconciled to loss of empire. They watched Russian and Slavic nationalism fill the ideological vacuum left by the collapse of communism. Turks' skepticism about the irreversibility of Russia's geopolitical retreat and about its transition to democracy and capitalism were fanned partly by the success of ultra-nationalist Vladimir Zhirinovsky's Liberal Democrats and Gennady Zyuganov's Communists in Russian elections. Russia's attitudes and policies, most starkly in the southern Caucasus, were interpreted as evidence of deeper intentions to revive its empire.[29] In a major speech before the Turkish Grand National Assembly (parliament) on September 1, 1993, Demirel (who had become president in May after serving as prime minister for eighteen months) asked, "Is the Russian Federation uneasy about the breakup of the Soviet empire? Are local conflicts there going to be pre-texts for the reconstruction of the empire? To what degree is Russia behind these conflicts?"[30]

Since that time, Turkish concerns have eased somewhat, thanks to the demonstrated inability of Russia's neo-imperialists to reconstitute the empire. On the other hand, "near abroad" instabilities—in the Caucasus, in particular—remain potential flash-points in Turkish-Russian relations.[31] The Armenian-Azerbaijani conflict is perhaps the most critical. Russia sees itself as guarantor of Armenia's security—a relationship formally rooted in the Russian-initiated CIS security treaty signed in Tashkent in 1992. A newer treaty of assistance provides Russia with a long-term military base and is extremely close to an outright military alliance against Azerbaijan.[32] Moscow has announced plans to modernize Armenia's air defense system by deploying S-300 missiles. Meanwhile, it is conceivable that Turkey would be willing to risk important interests in order to help Azerbaijan preserve its independence.

Needless to say, this polarization is extremely dangerous, carrying the seeds of a Turkish-Russian confrontation in the event of renewed Armenian-Azerbaijani hostilities. Such a scenario suggests ominous possibilities, particularly in view of the deteriorated state of Russia's conventional forces and its post-Soviet policy allowing for "first use" of nuclear weapons.[33]

Relative Shift in the 'Correlation of Forces'

One of the biggest challenges faced by the post-Soviet Russian polity was adjustment to the loss of superpower status. Russia's retreat as a world power—and its resulting inability to impose its will not only on the world but often even on its own periphery—produced among its decision-makers a deep sense of mistrust of Western intentions.[34] The outside world's heightened interest in Russia's "near abroad" reinforced this suspicion. Western involvement in the development of the rich natural resources there and NATO's sponsorship of PfP-related activities in Russia's "backyard" aroused much resentment. Turkey bore its share of Russian blame, generally being singled out as the most serious geopolitical threat to Russia on its southern periphery.

A root cause of Russia's negative perception of Turkey is the altered power relationship between the two countries. Turkey began to acquire the features of a "regional power" concomitantly with the breakup of the Soviet Union. Its size, population, democratic system of government, relatively high-performing free-market economy, and large NATO-backed military all propelled Turkey to the top echelon of the emergent regional state system.[35] At the same time, Russia was itself reassessed by many analysts to be no more than a "regional power."[36] A robust modernization effort by the Turkish armed forces in the 1990s caused serious concern in Moscow at a time when Russia's own conventional military force was drastically degrading.

Of special concern to Russia is the new Black Sea military balance.[37] The Black Sea is Russia's only outlet to the Mediterranean and would play a fundamental role in the defense of its southern interests during hostilities. However, Russia's strategic challenge in the Black Sea is not confined to Turkey's presumed naval superiority there. NATO, too, has increasingly encroached on the Black Sea and the southern Caucasus through the mechanism of the PfP. Turkey is a NATO ally with forces positioned directly across the sea from Russia's southern borders. This is a potentially threatening military situation for a much weakened Russia.

Russia declined to participate in the Black Sea Partnership '96 joint exercises under the PfP program. One reason, as reported in the Russian press, was that Moscow feared participation under the command of Turkish admiral Güven Erkaya would confirm the clear dominance of the Turkish navy in the Black Sea.[38]

The Black Sea Fleet has traditionally been Russia's strategic arm into the Mediterranean. In late March 1999 Russia dispatched eight warships to the Adriatic to monitor NATO's war against Belgrade.[39] On April 5, 1999, the first of these vessels sailed through the Turkish Straits, on its way to show the Russian flag off the Balkans coast, while sparking speculation as to whether Russia's real motive was to provide Serbia with intelligence support.

Turkey has recently encouraged confidence-building measures among the navies of the Black Sea countries. In July 1998 representatives of Turkey, Bulgaria, Georgia, Russia, Romania, and Ukraine met in Kiev to discuss measures such as exchanging military information and holding joint maneuvers. According to news agency reports, General Hüseyin Kıvrıkoğlu, chief of the Turkish general staff, suggested in early 1999 that the six Black Sea littorals set up a joint fleet for prospective peacekeeping purposes.[40]

Notwithstanding the enormous decline in Russia's power, Turkey gained only in a relative sense. In absolute terms, Russia continues to lead Turkey by a wide margin in virtually every measure of military power. However, prospects for Russia's near-term revival seem dim in view of its economic crisis. Thus, Russia will continue to look with apprehension at indications of growth in Turkish military power and NATO relations with neighboring countries.

What is Russia's place, then, in Turkey's security environment? For now Russia does not pose a conventional military threat to Turkey, despite its bases in Georgia and Armenia. Over the long term, however, Russia is capable of modernizing its conventional capability, and it remains a nuclear superpower whose military doctrine embraces the "first use" option. Finally, prolonged domestic instability in Russia might induce a future nationalist leadership to foster unity by engaging in foreign adventures, especially in the "near abroad." Thus, the long-term threat is potentially serious.

Issues in Controversy

Throughout most of the post-Soviet era, Turkey and Russia have had conflicting positions on pipelines for Caspian Sea oil, the hazards to the Straits posed by prospective increases in oil tanker traffic, Chechen and Kurdish separatism, and the adaptation of the CFE treaty. Problems regarding the Straits and CFE approached resolution in 1999, however. Russia's sale of S-300s to Nicosia was treated by Turkey primarily as a dispute with the Greek Cypriots, though it also strained Turkish-Russian relations.

Caspian Sea Energy Routes

According to a Turkish foreign ministry official, Ankara is interested in the energy potential of Azerbaijan, Kazakhstan, and Turkmenistan from three angles: as a customer for oil and gas, as a participant in energy production, and most importantly as a country offering unique access possibilities to Western markets.[41]

Russia has been in the "great game" with a proposed pipeline from Baku to its own Black Sea port of Novorossiisk, an alternative to Baku-Ceyhan as a route for Azerbaijani oil to move westward. Turkey and Russia initially entered the pipeline contest in a "zero sum" frame of mind, each convinced that only one side could win. However, over time Turkey came to appreciate that it could not completely shut out the Russians. Washington's advocacy of multiple pipelines since the mid-1990s—with a Turkish pipeline as part of the network—was the primary influence on Turkey's shift in attitude.[42] Washington has supported the Baku-Ceyhan alternative as the main export pipeline (MEP), while emphasizing that pipelines terminating at Novorossiisk and Supsa (Georgia) also could carry Azerbaijani oil. U.S. backing of Baku-Ceyhan is activated by a desire not simply to boost Turkey's regional role but also to reduce Caucasian dependence on Russia and to isolate Iran, another potential outlet for Caspian oil.

With U.S. backing, Turkey intensely lobbied Azerbaijan and other regional oil-producing countries. On October 29, 1998, the heads of state of Azerbaijan, Georgia, Kazakhstan, Uzbekistan, and Turkey were in Ankara for celebrations surrounding the seventy-fifth anniversary of the founding of the Turkish republic. There they signed a joint declaration endorsing Baku-Ceyhan as their preferred MEP and warning of humanitarian and environmental risks entailed in transporting oil via tankers through the Turkish Straits, as is necessary with oil piped to Novorossiisk and Supsa. A Turkish-Turkmenistani agreement on the same occasion endorsed the delivery of Turkmen gas by underwater pipelines in the Caspian Sea, which would link up on the Azerbaijani side of the Caspian to a gas pipeline following roughly the same route as Baku-Ceyhan. U.S. energy secretary William Richardson counter-signed both agreements.[43]

Russia all but openly opposes the Baku-Ceyhan route. In a clear allusion to U.S. lobbying, the Russian foreign ministry in October 1998 warned against "excessive politicizing" of the MEP route.[44] Russia seemingly prefers that the MEP go through Iran rather than Turkey in the event it cannot get the prize itself.[45]

The pipeline contest has implications for other Turkish-Russian issues, particularly the Straits and separatist activity in Russia's northern Caucasus and Turkey's southeast, which potentially threatens the safety and the security of the pipelines. These problems reinforce and magnify one another, making each more difficult to untangle from the rest.

The Straits Question

Transit of foreign ships through the Turkish Straits, comprising the Bosporus Strait, the Sea of Marmara, and the Dardanelles Strait, is regulated by the Montreux Convention of 1936. Freedom of transit is the guiding principle, subject to limitations only in the case of vessels of war. These limitations, and Article 21—which bestows on Turkey the right to close the Straits if threatened—allowed NATO Cold War strategists to plan to contain the Soviet Black Sea Fleet in peacetime and to bottle it up in wartime.

Traffic in the Turkish Straits—the only waterway from the Black Sea to the Mediterranean—has burgeoned over the years, jumping from 9,144 vessels in 1960 to 46,914 in 1995. In 1997, 50,942 merchant vessels transited the Bosporus and 36,453 the Dardanelles.[46] In the post-Soviet era, the Black Sea has gained greater commercial significance, partly reflecting the rush among the NIS to join the world economy. Meanwhile, the Bosporus is a navigational challenge. Only 700 meters wide at its narrowest point, it has four blind curves and is subject to violent currents and counter-currents.[47]

From the Turkish perspective, increased traffic in the narrow Straits raises issues of human, material, environmental, and maritime safety. Istanbul, a sprawling metropolis with a population of more than ten million, has come to the brink of disaster several times in recent history. In February and March 1994 alone there were five collisions, including one that resulted in the death of 30 seamen, 20,000 tons of spilled oil, and a slick that burned for five days and closed the Straits. With this type of possibility in mind, Turkey issued a decree on January 11, 1994, that effectively required vessels passing through the Straits to honor a new "traffic separation scheme" it had devised. The scheme requested the vessels to employ Turkish pilots during passage in order to reduce the possibility of accidents at sea. The new regulations went into force on July 1, 1994, and the International Maritime Organization (IMO) endorsed them in late 1995.

Russia, the Straits' primary foreign user, strongly objected to the Turkish action. It argued that Turkey had acted unilaterally, that is, without prior negotiations or consultation with Montreux Convention signatories, and that Turkey was limiting freedom of transit and thereby harming Russian interests. Russia was joined by others, particularly Bulgaria, Greece, and the Greek Cypriots, in a campaign ultimately aimed at repeal of the IMO's 1995 endorsement.[48] For their part, Turkish officials argued that freedom of transit and navigation does not imply "undisciplined passage" or absence of Turkish authority.[49]

Commentators in the Russian press denounced the "illegal" Turkish position as part of a premeditated strategy to discredit the Baku-Novorossiisk pipeline alternative, which would increase tanker traffic through the Straits, in favor of the Baku-Ceyhan alternative. Confronted with Turkish resistance, Russia sought Bulgarian and Greek cooperation in developing a pipeline from Burgas, Bulgaria, to Alexandroupolis, Greece, bypassing the Straits.

Turkey revised the 1994 regulations in November 1998 in order both to address technical problems and to clarify vague phraseology in the 1994 decree that had invited misinterpretation of Turkish intentions. Russia again objected, particularly because the revisions were issued unilaterally. At the same time, Russian foreign ministry spokesman Vladimir Rakhmanin conceded that "the dialogue conducted by Russia and other Montreux members with Turkey over the past few years was beneficial. Turkey took into consideration numerous recommendations in the new rules."[50]

Regional tensions over the issue have been defused since May 1999, when the IMO's Maritime Safety Committee concluded, in effect, that the significant drop in maritime accidents in the Straits between 1994 and 1999 vindicated Turkey's position. The question of the Straits thus has been removed from the IMO's agenda and, for the most part, from the Turkish-Russian agenda, at least for the time being.

Chechens and Kurds: Playing Cards?

Simultaneous Chechen and Kurdish separatist activity tempted domestic forces in both Russia and Turkey to try to manipulate these problems to weaken, if not dismember, the other country. Both governments rejected allegations of official complicity, but mutual perceptions of involvement by the other persisted.

The "great game" around the Caspian Sea oil pipelines further aggravated the political and security issues raised by these separatist movements. Both the Russian and Turkish alternatives would traverse territory vulnerable to separatists. This interplay was viewed by some members of the State Duma and the Russian media, often in the most explicit terms, as an opportunity to undermine Baku-Ceyhan. They saw the "Kurdish card" as perhaps Russia's most effective strategic asset in the struggle against realization of this route. Pledges by Kurdish figures in Moscow "to bomb the pipeline" found a receptive audience.[51]

Russian allegations of Turkish complicity in Chechen separatism were most vociferous during the 1994-1996 phase of the Russo-Chechen war. Many in the Russian media and some Duma members charged that the Turks were actively aiding the Chechens in order to undermine Russia's territorial integrity and to sabotage its chances of being the major venue for Caspian energy pipelines.

The official Turkish position from the outset of the war was to call for resolution of the Chechen issue by peaceful means based on the principle of respect for territorial integrity. All the same, Moscow was irritated, interpreting Turkish interest in the war and humanitarian initiatives as interference in its domestic affairs. Whether there was any truth to the Russian allegations of official Turkish involvement cannot be verified.[52] The commitment of some private Turkish citizens to the Chechen cause is verifiable, however, with the *Avrasya* episode of January 1996 being one outstanding example.[53] This episode highlighted the important place Turkey's *Kafkas* (Caucasian) diaspora occupies in Turkish society and its potential to influence Turkey's regional foreign relations.

State Duma support—especially from nationalists and communists—for Kurdish separatist aspirations in Turkey and specifically for the terrorist PKK was made clear in 1998. After Öcalan was forced out of Syria under Turkish military pressure in October 1998, he was smuggled into Russia in an operation reportedly led by Zhirinovsky. The 450-seat Duma overwhelmingly passed a resolution urging Yeltsin to grant him asylum; the vote was 298-0, with one abstention. Through its ambassador, Nabi Sensoy, Turkey sent a firm signal that it expected Öcalan not to be granted political asylum: "Moscow has no reason for seriously complicating Russian-Turkish relations or terminating them completely for the sake of giving political asylum to such a person."[54] Prime Minister Yevgeny Primakov's government emphasized that the Duma's position did not reflect official policy, however.[55] Upon Öcalan's departure from Russia for Italy, the Turkish ambassador praised the

Russian government's handling of the matter, which, he said, had strengthened bilateral relations.[56] Thus, Ankara was satisfied despite Russia's failure to comply with its request to extradite Öcalan to Turkey.[57]

Adapting the CFE Treaty: The Flank Issue

The CFE treaty is part of the bedrock of European and Turkish security. Negotiated between NATO and the Warsaw Pact in 1989-90, signed in 1990, and in force since 1992, the treaty needed adaptation to the new security landscape that emerged almost before the ink was dry. To that end, formal negotiations to replace CFE's bloc-to-bloc and concentric-zone structure with national and territorial limits for each state opened in Vienna in January 1997, and an updated CFE treaty was signed at the November 1999 Organization for Security and Cooperation in Europe (OSCE) summit in Istanbul.

Shortly after CFE was signed in 1990, Russia's "flank zone," defined in Article V of the treaty, emerged as an especially controversial issue and one of paramount importance for the future Turkish-Russian military balance in the region. Article V designates Russia's northern Caucasus and Leningrad military districts as "flank zones" and sets ceilings on the amount of "treaty-limited equipment"—such as armored combat vehicles and heavy artillery—that Russia can hold there. It was included in the original treaty in large part to prevent Moscow from taking weapons removed from Eastern Europe and piling them up on its flanks in the Baltics or the Caucasus, threatening NATO members Norway and Turkey, respectively. Therefore, preservation of Article V was initially one of Turkey's primary objectives in the Vienna negotiations to update CFE.

Turkish-Russian disagreements over Article V began in early post-Soviet years. Arguing that the collapse of the Soviet Union had drastically changed the political and military circumstances, Russia formally asked the treaty signatories in October 1993 to revise the flank provisions to allow it further deployments.[58] Instability in the southern Caucasus and the 1994-96 Russo-Chechen war seemed to give special credence to Moscow's arguments. Turkey, the one NATO country directly exposed to Russian forces in the Caucasus, opposed any revision. Nevertheless, Russia continued to deploy treaty-limited equipment in the northern Caucasus in excess of the permitted ceilings, even after the November 17, 1995, deadline for compliance had passed.

At the first "treaty review conference," in Vienna in May 1996, a compromise was reached, effectively allowing Russia until May 31, 1999, to comply with CFE flank restrictions. In addition, the size of the northern Caucasus flank was reduced, effectively increasing the surrounding area not subject to limitation. Turkey's agreement to the compromise probably was a result of pressure from Washington, which hoped to win Russian consent for NATO's eastward expansion. Russian officials and the public saw the new arrangement as a diplomatic victory.[59]

Another breakthrough was achieved at bilateral talks regarding the updated treaty in November 1998 in Moscow and January 1999 in Ankara, where the parties agreed on a further and perhaps more durable compromise solution.[60] Russia dropped its demand for removal of all Article V ceilings. In turn, Turkey signaled it would not object to Russian deployment of certain kinds of treaty-limited equipment in the flank zone in numbers exceeding the treaty ceilings. Turkey thus was content to ensure continuation of the flank regime and affirmation of the legally binding status of the agreement at least in principle.

The Turkish-Russian understanding was endorsed at the negotiating forum in Vienna in March and incorporated into the final draft signed at the November 1999 OSCE summit. A major source of bilateral discord thus appears to have been resolved—again, at least for now.

Toward Economic Interdependence?

Turkish-Russian economic relations have been among the most impressive achievements in post-Soviet Eurasian regional cooperation.[61] They include three main areas: trade, construction, and tourism. The progressive increase in the total value of these activities—except in 1998 when Russia plunged into a grave economic crisis—fostered the feeling that the two countries might indeed be moving toward economic interdependence.

The original impetus for economic cooperation came in the final years of the Gorbachev era. Albert Chernishev, Soviet (and then Russian) ambassador to Ankara from 1987 to 1994, actively sought to entice Turkish businessmen to invest in the Soviet Union. He found a receptive audience. Özal's liberalizing economic reforms had already changed the worldviews and business strategies of Turkish businessmen. They yearned to compete for profits beyond Turkish borders—especially with the help of government credits and tax breaks. Özal had founded the Turkish Eximbank specifically with this objective in mind. In short, Turkish businessmen were offered attractive inducements by both Soviet and Turkish *perestroika*s to enter the Soviet market.

Construction firms were the first among larger Turkish companies to do business in Russia. In 1991 they competed with Germany in a Soviet tender for the construction of housing for Soviet forces being withdrawn from East Germany and won an important portion of the project—to the chagrin of the Germans, who had paid the Soviets compensation for vacating East Germany.

The Soviet collapse introduced an altogether new dimension to Turkish-Russian economic ties: the so-called "luggage trade," referring to goods purchased in Turkey by Russian tourists for re-sale in Russia. This type of trade soared in the early and mid-1990s to meet the rising demand of Russian consumers. But efforts by Duma hardliners to restrict the luggage trade and Russian consumers' desire to diversify sources of supply had diminished the volume of such trade even before Russia's 1998 economic crisis.

Because it is unrecorded, reliable statistics on luggage trade are not available. Market analysts and official sources in Turkey estimate it to have been anywhere between $6 billion and $10 billion annually during the peak years, 1991 to 1996. Those same sources say that, since the onset of the Russian economic crisis, luggage trade has shrunk to probably one-third its earlier peak value.

Hard figures are available for official trade, though their accuracy is open to question. Russian figures are noticeably lower than Turkish figures, possibly due to differences in accounting practices. According to Turkish figures, the total value of Turkish-Russian trade stood at $3.5 billion in 1998. Of this total, $1.347 billion represented Turkey's exports to Russia—a 34 percent decline from the previous year—and $2.152 billion its imports from Russia.

Two categories have dominated Turkish imports from Russia: natural gas, and iron and steel. Turkey depends on imported fossil fuels to meet rising domestic demand for energy and currently imports six billion cubic meters of natural gas annually from Russia. Plans are under way to raise this volume to thirty billion by modernizing the Ukrainian-Bulgarian pipeline that transports Russian gas to Turkey and by constructing the "Blue Stream" pipeline directly from Russia to Turkey under the Black Sea.[62]

Turkey's almost total reliance on Russian natural gas imports has provoked concern in some circles in Turkey. After the mid-1990s Turkish governments stepped up efforts to purchase gas from Iran and Turkmenistan. The Iranian option is complicated due above all to Washington's objections. The Turkmenistan option is complicated by the question of how to transport the gas: through Iran or via pipelines under the Caspian Sea? Until these issues are resolved, Turkey will have to rely mainly on Russia.

Construction activity by Turkish firms is another important element in bilateral economic relations. According to Turkish sources, the volume of this activity reached a total of $6.1 billion in 1996. In 1989 the Turkish Eximbank opened a credit line of $950 million to Russia to help subsidize the activities of Turkish businessmen there.

Another interesting development has been the remarkable and steady growth in the number of Russian tourists visiting Turkey. According to Turkish statistics, more than a million Russians visited Turkey in 1996.

Turkish-Russian economic relations face systemic vulnerabilities. The blow they suffered from the 1998 Russian economic crisis and its global reverberations is a good indicator of this, as are political factors such as the Duma's intervention in the Öcalan affair. Moreover, some Russian nationalists have complained that Turkish profits originating in Russia are being used to harm Russian interests,[63] suggesting Turkish firms could someday become a target of a nationalist backlash in Russia.

Conclusion

The "virtual rapprochement" achieved between Turkey and Russia in the 1990s was both a frustrating and a promising experience. It represented a highly complex and uncertain relationship in a turbulent period marked by parallel upheavals in Russian governance and in the international system. The daunting challenges Russia faced after 1991 severely constrained possibilities for full-blown Turkish-Russian rapprochement. Russia took the loss of empire and superpower status unusually hard, especially when compared to other imperial losers in the twentieth century. Its deep sense of loss translated into suspicion and fear directed against nearly every foreign actor that took an interest in former Soviet imperial lands. Turkey sits near the center of this dark worldview entertained especially by Russian communists and radical nationalists.

In contrast, Turkish domestic political forces have not impeded relations. There has been no openly anti-Russian faction in the Turkish parliament in the post-Soviet era—not even the *Milliyetçi Hareket* (Nationalist Movement) Party (MHP), long known for its ultranationalist ideology and its strong support for the Turkic peoples of the region. Thus, Turkish-Russian relations remained on course even with MHP as part of Turkey's governing coalition since June 1999 and in the face of renewed Russian-Chechen fighting in late 1999.

A significant amount of post-Soviet tension and mistrust between Turkey and Russia was systemically determined, a direct result of challenges generated by Russia's turbulent internal transition and the pains encountered in the adjustment of both Russia and Turkey to the post-imperial system in Eurasia. To a large extent, bilateral difficulties were unavoidable. But can they be avoided in the future? Can Turkey and Russia reach an accommodation?

It is possible that both sides might have learned to moderate their zero-sum approach to the new geopolitical landscape in Eurasia. For this to be decidedly so, Russia would have to accept a liberal system of international relations in lands where historically it was the hegemon. In practical terms, this would mean a willingness to reorient its thinking away from treating those lands as its "backyard" and a readiness to cooperate with Turkey in developing Eurasia and in resolving regional conflicts.

Turkey, for its part, would have to show greater willingness to consider the possibility that Russia can be a positive force for regional peace and stability. Turkey has already discovered the limited practical value of the vague "Turkic world" concept. Indeed, internal dynamics within the "Turkic world" itself betrayed the Turkish dream, as Turkic states effectively rejected the notion of Turkey as their leader and role model. Turkey needs to encourage the present trend of friendly relations with the Central Asian NIS, but not deliberately at Russia's expense. A Turkish-Russian reorientation toward political—perhaps even military—cooperation to promote peace and stability in Eurasia can be built only on the principles of transparency and reciprocity. In that regard, Turkish-Russian cooperation should not confine itself merely to Eurasian affairs. For example, Ankara should be sensitive to Russia's security concerns about NATO.

"New thinking" is needed, and it should take into account new developments like the scaling down of Turkey's exclusivist aspirations in the former Soviet south and the enormous amount of good will generated in Turkey for Russia and the Russian people since the time of Gorbachev. Turks regard Mikhail Gorbachev not merely as a Russian leader who ended the empire, but as a friend who opened up the charms of this formerly secretive, sullen polity to the ambitions and prosperity of tens of thousands of Turkish businessmen.

Is there a role for the United States in Turkish-Russian accommodation? Perhaps not. U.S.-Russian relations have suffered as a result of differences over issues such as Iraq, Kosovo, NATO enlargement, and the U.S. national missile defense program. Moreover, Washington's support of Baku-Ceyhan has intensified Moscow's resentment. It is difficult to see how the United States can facilitate Turkish-Russian accommodation.

But the United States can contribute indirectly to Turkish-Russian rapprochement by helping Russia to weather its enormous internal instabilities. Unless Russia attains domestic stability with an open, democratic process and sustained economic reform—and ceases to insist on being accorded the status and privileges of a great power—its relations with its neighbors are likely to be far more contentious than conciliatory.

Notes

1   "Turkey Spokesman: Turkey 'Must Immediately Withdraw' from Iraq," ITAR-TASS World Service, November 11, 1997, in Foreign Broadcast Information Service Daily Report, Military Affairs (FBIS-UMA), 97-315, November 14, 1997.

2   Alexei G. Arbatov, "Russian National Interests," in Robert D. Blackwill and Sergei A.Karaganov (eds.), *Damage Limitation or Crisis* (Washington, D.C.: Brassey's, 1994), p. 71.

3   During one of the high points of the Russo-Chechen war in January 1996, the Turkish ferryboat *Avrasya* was hijacked at the Turkish port of Trabzon by gunmen who called themselves "Caucasian Turks" and declared their aim to be "to stop the massacre of the 250 Chechens in Dagestan. They are being massacred now. ... This action is entirely against Russia and Yeltsin." The gunmen eventually gave themselves up to Turkish security forces to face prosecution in Turkish courts. The passengers, mostly Russian, were released unharmed. See "Hijacking of Trabzon-Sochi Ferry," BBC Monitoring Summary of World Broadcasts Part I, The Former USSR (SWB) (January 18, 1996), SU/2512 B/12-14.

4   Alexei Vassiliev, "Turkey and Iran in Transcaucasia and Central Asia," in Anoushiravan Ehteshami (ed.), *From the Gulf to Central Asia: Players in the New Great Game* (Exeter, England: University of Exeter Press, 1994), p. 132.

5   "Russia: Turkish Prime Minister Visits as Government Seeks Trade Rather than War over Transcaucasia," *Independent*, May, 25, 1992, in Reuters, May 25, 1992.

6   "Prime Minister Signs Treaty of Friendship with Russian Prime Minister," *Middle East Economic Digest*, in Reuters, June 12, 1992.

7   "Russia: Russia and Turkey Sign Bilateral Treaty," Reuters, May 27, 1992; "Turkish Premier in Russia: Bilateral Treaty Signed," SWB, SU/1391 A4/1 (mimeographed text of the treaty from the Turkish Ministry of Foreign Affairs on file with author).

8   "Turkey: Chernomyrdin, Yılmaz Stress Growing Trade Ties," *Turkish Daily News (TDN)*, December 17, 1997, in Reuters, December 17, 1997.

9   "Russia: Chernomyrdin Proposes Strategic Partnership at Meeting with Turkish Businessmen," ITAR-TASS News Agency, December 16, 1997, in *BBC Monitoring Service: Former USSR*, December 17, 1997, in Reuters, December 17, 1997.

10 "Russia: Premier Chernomyrdin Says Russia Favours Steady Relations with Turkey," ITAR-TASS News Agency (World Service), December 15, 1997, in *BBC Monitoring Service, Former USSR*, 17/12/97, in Reuters, Dec 17, 1997.

11 "Turkey: Turkish and Russian Premiers Stress Importance of Bilateral Ties," TRT-TV Ankara, December 15, 1997, *BBC Monitoring Service: Central Europe and Balkans*, 17/12/97, in Reuters, December 17, 1997.

12 Akdes Nimet Kurat, *Turkey and Russia* (Ankara: Kültür Bakanlığı/1194, 1990); Ivo J. Lederer, "Russia and the Balkans" in Ivo J. Lederer (ed.), *Russian Foreign Policy* (New Haven, Conn.: Yale University Press, 1962), pp. 417451; David M. Goldfrank, "Policy Tradition and the Menshikov Mission of 1853," in Hugh Ragsdale and Valerii Nokolaevich Ponomarev (eds.), *Imperial Russian Foreign Policy*, (Washington, D.C.: Woodrow Wilson Center Press and Cambridge University Press, 1993), pp. 119-158.

13 David Thomas, *Europe Since Napoleon* (Middlesex, England: Pelican Books, revised ed., 1966), p. 243; V.N. Vinogradov, "The Personal Responsibility of Emperor Nicholas I for the Coming of the Crimean War: An Episode in the Diplomatic Struggle in the Eastern Question," in Hugh Raggsdale and Valerii Nikoaevich Ponomarev (eds.), *Imperial Russian Foreign Policy* (Washington, D.C.: Woodrow Wilson Center Press and Cambridge University Press, 1993), pp.159-160.

14 Firuz Kazemzadeh, "Russia and the Middle East," in Ivo Lederer (ed.), *Russian Foreign Policy* (New Haven, Conn.: Yale University Press, 1962), p. 495.

15 Serge A. Zenkovsky, *Pan-Turkism and Islam in Russia* (Cambridge: Harvard University Press, 1960), pp. 106-112.

16 Graham E. Fuller, "Russia and Central Asia: Federation or Fault Line?" in Michael Mandelbaum (ed.), *Central Asia and the World* (New York: Council on Foreign Relations Press, 1994), pp. 112-113.

17 Arbatov, "Russian National Interests," p. 60.

18 Dale F. Eickelman, "Introduction: The Other 'Orientalist' Crisis," in Dale F. Eickelman (ed.), *Russia's Muslim Frontiers: New Directions in Cross-Cultural Analysis* (Bloomington: Indiana University Press, 1993), p. 5.

19 George S. Harris, "The Russian Federation and Turkey," in Alvin Z. Rubinstein and Oles M. Smolansky (eds.), *Regional Power Rivalries in the New Eurasia: Russia, Turkey and Iran* (Armonk, N.Y.: M.E. Sharpe, 1995), p. 16. Quotation marks within passage indicate a quote used by Harris from another source.

20 "Prime Minister Signs Treaty of Friendship with Russian Prime Minister," *Middle East Economic Digest*, in Reuters, June 12, 1992.

21 "Turkish Premier Concludes Visit to Russia," SWB, SU/1792 B/9.

22 Dr. Sergei A. Karaganov, deputy director of the Institute of Europe, Academy of Sciences of Russia, Moscow, interview with author, August 22, 1996. Quotation with permission of Dr. Karaganov.

23 "Turkey: Aliyev: No Borders Between Turkey, Azerbaijan," Anatolia News Agency, September 29, 1998, in Foreign Broadcast Information Service Daily Report, West Europe (FBIS-WEU), 98-272, September 30, 1998.

24 "Turkey: Security Corridor to Parallel Caspian Energy Path," *TDN*, April 28, 1998, in Reuters, April 28, 1998.

25 "Azerbaijan: Russia Said Arming Armenia Against Turkey," *Zerkalo* (Baku), December 26, 1998, in Foreign Broadcast Information Service Daily Report, Central Eurasia (FBIS-SOV), 98-364, December 30, 1998.

26 Ibid.

27 "Minister Abiyev on NATO, Related Issues," *Obshchaya Gazeta* (Moscow, electronic version), February 11-17, 1999, FBIS-SOV, 1999-021, February 11, 1999.

28 Liz Fuller, "Georgia/Turkey: Agreements Secure Bilateral Trade and Defense,"http://search.rferl.org/nca/features/1999/03/f.ru99031050916.htm.

29 For striking similarities between the views of Turkish officials in the early post-Soviet era and some distinguished U.S. analysts of Russia, see Henry Kissinger, *International Herald Tribune,* July 6, 1992 (editorial) and Zbigniew Brzezinski, "The Premature Partnership," *Foreign Affairs* 73, no. 2 (March-April 1994): 67-82. Interestingly, Strobe Talbott, U.S. deputy secretary of state, the staunch advocate of Washington's "Russia first" policy, approached their ranks when he referred to the "imperialist impulses" among some in Moscow. S. Frederick Starr, "Power Failure: American Policy in the Caspian," *National Interest* (Spring 1997): 31 (quoting Talbott).

30 Duygu Bazoğlu Sezer, "Turkey's Political and Security Interests and Policies in the New Geostrategic Environment of the Expanded Middle East," Occasional Paper no. 19, The Henry L. Stimson Center (Washington, July 1994), p. 7.

31 Shireen T. Hunter, *The Transcaucasus in Transition: Nation-Building and Conflict* (Washington, D.C.: Center for Strategic and International Studies, 1994).

32 Stephen Blank, "Instability in the Caucasus: New Trends, Old Traits," *Jane's Intelligence Review* 10, no. 4 (April 1998): 14-21 (part 1); Stephen Blank, "Instability in the Caucasus: New Trends, Old Traits," *Jane's Intelligence Review* 10, no. 5 (May 1998), pp. 18-21 (part 2).

33 Richard F. Staar, "Russia's New Blueprint for National Security," *Strategic Review* 26, no. 2 (Spring 1998), p. 37.

34 Ibid.

35 Eric Rouleau, "The Challenges to Turkey," *Foreign Affairs* 72, no. 5 (November-December 1993), pp. 110-126.

36 "Russia: Brzezinski Interviewed on Russia's Future," *Komsomolskaya Pravda* (Moscow), January 6, 1998, in FBIS-SOV, 98-023, January 23, 1998; Robert Legvold, "Foreign Policy," in Timothy J. Colton and Robert Legvold (eds.), *After the Soviet Union: From Empire to Nation* (New York: W.W. Norton, 1992), p. 149.

37 "Turkey: Russia Reveals Plan for Black Sea 'Parity' With Turkey," *Milliyet*, July 31, 1997, in FBIS-WEU, 97-212, July 31, 1997; Viktor Vodolazhskiy, "Russia: Status of Black Sea Fleet Division Process Viewed," *Rossiyskaya Gazeta* (Moscow), October 16, 1996, FBIS-SOV, 96-202, October 16, 1996.

38 "Russian Fleet Doesn't Take Orders from Turkish Navy," *Current Digest of the Post-Soviet Press* 48, no. 37 (October 9, 1996), p. 25.

39 "Turkey: Atacanlı–'Russia Made an Announcement about Transit of Eight Warships from Turkish Straits between April 3 and 8' " Anatolia News Agency, April 1, 1999, in Reuters, April 1, 1999.

40 "Ukraine: Ukraine Ponders Turkey's Proposal for Joint Naval Force on Black Sea," ITAR-TASS, January 20, 1999, in BBC Monitoring Service, Former Soviet Union—Political, January 20, 1999.

41 Temel İskit, "Turkey: A New Actor in the Field of Energy Politics," *Perceptions* 1, no. 1 (March-May 1996), p. 67.

42 Ibid., p. 69.

43 *TDN*, October 30, 1998.

44 "Transcaucasia and Central Asia: …While Russia Expresses Displeasure," *RFE/RL Newsline* 2, no. 210, Part I (October 30, 1998).

45 Uğur Akıncı, "Turkey: PFC Report—Baku-Ceyhan Pipeline Is Bad Choice," *TDN*, May 19, 1998, in Reuters, May 19, 1998.

46 *Rapport Annuel sur le Mouvement des Navires a Travers les Detroits Turcs* (Ankara, Aout 1998), pp. 47-48. For statistics on previous years, see back issues.

47 Ferenc A. Vali, *The Turkish Straits and NATO* (Stanford, Calif.: Hoover Institution Press, 1972), p. 8.

48 Working papers submitted to IMO Maritime Safety Committee (MSC), 70th session, agenda item 11, respectively, MSC 70/11/15, 16, October 23, 1998; MSC 70/11/11, October 9, 1998; MSC 70/11/13, October 9, 1998; MSC 70/11/12 October 1998.

49 Michael Rank, "Russia: Russia, Turkey Clash over Control of Bosporus," in Reuters, July 25, 1997.

50 "Russia: Russia Expresses Regret over Turkey's Change of Navigation Rules," Interfax News Agency, November 20, 1998, in *BBC Monitoring Former Soviet Union—Political*, November 20, 1998, in Reuters, November 20, 1998.

51 "Russia: Seleznev Says Russia, Turkey 'Will Jointly Fight Terrorism,'" ITAR-TASS, July 20, 1998, in Reuters, July 22, 1998; "Azerbaijan, Georgia:

Threats to Western Pipeline Route Examined," *Zerkalo* (Baku), May 17, 1997, in FBIS-SOV, 97-121, May 17, 1997.

52   "Duma Deputy—'Dudayev Receives Arms from Turkey and Iran'" SWB SU/2260 B/7, March 24, 1995.

53   See note 3, supra.

54   "Russia: Turkey Expects Russia to Find, Oust Kurdish Leader Öcalan," Interfax News Agency, November 10, 1998, in FBIS-SOV, 98-314, November 10, 1998.

55   "Turkey: Russia Says No Change in Stand against Sheltering Öcalan," Anatolia News Agency, in FBIS-WEU, 98-308, November 4, 1998.

56   "Turkey: Ambassador Says Relations with Russia 'Strengthened'" Anatolia News Agency, November 14, 1998, in FBIS-WEU, 98-318, November 14, 1998.

57   "Turkey: Turkey Said to Ask Russia 'Officially' for Öcalan," *Sabah*, October 27, 1998, in FBIS-WEU, 98-300, October 27, 1998.

58   Jeffrey D. McCausland, "Conventional Arms Control and European Security," *Adelphi Paper* 301 (London: International Institute for Strategic Studies, 1996), pp. 37-40.

59   "Russia Allowed Time to Fulfill CFE Treaty," *Moscow Times*, June 4, 1996, p. 5; "Russia: Grachev Praises Vienna Conference on CFE Treaty," Interfax News Agency, June 9, 1996, in FBIS-SOV, 96-112, June 10, 1996: 37; "Russia: CFE Compromise Seen as 'Major' Success," *Krasnaya Zvezda* (Moscow), June 7, 1996, in FBIS-SOV, 96-112, June 10, 1996, p. 26.

60   "Turkey: Adaptation of CFE to Changing Security Conditions—Turkey Holds Regular Bilateral Consultations," Anatolia News Agency, January 1, 1999, in Reuters, January 30, 1999; "Russia: Russia and Turkey Reach Agreement on Conventional Forces Treaty," ITAR-TASS News Agency, February 11, 1999, in Reuters, February 11, 1999.

61   Figures quoted in this section were obtained from the Turkish foreign ministry in April 1999 but do not necessarily represent official figures.

62   Dmitry Zhdannikov, "Russia: Interview—Black Sea Gas Pipe Start Seen in Autumn," Reuters, March 23, 1999.

63   "Turkey: Minister Taner—Russia More Important Market than EU," Anatolia News Agency, April 24, 1998, in FBIS-WEU, 98-115, April 25, 1998.

Gareth M. Winrow

Turkish Policy toward Central Asia and the Transcaucasus

Turkish policy-makers were faced with new opportunities and challenges in Central Asia and the Transcaucasus after the demise of the Soviet Union. Initially they sought to build ties with the newly independent Turkic states—Azerbaijan, Kazakhstan, Kyrgyzstan, Turkmenistan, and Uzbekistan—by stressing the significance of perceived common cultural, historical, ethnic, linguistic, and religious ties. The limitation of this policy's effectiveness was soon acknowledged as Turkish decision-makers were forced in their dealings with these states to concentrate on more immediate economic and political issues. One of the most significant of these issues was Caspian Sea-based energy resources, which also prompted Turkey to improve relations with non-Turkic Georgia.

While one may still examine Turkish policy toward post-Soviet Central Asia and the Transcaucasus separately, as in this chapter, the increasing importance of Caspian pipeline politics has led commentators and politicians in Turkey and elsewhere to think of the Caspian littoral states—including Iran and Russia—and the Transcaucasus as constituting one "Caspian region." Turkish policy-makers appear to be less concerned about geographically remote and relatively energy-poor Kyrgyzstan and predominantly non-Turkic, Farsi-speaking Tajikistan. How they perceive Uzbekistan—a non-Caspian Turkic state like Kyrgyzstan—is somewhat unclear. With Uzbekistan's energy resources, population, and location, and given president Islam Karimov's ambitions to make it a major regional actor, Ankara may yet elevate Turkish-Uzbek relations to the same level of importance as relations with Caspian littorals Kazakhstan and Turkmenistan.

A "great game" is taking place not in Central Asia—the site of the original "great game" of great power rivalry in the nineteenth century—but in the Caspian region. A number of states and energy companies are participants. Turkey is also a key player. It has been argued that Turkey is a "pivotal state" because of its critical geographical location astride the Balkans, the Black Sea, the Mediterranean, the Middle East, and the Transcaucasus. In addition to this regional and geostrategic "pivotalness," Turkey could also play a pivotal role politically if the

Turkic states look to Ankara for regional leadership and begin to regard Turkey as a political and economic role model.[1] The potential geo-economic pivotalness of Turkey should also be underlined, bearing in mind the possibility that Caspian oil and gas will be transported westward through Turkish territory.

Turkey and Central Asia

Turks were euphoric when the unexpected unraveling of the Soviet Union enabled them to develop relations with long-forgotten Turkic cousins in Central Asia and Azerbaijan. Fearful of the possible spread of Iranian influence, U.S. secretary of state James Baker, in Central Asia in early 1992, urged Central Asians to adopt the "Turkish model" of secularism, liberal democracy, and a market economy.[2] In February 1992 Turkish prime minister Süleyman Demirel declared that a "gigantic Turkish world" was emerging from the Adriatic to the Great Wall of China.[3] When visiting Central Asia in May 1992, Demirel spoke of forming an "association" of independent Turkic states,[4] perhaps suggesting some form of Turkic commonwealth. The late president Turgut Özal announced that the next century would be "the century of the Turks."[5] These high expectations were dashed to a considerable extent when the first Turkic summit in Ankara in October 1992 produced only ambiguously worded declarations of intent with little substance.

Nevertheless, Turkey had already begun to develop extensive cooperation with the Turkic states, setting up telecommunications and air links, providing scholarships for Turkic students to study at Turkish universities and schools, and organizing training courses for Turkic diplomats and businessmen. Religious and military officials established contacts with Turkic counterparts. The Turkish Eximbank swiftly offered credits worth more than $600 million to boost trade and support construction of hotels and factories in Central Asia, and the government formed the Turkish International Cooperation Agency (TİKA by its Turkish acronym) to coordinate public-and private-sector cooperation with the new states, especially in education, culture, and technical fields.

From the outset, though, there were problems, often of an interpersonal nature. In 1997, State Minister for Turkic Affairs Ahat Andıçan claimed that Turkish officials tended to underestimate the Central Asians, failing to appreciate the high levels of education and technical expertise Central Asians had achieved during the Soviet era.[6] According to another source, Central Asians objected to Turkey's "excessive emphasis" on a Turkic commonwealth, just as they were seeking to foster their own national identities.[7]

By April 2000 six Turkic summits had convened. In practice, the summits concentrate only on economic and cultural issues. Immediately before the fifth summit in Astana, Kazakhstan, in June 1998, Uzbekistan's Karimov explicitly declared that the summits should not consider political or security matters because of the absence of Iran and Tajikistan.[8] Karimov and Turkmenistani president Saparmurat Niyazov refused to attend the sixth summit in Baku, Azerbaijan, in April 2000, and the Uzbek and Turkmenistani parliamentary speakers took their place. The leaders' absence reflected political disputes with other Turkic states. Niyazov had clashed with Azerbaijani president Haydar Aliyev over ownership of some Caspian oilfields, and Karimov had accused Turkey of harboring political opponents to his regime.

Pan-Turkic groups in Turkey are centered around the *Milliyetçi Hareket* (Nationalist Movement) Party (MHP). With the support of these groups, the Turkic States and Communities Friendship, Brotherhood, and Cooperation Foundation (TÜDEV) was established. Since 1993, this foundation has organized annual Turkic congresses in Turkey. There, delegates from across the "Turkic World"—including Bashkortostan, Tatarstan, and Yakutia in the Russian Federation—have discussed how to expand cooperation among Turkic peoples. Leading Turkish officials such as Özal, Demirel, and former prime minister and foreign minister Tansu Çiller have addressed these meetings. In practice, though, these gatherings have little impact on official Turkish policy. The extremely small pan-Turkic groups in Central Asia also are politically marginal in their homelands.

Central Asians have not adopted the "Turkish model." While Turkey's version of liberal democracy has itself come under criticism in the West, Central Asia's clearly authoritarian regimes—headed, in most cases, by Communist-era rulers—remain entrenched. Any potentially serious political opposition is crushed. This has led to the aforementioned problems in Turkish-Uzbek relations, for example, even as Turkey has generally tried to assuage Karimov's feelings. According to the press center of the Uzbek opposition party Erk, party leader Mohammed Salih on three occasions was temporarily expelled from his exile in Turkey immediately before Karimov visited Turkey or a high-ranking Turkish official visited Uzbekistan.[9] In summer 1999 Uzbek authorities closed twelve Turkish schools in Uzbekistan and recalled Uzbek students studying in Turkey. This move came in reaction to Ankara's refusal to hand over a Turkish citizen accused of masterminding bomb attacks in Tashkent in February 1999.

The Central Asians did not adopt Turkey's relatively free-market economic system, either. In part, they may have been made skeptical by Turkey's own economic problems, including high budget deficits and soaring inflation.

Meanwhile, Turkey's credentials as a model secular state were brought into question in Central Asia after the formation in 1996 of a coalition government led by the pro-Islamist *Refah* (Welfare) Party (RP).[10] Moreover, probably no Turkish entity cuts a higher-profile presence in the Turkic states than the schools run by energetic followers of Fethullah Gülen, leader of the Islamic Nurcu religious sect in Turkey. Gülen's followers have opened more schools in the Turkic states than the Turkish Ministry of Education. At the same time, Central Asian leaders have clamped down heavily on politicized Islam, fearing possible spread of Taliban-inspired radicalism.

Turkish economic relations with the Turkic states are growing but are less robust than Turkish economic relations with Russia. In 1996 Turkey was reportedly the second-largest investor in Central Asia after Russia, investing $1.6 billion in Turkmenistan, $1.5 billion in Kazakhstan, $928.4 million in Uzbekistan, and $279 million in Kyrgyzstan.[11] Private Turkish construction firms in Turkmenistan had carried out projects worth $2.3 billion by the end of 1997. As a point of comparison, work undertaken by Turkish firms in Russia to that point amounted to more than $12.3 billion.[12] Likewise, trade with Turkic states is less than that with Russia. Without taking into account the considerable unregistered luggage trade, Turkey's 1999 exports to Russia totaled $587 million, and imports from Russia amounted to $2.37 billion. In the same year exports to Turkic states collectively were valued at just $573 million, and imports came to only $457 million.[13] Exports to Central Asia consist primarily of processed foods, textiles, machinery, and transport equipment. Imports are mainly textiles and metal products.[14] Turkish officials and businessmen hope to boost this trade considerably once Central Asians generate earnings by exporting energy to Turkey and other hard-currency markets. However, Central Asian oil and gas will not reach the world market in significant amounts in the near term, however.

Central Asia is not an area of major Turkish strategic concern, especially in comparison to the nearby Transcaucasus. In general, Central Asian Turkic leaders—concerned about the possible destabilizing impact of the Taliban's success in Afghanistan and anxious not to be plunged into the type of civil war that has ravaged Tajikistan—have looked to Moscow for a protective security umbrella.

Turkish officials have repeatedly voiced concern about developments in Central Asia as a whole, including Tajikistan, Afghanistan, Mongolia, and the Turkic province of Xinjiang in China. In August and September 1998 former Afghan president Burhanuddin Rabbani and Afghan warlord General Abdul Rashid Dostum, an ethnic Uzbek, visited Ankara, seeking pressure on Pakistan to cease supporting the Taliban.[15] In practice, though, there may be little Turkey can do to influence events in Afghanistan or in Xinjiang, where Chinese authorities repress Uighur Turks who oppose *de facto* direct rule from Beijing.

Mainly because of the importance of Caspian energy, Turkish politicians and businessmen follow developments in Kazakhstan and Turkmenistan more closely than they do events elsewhere in Central Asia.

Turkey and the Transcaucasus

Geographic proximity, unresolved ethnic and regional disputes, Russian involvement in the second Chechen war commencing in 1999, close Russian-Armenian relations, and Caspian energy reserves make the Transcaucasus an area of particular security concern for Turkey. The Turkish armed forces and the Ministry of Foreign Affairs are especially anxious that Russia does not reacquire a dominant influence there. Stability in the Transcaucasus clearly would be in Turkey's interest, particularly since it would facilitate construction of regional oil and gas pipelines.

Tensions between Turkey and Russia in the Transcaucasus peaked in the years 1993-96. Russian security forces meddled in Azerbaijan, provoking the overthrow of pro-Turkish president Ebulfez Elchibey in 1993. Russian combat units in Georgia assisted the Abkhazians in their failed secessionist bid in 1994. During the 1994-96 Chechen war, solidarity groups based in Turkey and composed of Turkish citizens of Caucasian origin delivered food, money, and probably weaponry to the Chechens, prompting Russia to retaliate by allowing Kurdish groups associated with the Kurdistan Workers Party (better known by its Kurdish initials PKK) to hold meetings in Moscow.

After the Russian military debacle in Chechnya in 1994-1996, tensions eased, perhaps because Turkey got a first-hand look at the Russian military decline. Moreover, in the period between 1996 and 1999, many in Moscow—eager to achieve construction of a major oil pipeline between Azerbaijan and the Russian Black Sea coast—appeared to come around to share Turkey's interest in fostering stability in the Transcaucasus. The 1998 agreement to withdraw all Russian border troops from Georgia by July 1999 also helped to improve Turkish-Russian relations.[16]

But problems in Turkish-Russian relations resurfaced somewhat with the outbreak of a second Chechen war in late 1999. Many Turkish officials fear that Russia could attempt to exploit the war in order to reassert Russian dominance in Azerbaijan and Georgia. Meanwhile, many in Moscow see Turkey as a willing vehicle for expansion of the North Atlantic Treaty Organization's (NATO's) presence in the Transcaucasus. In June 1998 deputy chief of the Turkish general staff Çevik Bir proposed creation of a peacekeeping force in the Transcaucasus under NATO's Partnership for Peace (PfP) program.[17] However, neither Turkey nor NATO actively pursued this idea.

Turkey also is concerned about closer military cooperation between Russia and Armenia. In February 1999 Russian air force General Anatoly Kournishev declared that Russia was stationing S-300 missiles and MiG-29 fighters in Armenia to protect it against threats from Turkey and NATO.[18]

Turkish-Armenian relations are heavily weighted by the history of the late Ottoman years, when massacres of Armenians, particularly in 1915 and 1916, created psychological scars still unhealed. In contemporary times, relations are constricted by the problem of Nagorno-Karabakh, the Armenian-populated enclave in Azerbaijan. Armenia came to occupy some twenty percent of Azerbaijan's territory as a result of fighting sparked by Nagorno-Karabakh's bid for independence. Although a cease-fire has been in place since 1994, diplomatic efforts to resolve the problem remain stalemated. Turkey recognized Armenia's independence, like that of all former Soviet states in December 1991, but it says it will not establish full diplomatic relations until Yerevan withdraws its forces from all territory occupied in Azerbaijan and agrees to respect Azerbaijani sovereignty over Nagorno-Karabakh. Some Turkish and Armenian businessmen have saught to normalize ties and open the closed borders. A joint Turkish-Armenian business development committee was established in May 1997. However, in spite of pressure from business lobbies, relations probably will not improve until real progress is made toward resolving the Nagorno-Karabakh dispute.

Continued close ties between Russia and Armenia have left Azerbaijani president Haydar Aliyev little choice but to maintain the warm relationship with Turkey that his predecessor Elchibey developed. In February 1999 Azerbaijan announced that it would withdraw from the Russian-led, post-Soviet Commonwealth of Independent States (CIS) collective security treaty because of lack of Russian support over Nagorno-Karabakh.[19] More surprisingly, the previous month, Aliyev's foreign affairs adviser, Vafa Guluzade, publicly proposed that Baku ask Turkey, the U.S., or NATO to establish a base in Azerbaijan on the Aphseron peninsula by the Caspian Sea to counter the Russian presence in Armenia. Aliyev, however, rejected the idea.[20] Reluctant to provoke the Russians, Turkish foreign ministry officials were presumably relieved to hear—and perhaps had a role in shaping—Aliyev's reaction.

Relations between Turkey and Azerbaijan are close. Turkey has been a firm supporter of Azerbaijan's position on Nagorno-Karabakh. Azerbaijan, in turn, has strongly supported the idea that the main export pipeline for its Caspian Sea oil should traverse Turkey. Aliyev has frequently visited Turkey for official reasons, as well as for medical treatment and vacations. In 1999, Turkey awarded him the highest distinction it bestows on foreigners, the Atatürk Peace Prize.

Nevertheless, Turkish-Azerbaijani ties have not been smooth at all times during Aliyev's presidency. In March 1995 ultranationalist groups connected with the Turkish mafia and rogue elements in Turkish intelligence tried but failed to overthrow Aliyev in a planned coup designed to restore Elchibey. Relations also suffered when a Turkish parliamentary report suggested that Aliyev's son Ilham, deputy head of the State Oil Company of Azerbaijan (SOCAR), had possible mafia links. Prime Minister Yılmaz rebutted this charge on Ilham Aliyev's behalf, but the incident provoked resentment in Baku's governing circles.[21]

Immediately after the Soviet breakup, central authorities in Georgia were suspicious of Turkey's possible links with Muslim-populated Ajaria, a region seeking more autonomy from Tbilisi, and were wary of the sympathies of a large number of Turkish citizens of Abkhazian origin for the Abkhazian separatist cause. Relations between Tbilisi and Ankara greatly improved, however, when it became clear that Georgia was a prospective transit country for the passage of Caspian oil and gas from Azerbaijan to Turkey. In early March 1999, Georgia and Turkey signed several defense agreements. These symbolized growing bilateral ties but appeared to have minimal operational significance. Georgian leader Eduard Shevardnadze made clear that Turkey would not establish military bases in Georgia.[22]

In order to acquire a better understanding of the importance of Turkey's ties with certain states in the Transcaucasus and in Central Asia, one must examine closely the Caspian energy issue. Energy issues have assumed priority for Turkey in its relations with the states of the region. Two goals are most important for Turkey: serving as a transport route for westward-bound Caspian oil and acquiring gas. Success in achieving these goals would satisfy Turkey's twin cravings for enhanced strategic importance and for fuel to power its growing economy.

Oil, Gas, and Pipelines

Ankara has been pressing the case that the main export pipeline for Caspian Sea oil should run through Turkey. Specifically, Turkey's proposal envisions the pipeline originating in Baku, Azerbaijan; traversing Georgia; and then heading south through Turkey to a terminal on the Turkish Mediterranean coast at Ceyhan.

The U.S. has strongly advocated the choice of Baku-Ceyhan as the main Caspian export line. This was symbolized on the margins of the November 1999 summit of the Organization for Security and Cooperation in Europe (OSCE) in Istanbul, when U.S. president Bill Clinton witnessed the signing of a commitment to Baku-Ceyhan by the leaders of Azerbaijan, Georgia, and Turkey. As a non-Russian, non-Iranian outlet for Caspian oil, Baku-Ceyhan makes strategic sense for the U.S.

In fact, Washington envisions Baku-Ceyhan as part of a larger "east-west energy corridor" that would also include a trans-Caspian pipeline (TCP) carrying gas from Turkmenistan across the Caspian to Azerbaijan and then following a route parallel to Baku-Ceyhan. However, Washington has insisted that it will not subsidize Baku-Ceyhan (or, for that matter, TCP) and that the project therefore must be commercially viable.

Environmental and strategic motives largely impel Turkey's effort to be the primary westward outlet for Caspian oil. Potential commercial gains are relatively limited. The narrow, crooked Bosporus waterway, which bifurcates Turkey's largest city, Istanbul, and its ever-swelling population of now more than ten million, has been the scene of numerous oil-tanker accidents. Since the other two main export line proposals each terminate on the Black Sea—one at Georgia's Supsa, the other at Russia's Novorossiisk—the likely outlet for their oil would be the sea route from the Black Sea through the Bosporus. Turkey fears an increase in tanker traffic in the Bosporus could create an environmental and humanitarian disaster.

Declaring that the Bosporus should not be regarded as an "oil pipeline," Turkish officials insist that the 1936 Montreux Convention grants them the right to regulate, and therefore limit, tanker traffic along the Turkish Straits. Russia, whose economic well-being depends on assured passage from the Black Sea and which harbors the hope that Baku-Novorossiisk will emerge as the main export line for Caspian oil, naturally disputes Turkey's interpretation and opposes any restriction on shipping in the Bosporus not specifically cited in Montreux. Some Turkish politicians have suggested that Turkey not only impose stricter traffic regulations but also require use of double-hulled vessels, with the apparent aim of making the cost of shipping oil through the Straits prohibitively high.

Although Turkish environmental and safety concerns seem justified, suspicion lingers in some quarters that Turkey has raised these issues merely to scuttle any alternatives to Baku-Ceyhan. This skepticism was fed by a 1997 statement by the Turkish state minister responsible for maritime affairs, Burhan Kaya, who warned that Turkey might increase transit fees for tankers by 500 percent if the Baku-Ceyhan pipeline were not realized.[23]

Strategic factors—geopolitics and international prestige—are probably the main considerations in Turkey's pursuit of the Baku-Ceyhan pipeline. Many Turkish generals, diplomats, and politicians believe construction of Baku-Ceyhan—as well as gas pipelines from Azerbaijan, Turkmenistan, and perhaps elsewhere in Central Asia—would enable the newly independent post-Soviet states to decrease their dependence on Russia and strengthen their ties with Turkey. Turkey thus would be an even more important player in the Caspian region, and Russian influence would decrease.

Compared with the opportunity to increase its geostrategic significance and protect its environment, commercial considerations appear to be less important in Ankara's Baku-Ceyhan bid. In order to make the project more attractive to investors, Turkey has already agreed that transport fees imposed on oil piped to Ceyhan would be kept low. As a further inducement, Turkey has promised to guarantee construction costs of the pipeline on Turkish territory above $1.4 billion (the Turkish estimate of what construction of that portion of the pipeline should cost), further cutting into Turkish income from transit fees.

Although oil consumption is not a primary motive for its involvement in the Baku-Ceyhan project, Turkey would benefit domestically from easy access to a new energy source. Turkish energy officials estimate that approximately 300,000 barrels of oil per day flowing along a Baku-Ceyhan pipeline may find its way to Turkish consumers.

For many reasons, however, the prospect that Baku-Ceyhan actually will be built is questionable. The most important variable is oil volume: Despite initially optimistic projections about its reserves, it is not yet clear whether Azerbaijan has sufficient oil to justify the building of Baku-Ceyhan. Kazakhstan has indicated that it is prepared to ship some of its Caspian oil through Baku-Ceyhan, which could make up for a shortfall. However, it is also unclear whether Kazakhstan has sufficient volume to dedicate to making Baku-Ceyhan viable or, if it does, whether the oil companies working in Kazakhstan will opt for that route. According to industry estimates, Baku-Ceyhan will have to carry roughly a million barrels of oil per day to justify its construction.

A second concern, related to volume, is the likely cost of a Baku-Ceyhan pipeline. Industry officials have maintained the cost could run as high as $4 billion; U.S. officials have said $2.4 billion, and Turkish officials put the figure as low as $1.7 billion if parallel oil and gas pipelines are built. Turkey's decision to cap costs for pipeline construction on its own territory at $1.4 billion should alleviate this problem somewhat.

Even if sufficient oil is found and the cost of pipeline construction kept sufficiently under control to justify it commercially, construction and functioning of Baku-Ceyhan still is not assured. Security problems could dissuade potential investors or sabotage a completed line. The Turkish portion of a Baku-Ceyhan line would run through the Kurdish-populated east, where it could be threatened by a resurgence of PKK violence. The section of pipe running across Georgia might be attacked by Abkhazian separatists or the disgruntled Armenian minority seeking autonomy in Georgia's Javakhetia district. Given Russia's well-known opposition to Baku-Ceyhan, one can also speculate on covert or overt operations Moscow may undertake to block its construction or undermine its operation.

Making Baku-Ceyhan's prospects even less certain is the fact that it is not necessarily the only alternative for transporting Caspian oil to the west, as already noted. A pipeline connecting Baku and Novorossiisk on Russia's Black Sea coast began operation in January 1998, carrying small quantities of so-called "early oil" produced in Azerbaijan. The security and general viability of this pipeline is, however, problematic. In February 1999 alone, its flow was interrupted three times because of a fire and other so-called "technical problems" on the section of the pipeline that traverses Chechnya.[24] It was closed in summer 1999 because of Russian-Chechen disagreements over cost-sharing and profit-taking arrangements regarding the Chechen section of the pipeline. A Chechnya-bypass line through Daghestan was completed in spring 2000, but its long-term viability is subject to question. Moreover, facilities at Novorossiisk—where poor winter weather interferes with loading oil—would not be able to handle significantly increased amounts of Kazakh and Azerbaijani oil. In 1999 early oil also began to flow along a pipeline connecting Baku with the Georgian Black Sea port of Supsa. Both the Baku-Novorossiisk and Baku-Supsa pipelines are considerably smaller than the envisioned Baku-Ceyhan line.

Possible Bosporus-bypass routes—which would carry Caspian oil by tanker from Supsa or Novorossiisk to Odessa, Ukraine, or Constanta, Romania, and then pipe it overland across Europe—do not appear commercially feasible because of high costs and logistical problems involved in loading and offloading the oil. The same is true of the Burgas-Alexandroupolis and Burgas-Durres options, whereby oil would be brought by tanker to Bulgaria, thence piped to a Greek outlet on the Aegean Sea or an Albanian outlet on the Adriatic, and then shipped to Europe via tanker.

Ultimately, Iran may play the spoiler of Turkish dreams for Baku-Ceyhan. Despite U.S. opposition, the leading international oil consortium in Azerbaijan reportedly has not discarded the option of constructing a pipeline across Iran from Baku to the Persian Gulf, particularly if Washington relaxes its policies toward Iran.[25] "Swap deals" also could be arranged in which Caspian oil is transported to refineries in northern Iran while an equivalent amount of Iranian oil is shipped from Iranian ports in the Gulf.

Final determination of the pipeline route will be made not by governments but by the main oil consortium in Azerbaijan—the Azerbaijan International Operating Company (AIOC)—many of whose members likely would fund the project. AIOC's top shareholder is the British concern BP Amoco, but it also includes U.S., Turkish, Azerbaijani, Russian, and other elements. Given the possibility that recoverable oil reserves in the Caspian are not as substantial as first supposed, AIOC may decide not to build a major export pipeline. Rather, it may be content to continue to use the Baku-Novorossiisk and Baku-Supsa "early oil" pipelines indefinitely, while adding Iranian "swap deals" to the mix. This would be a disappointing result for Turkish officials seeking to boost Turkey's strategic importance in the region.

Even with the best possible policy management by Turkey, the viability of Baku-Ceyhan is open to doubt, as suggested above. Nevertheless, it is worth noting that throughout much of the second half of the 1990s, as the issue of Caspian oil exports was emerging, Ankara had problems coordinating its energy policy. The presidency, prime ministry, foreign ministry, energy ministry, the state-owned petroleum agency, the state-owned pipeline company, and, at times, the armed forces all were involved in decision-making. Frequent changes of government and rapid turnover of relevant personnel undermined policy consistency. Stories of favoritism, corruption, and cliques appeared in the Turkish press. Various private construction companies and other Turkish businesses reportedly sought to place their men in prominent positions in the energy ministry and the state-owned energy agencies.[26] In 1998, however, things improved as an interagency Baku-Ceyhan working group was formed to coordinate policy activities and negotiate with the AIOC and Azerbaijani and Georgian governments to conclude technical and legal agreements. President Demirel's decision to become personally engaged in the issue also boosted Turkey's ability to speak with one coherent voice on Baku-Ceyhan-related issues.

TCP—the other part of the U.S.-envisioned "east-west energy corridor"—would serve Turkish interests in a manner very different from Baku-Ceyhan. The main purpose of TCP would be to deliver gas, not geostrategic importance. Turkey's growing economy is badly in need of new energy sources, particularly natural gas. According to official Turkish estimates, Turkey's need for imported natural gas may roughly triple in the first five years of the new century, from approximately 16 billion cubic meters (bcm) in 1999 to an estimated 45 bcm by 2005 and 53 bcm by 2010. Most independent analysts say the Turkish figures are exaggerated, but only somewhat. Meanwhile, Turkmenistan has potentially vast quantities of natural gas to export and, seemingly, a strong strategic incentive to export it by a non-Russian route.

TCP would not be bereft of strategic importance for Turkey. It is envisioned that up to 14 bcm of gas ultimately will be delivered to central Europe via an extension of the pipeline.

Nevertheless, a number of factors make TCP an uncertain prospect. For one, Turkey also is involved in a major gas pipeline deal with Russia. Known as "Blue Stream," this project would entail two parallel underwater pipelines across the Black Sea directly connecting Russia and Turkey; these would be the world's deepest underwater pipes. Total capacity of Blue Stream would be 16 bcm per year. Planning for Blue Stream is much further along than planning for TCP. If Blue Stream proves feasible, TCP may be unnecessary in the near term. TCP also is anticipated to deliver about 16 bcm per year.[27] Turkish officials claim they need both projects, and that may well be true over the long term. For now, however, their statements are widely seen as merely a diplomatic effort to handle a sensitive situation in which Ankara seemingly has tilted toward a project opposed by the U.S., Blue Stream, and away from the U.S.-preferred TCP project. TCP is backed by U.S. commercial interests and also would contribute to Washington's vision of a Central Asia less dependent on Russia.

Further competition to TCP may come from other sources, including major gas deposits uncovered in 1999 in the Shah Deniz fields in Azerbaijan itself, delivery of which to Turkey would be cheaper and less complicated than gas from TCP. Natural gas deliveries from Iran, volume of which eventually could be as much as 10 bcm annually, are scheduled to begin in June 2001. Probably in deference to U.S. concerns about Iran, Turkey has moved slowly on completion of its portion of a gas pipeline to Iran and therefore missed the originally planned December 1999 target for taking deliveries. Tehran agreed to the mid-2001 rescheduling, and Ankara has agreed to a "take-or-pay" arrangement—that is, it must pay whether or not it takes delivery—so it is likely the gas really will flow at that time. Turkey also has signed agreements to import gas or liquefied natural gas (LNG) from several other sources, including Algeria, Egypt, Iraq (when sanctions are lifted), Iran, Nigeria, and Qatar.

Aside from competitors and the logistical complications of the TCP project—which would traverse a major sea and two other countries before reaching Turkey—its realization faces other impediments as well. Russian opposition, Azerbaijani-Turkmenistani legal disputes regarding the Caspian, and the difficult bargaining style of Turkmenistani president Niyazov all cast doubt on TCP's prospects.

Some Turkish energy bureaucrats complain that their government gives gas deals involving Russia undue priority over other energy projects. This, they say, is because of effective lobbying by private Turkish construction companies such as GAMA, ENKA, and Tekfen, which hold substantial Russian investments. Several such companies wield considerable influence within former prime minister Mesut Yılmaz's Motherland Party (ANAP), which held the prime ministry and the energy ministry for one-and-a-half years in 1998-99. After a half-year hiatus,

ANAP regained the energy ministry as a junior partner in Prime Minister Bulent Ecevit's three-party coalition government formed in June 1999.

U.S. Interests

When referring to U.S. interests with regard to Turkish policy in Central Asia and the Transcaucasus and Turkey's Caspian energy concerns, one must differentiate between the positions of the U.S. administration, Congress, and energy companies. The Bush and Clinton administrations emphasized Turkey's pivotal role. In February 1998 testimony before the House Foreign Relations subcommittee on Asia and the Pacific, Assistant Secretary of Energy for Policy and International Affairs Robert Gee declared in no uncertain terms that Turkey needs support because it is an "anchor of stability" in a troubled region.[28]

The Clinton administration—eager to create an east-west energy transport corridor from the Caspian to Europe, which would exclude Iran and only minimally incorporate Russia—vigorously backs Baku-Ceyhan and actively promotes the trans-Caspian gas pipeline option. In return, U.S. officials hope Turkey will not follow through with the Blue Stream project and will continue to delay implementation of its gas import deal with Iran. In October 1998 the U.S. Eximbank, the U.S. Trade and Development Agency, and the U.S.-based Overseas Private Investment Corporation (OPIC) awarded the Turkish state pipeline company BOTAŞ a project credit of $823,000. Its purpose was to enable Turkey to tap U.S. expertise on technical, financial, environmental, and legal matters when negotiating for the construction of an oil pipeline to Ceyhan.[29] Another indication of the Clinton administration's serious intent was the February 1999 opening in Ankara of a U.S. Caspian Finance Center—the first of its kind—to assist U.S. companies interested in investing in the Caspian energy market.[30]

The U.S. Congress, influenced by an active pro-Armenian lobby, has a different perception of developments in the Transcaucasus. This affects U.S.-Turkish relations and also hinders the activities of U.S. energy companies working in Azerbaijan. The Clinton administration has attempted, in vain so far, to have Congress rescind Section 907 of the 1992 Freedom Support Act, which prohibits the U.S. government from providing aid to Azerbaijan because of its blockade of Armenia resulting from the Nagorno-Karabakh dispute. In part yielding to White House pressure, in October 1998 Congress declared the U.S. Eximbank and OPIC exempt from provisions of Section 907. These agencies may now assist U.S. energy companies working in Azerbaijan by offering limited financial support and providing "political risk" insurance.[31] In late 1999 these exemptions were renewed for another year.

Naturally, U.S. energy companies are primarily interested in profits and not geopolitics or geoeconomics. Projects must be commercially attractive to secure their financial backing. This backing will be crucial for the implementation of any of the Caspian energy schemes. The U.S. administration has only been able to offer political support and limited economic incentives. Ultimately, therefore, Turkey must convince U.S. and British energy companies, which have a preponderant stake in AIOC, that a Baku-Ceyhan pipeline is commercially attractive. Close U.S.-Turkish relations, in and of themselves, cannot clinch a deal in the Caspian pipeline game.

Conclusion

In the wake of Soviet collapse, Turkish officials quickly moved to develop and consolidate ties with the newly independent Turkic states in Central Asia and the Transcaucasus. The Turkic republics, though, were at no time willing to bind themselves exclusively to Turkey. For example, they were not prepared to jeopardize their relations with the international community by recognizing the "Turkish Republic of Northern Cyprus," as Ankara greatly wished.

Because of the growing importance of Caspian energy for Turkey, it appears that Turkish officials tend to focus more on developments in what is now commonly referred to as "the Caspian region." This region covers the Transcaucasus, southwestern Russia, Iran, and the western Central Asian states of Kazakhstan and Turkmenistan. Policy-makers in Ankara may also increasingly come to perceive Uzbekistan to be a part of this region. When the Ankara Declaration, which focused on pipeline routes, was signed in Turkey in October 1998, Uzbekistan's Karimov took full part in the official proceedings together with his Turkish, Azerbaijani, Kazakhstani, and Turkmenistani counterparts. Distant Kyrgyzstan is less attractive for Turkish politicians and businessmen and may gravitate more toward China.

It probably is not wise to attempt to predict the future of Turkey's relations with states in the Caspian region, especially in the face of the fluid and ever-changing nature of pipeline politics. The death of Azerbaijani leader Aliyev—whose health is believed to be in serious decline—could have considerable repercussions for Turkey and other states (and energy companies) interested in regional security and Caspian energy. The rise to power of Vladimir Putin in Russia and the end of the Demirel presidency in Turkey may also have a bearing on future developments. What does appear clear, though, is that Turkish officials and entrepreneurs are determined to ensure that Turkey remains a major player in the Caspian region.

Notes

1 Alan O. Makovsky, "Turkey," in Robert Chase, Emily Hill and Paul Kennedy (eds.), *The Pivotal States: A New Framework for U.S. Policy*

    in the Developing World (New York and London: W.W. Norton, 1999), pp. 88-119.

2   Heinz Kramer, "Will Central Asia Become Turkey's Sphere of Influence?" *Perceptions* 1, no. 1 (March-May 1996), p. 115.

3   *Cumhuriyet*, February 24, 1992.

4   *Turkish Daily News (TDN)*, May 4, 1992.

5   Ibid., October 31, 1992.

6   Interview with State Minister Ahat Andıçan in *Nokta*, August 24-30, 1997, pp. 26-27.

7   Mustafa Aydın, "Turkey and Central Asia: Challenges of Change," *Central Asian Survey* 15, no. 2 (June 1996), pp. 165-166.

8   *Turkistan Newsletter (TN)* 98, no. 2-110, June 11, 1998.

9   *TN* 98, no. 2-044, March 12, 1998.

10   Although RP leader Necmettin Erbakan toured various Islamic countries—including Iran—as prime minister, he strikingly did not visit a single Turkic state. It is not clear if this omission was his choice or that of the Turkic states.

11   *Yeni Yüzyıl*, February 13, 1997.

12   "The Turkish Economy in Figures," *DEİK* (*Foreign Economic Relations Board* [*of Turkey*]) *Bulletin*, February 1998.

13   Figures are from the *Foreign Trade Statistics Bulletin*, March 10, 2000, published by the Turkish State Institute of Statistics: http://www.turkey.org/f_business.htm

14   Gül Turan and İlter Turan, "Turkey's Emerging Relationship with other Turkic Republics," in Libby Rittenberg (ed.), *The Political Economy of Turkey in the Post-Soviet Era: Going West and Looking East?* (Westport, Connecticut and London: Praeger, 1998), p. 197.

15   *TDN*, September 7-8, 1998.

16   *RFE/RL Newsline* 2, no. 224, part 1 (December 21, 1998). Georgia finally took over sole responsibility for guarding its borders in September 1999. However, Russian troops remained stationed on four bases there.

17   Kelly Couturier, "Turkey Assuming Lead Peacekeeping Role," *Washington Post*, July 16, 1998.

18   *TDN*, February 20, 1999.

19   *Turkistan Economy Bulletin (TEB)* 99, no. 18 (February 12, 1999).

20   *TDN*, February 1, 1999.

21   Saadet Oruç, *Turkish Probe*, February 22, 1998.

22   *RFE/RL Caucasus Report* 2, no. 10 (March 9, 1999).

23   *TN* 98, no. 118, November 9, 1998.

24   *TEB* 99, no. 18, February 12, 1999; and *TEB* 99, no. 19, February 15, 1999; *RFE/RL Newsline* 3, no. 37, part 1 (February 17, 1999).

25   Onnic Marashian, "Pipeline Routes and Pipeline Politics," in *The Geopolitics of Oil, Gas and Ecology in the Caucasus and Caspian Basin*, Conference Report (Berkeley Soviet and Post-Soviet Studies Program, Center for Slavic and East European Studies, May 16, 1998), p. 41.

26   *TDN*, March 4, 1999.

27   *Yeni Yüzyıl*, October 30, 1998.

28   *TN* 98, no. 2-031, February 18, 1998.

29   *TDN*, October 28, 1998.

30   *TEB* 99, no. 018, February 12, 1999.

31   *Energy and Politics*, no. 37, part 2 (November 3, 1998).

Tozun Bahcheli

Turkish Policy toward Greece*

A n extraordinary warming of relations between Greece and Turkey in the wake of the devastating earthquake of August 17, 1999,
in western Turkey raised expectations of lasting improvement in Greek-
Turkish relations. Ironically, this unexpected development occurred in
the final months of an otherwise troubled decade that witnessed dangerous confrontations between the two neighbors both in the Aegean
Sea and in Cyprus. In January 1996 Greece and Turkey almost went to
war over an uninhabited Aegean islet close to Turkey's coast. During
much of the 1990s, Turkish officials accused Greece of acting against
Turkey in virtually every area vital to its interests: Cyprus, the Aegean,
European Union (EU) relations, and Kurdish separatism. Ankara's relations with Athens deteriorated markedly over the Abdullah Öcalan
affair in February 1999. The discovery that Greece had sheltered Öcalan—
leader of the separatist Kurdistan Workers Party (PKK, by its Kurdish initials) and thus Turkey's public-enemy number-one—in its embassy in
Nairobi, Kenya, enraged the Turks, whose leaders had long accused Athens of supporting PKK terrorism against Turkey. President Süleyman
Demirel vented Ankara's anger by urging that Greece be designated a
"rogue state" and warned that Turkey would use its right of self-defense if
Athens continued to support Kurdish insurgents.[1]

For their part, Greek leaders accused Turkey of generally assuming
a more aggressive stance toward Greece in the post-Cold War era and
of making new territorial claims in the Aegean. An intensified arms
race between the two rivals, and the extension of their competition to
regions where they were barely active during the Cold War—the
Balkans, the Caucasus, and the Middle East—helped fuel the rivalry
through much of the 1990s.

In the weeks following the earthquake, the Greek and Turkish media—particularly the press—gave ample coverage to acts and statements
of friendship on the part of ordinary citizens, nongovernmental organizations, and officials. The enthusiastic and generous response of the
Greek people and government in assisting Turkish victims struck a positive chord in the Turkish public and in Ankara. Turks were also

*The author would like to thank the United States Institute of Peace in Wash-
ington, D.C., for a grant that helped facilitate this research.

pleased when Athens reversed its opposition to previously earmarked EU assistance to Turkey and endorsed new aid initiatives. When a considerably less severe earthquake struck Athens on September 7, Turkey reciprocated by providing swift assistance to Greek victims.

This "seismic diplomacy," as the media dubbed it, raised expectations that relations might enter a new era of cooperation. Even before the earthquakes, Turkish foreign minister İsmail Cem and Greek foreign minister George Papandreou had begun a tentative dialogue and cooperated in providing humanitarian aid to Kosovo during the North Atlantic Treaty Organization (NATO) military campaign against Yugoslavia in spring 1999. With the mutual aid during the earthquakes energizing bilateral dialogue, Greece lifted its veto on Turkey's candidacy for EU membership at the EU's Helsinki summit in December 1999. This further boosted Greek-Turkish ties and perhaps suggested a newfound Greek willingness to "decouple" bilateral issues from the Cyprus problem, as Ankara prefers.

A series of bilateral meetings during the summer and fall of 1999 tackled largely noncontroversial issues related to economic and cultural ties, border security, terrorism, and organized crime. Subsequently, nearly a dozen agreements related to these issues were signed during the visits of Papandreou to Ankara and of Cem to Athens in January and February 2000, respectively. In a further sign of this developing rapprochement, Greek prime minister Costas Simitis accepted Turkish prime minister Bülent Ecevit's invitation to visit Turkey. At the same time, as commentators and officials in both countries cautioned, a wide divergence of interests continued to exist, and it may be premature to envisage a pronounced change in Greek or Turkish policies in key areas of contention such as Cyprus and the Aegean.

Between War and Managed Rivalry

That Turkey and Greece were adversaries for long periods in their history has deeply influenced their relationship and their leaders' reactions to disputes. The mistrust traditionally exhibited is a product of an acrimonious historical legacy. Nevertheless, Greeks and Turks have shown that they are not entirely prisoners of memory. Their history of conflict has not ruled out periods of peace and reconciliation, or even close and interdependent relations. Only eight years after their last war (1919 to 1922), which was fought with great ferocity and bitterness, Greece and Turkey began a period of détente.

Greek-Turkish reconciliation was introduced in 1930 by two powerful, visionary leaders, Kemal Atatürk and Eleftherios Venizelos. It yielded agreements in the political, economic, and security spheres and weathered occasional irritants. In the post-World War II era prospects for closer relations were further enhanced when both Turkey and Greece joined the Western alliance system and simultaneously became NATO members in 1952.

Amid these auspicious developments, Cyprus emerged as a major arena where Greek and Turkish interests clashed, beginning in the mid-1950s. Turks insist their policy in Cyprus (and the Aegean) was merely reactive. From their viewpoint, it was Greece and the Greek Cypriot leadership that repeatedly reopened the issue of sovereignty over the island, even after the Zurich-London agreements created Cypriot independence in 1959. Later, in the Aegean, Ankara accused Athens of wanting to bring about unilateral changes to the status quo by claiming the right to extend its territorial seas from six to twelve miles.

While these disputes seriously damaged relations, and even brought them to the brink of war on several occasions, the two neighbors also showed a capacity to cool tempers and to adopt measures that would discourage future confrontations. The Aegean confrontation of 1976 ushered in a decade of relative stability with the post-crisis adoption of the Berne Declaration. Another Aegean confrontation in 1987 had a profoundly sobering effect and led to the short-lived dialogue known as the "Davos process." But these respites from crisis failed to yield any sustained negotiating process, as Turkey would have liked. In fact, again in January 1996, the two neighbors briefly confronted each other over an uninhabited islet but without, this time, any subsequent improvement in the climate of relations. Moreover, the UN-sponsored Cyprus negotiations—to which Greek leaders attached a much higher priority than did Ankara—failed to achieve progress and generally undermined Greek-Turkish relations. Indeed, more often than not, tensions over Cyprus preoccupied the two countries. Just in the years 1997 through 1999, these tensions were fed by such developments as violence along the Green Line separating the two Cypriot communities, Cyprus's bid for accession to EU membership, and—before its cancellation in 1999—the proposed deployment of Russian-made S-300 surface-to-air missiles in Greek Cyprus. Thus Greek-Turkish relations remained strained through most of the 1990s.

Turkish Interests and Approach in the Aegean

It is conceivable that, without the legacy of past conflicts and the poisoning effect of the ongoing Cyprus issue, Ankara and Athens would find reasonable compromises to resolve their Aegean disputes. After all, even the best of neighbors are often enmeshed in sovereignty issues involving such complex areas. Nevertheless, the willingness of both Turkish and Greek leaders to consider war on three occasions in the last quarter of the twentieth century attests to the enormity of the two states' stake in the Aegean. For Turkey, the key concerns are access to its Aegean ports and sovereign control of significant maritime and air space. These are matters of great strategic consequence, but they also relate more simply to the important question of how to share the resources of common seas.

The Aegean issues that divide Turkey and Greece are limits on territorial sea, sovereign rights over the continental shelf and airspace, management of military and civil air-traffic control zones, and the militarization of Greek islands in the eastern Aegean. Turkey is seriously disadvantaged in pressing its claims by the fact that the great majority of Aegean islands and islets (which number more than 2,000) are Greek and that some of these are very close to the Turkish coast. This contributes to the Turks' perception that they are "hemmed in."

To the great disappointment of Turkish leaders, international maritime laws have been modified seemingly in Greece's favor in recent decades. Article 3 of the 1982 Law of the Sea (LOS) Convention provides for the right of states to establish territorial seas of "a maximum breadth of twelve miles from the baselines."[2] Greece was one of the first LOS signatories; Turkey has not signed LOS and does not intend to do so. Nevertheless, Greece thus far has refrained from extending its territorial sea in the Aegean beyond six miles.

While most Aegean quarreling has centered on the continental shelf, the territorial sea issue is the one that is most vital for Turkey. The two issues are not unrelated, since all of the shelf claimed by Greece would accrue to it automatically, were it able to implement a twelve-mile territorial claim. Greek extension of its Aegean territorial waters would make Turkey's access to its major ports, Istanbul and Izmir, more difficult. As Andrew Wilson pointed out in his 1980 study, *The Aegean Dispute*, "Already the application of the six-mile limit restricts Turkey to only three places where shipping may enter or leave Turkish territorial waters from international waters."[3]

If the territorial sea claimed by both countries were increased to twelve miles, the Greek share of the Aegean would go up to 64 percent, whereas Turkey's share would increase to less than 9 percent.[4] The proportion of international waters would drop from 56 percent to 26 percent.[5] Athens has tried to alleviate Ankara's concerns about port access by arguing that Turkish shipping would be fully protected by the right of innocent passage. Turkish leaders find such assurances inadequate.

Ankara has repeatedly declared that an extension to twelve miles would constitute a *casus belli*, that is, a justification for war. After the Greek parliament ratified the International Law of the Sea on June 1, 1994, the Turkish parliament followed on June 8 with a resolution authorizing the government to use all measures—widely understood to include physical force—to protect Turkey's rights in the Aegean, if necessary.

The access issue applies also to aircraft, as Turkey feels similarly confined by the airspace of Greece's islands. It has rejected the ten-mile airspace claimed by Athens by arguing that Greece is entitled to exercise sovereignty only over six miles, corresponding to its territorial seas—a position also taken by the U.S. and all NATO countries aside from Greece. Ankara challenges the claimed airspace by regularly sending its military aircraft to a distance of six miles from Greek island coasts. Typically Athens responds to what it considers violations of its airspace by sending its own aircraft to intercept. These aerial challenges have long worried their NATO allies, but Athens and Ankara thus far have managed to prevent mock dogfights from escalating into more serious exchanges.

Ankara has occasionally quarreled with Athens over lesser issues related to flights in the Aegean, repeatedly accusing Greece of abusing its purely technical Flight Information Region (FIR) responsibilities to try to gain sovereign rights. Again, like the U.S. and other NATO states, Turkey does not accept the Greek claim that it is obliged to notify Greek authorities when its military aircraft enter Aegean airspace. Turkey has much regretted its acceptance in 1952—when Greek-Turkish relations were harmonious—of International Civil Aviation Organization (ICAO) arrangements that assigned FIR responsibilities in the Aegean to Greece.

While the FIR issue has been an irritant, the stakes for both Turkey and Greece have been greater in the Aegean continental shelf. The shelf—comprising the seabed and subsoil of the submarine area beyond the territorial sea, to the point where the land mass is deemed to end—has proved to be one of the most difficult and potentially explosive issues facing the Aegean neighbors.

Athens has long held that delimitation of the continental shelf is the sole Aegean issue requiring formal resolution (as opposed to simple Turkish acquiescence to Athens's positions) and that the problem must be adjudicated by the International Court of Justice (ICJ) at The Hague. Greek leaders assert that their islands are surrounded by continental shelf beyond that of the Greek mainland. In the Turkish view, the Greek Aegean islands lie within Turkey's continental shelf as a natural extension of the Anatolian peninsula. According to Wilson, application of Greece's formula would confer on it about 97 percent of the Aegean seabed, leaving Turkey with less than 3 percent, specifically a narrow strip off Anatolia.[6] It is obvious even to Greek officials that Turkey would reject any such apportionment. Turkish leaders assert that "equity" should be the key principle in finding solutions for all Aegean problems. In accordance with this position, Ankara has proposed—and Athens has rejected—drawing a median line through the Aegean archipelago, leaving each side with roughly half of the sea's continental shelf.

Unlike Athens, which apparently feels confident about its legal position, Ankara fears that its cases on these issues is legally weak and demurs on Athens's desire to pursue an ICJ decision. However, Turkish leaders do feel confident on the issue of demilitarization of Greece's eastern Aegean islands, and they have periodically brought up the issue to demonstrate Greece's seeming contravention of the treaties of Lausanne (1923) and Paris (1947).

Ankara's approach to resolving its Aegean problems is driven by a determination generally to avoid the ICJ or indeed any other third party adjudication or arbitration, except "as a last resort." There is simply too much at stake. Turkish leaders calculate that, given Turkey's military strength vis-à-vis Greece, they can obtain far better terms in bilateral negotiations. In accordance with this approach, Ankara strongly resists Greek attempts to "internationalize" (and "Europeanize") Aegean issues. Turkish leaders traditionally react angrily to Athens's attempts to enlist the support of its EU partners.

Turkey has periodically tried, but failed, to induce Greece into bilateral negotiations on Aegean issues. There were intermittent talks on Aegean and other issues, particularly after the adoption of the Berne agreement in 1976. These ended with the election of Greece's first Panhellenic Socialist Movement (PASOK) government under the populist Andreas Papandreou in 1981. Talks concerning Aegean issues were briefly revived during the "Davos process" in 1988 and 1989 but proved inconclusive.

While both countries have generally avoided serious provocations in the Aegean, mutual suspicions sometimes create tensions and even confrontations. A case in point was Ankara's concern about Greek attempts to populate remote Aegean islands in 1995.[7] But Athens accused Ankara of a greater transgression in challenging Greek sovereignty over an unpopulated islet off the Turkish coast—known as Imia to Greeks and Kardak to Turks—in early 1996. Indicating a hardened policy after that incident, Turkish leaders announced a new position that there are more than a hundred uninhabited Aegean islets whose legal status is unclear, and thus represent "gray areas" of uncertain sovereignty. This policy departure sowed new doubts in Greek leaders' minds concerning Turkish intentions.

In an appeal to Greece on March 24, 1996, not long after Turkey and Greece nearly went to war over Imia-Kardak, Prime Minister Mesut Yılmaz announced Turkey's willingness to accept third-party mediation. The following year, Yılmaz (again prime minister after a one-year hiatus) urged that the two countries "resolve everything possible through negotiations and leave the rest to international arbitration and, as a last resort, to the International Tribunal in The Hague."[8] But these overtures did not move Athens to change its own approach.

For Ankara the prerequisite of any agreement is that Aegean territorial seas and corresponding airspace must be limited to six miles. Once this principle is accepted, it is conceivable that both negotiations and recourse to the ICJ could be utilized to resolve the continental shelf issue. However, this remains a theoretical possibility, given the profound gap in the Turkish and Greek approaches, as well as the two states' overall rivalry.

Rivalries in a New Strategic Landscape

One of the consequences of the end of the Cold War was the expansion of the geographical bounds of Greek-Turkish rivalry. Athens and Ankara vied to expand their influence and garner new allies in the Balkans, the Black Sea region, the Caucasus, and the Middle East. New strategic relationships, such as that formed by Turkish-Israeli military cooperation, have sharpened the rivalry.

In spite of a newfound impetus for rivalry in the Balkans, Athens and Ankara clearly had common anxieties concerning the disintegration of Tito's Yugoslavia and the ensuing instability. However, once the collapse of most of the Yugoslav federation became inevitable, and with new governments in the region replacing the communist ones, Greek-Turkish rivalry became more pronounced. Ankara capitalized on Greek hostility toward the new Macedonian state by establishing close relations with it. Turkey was among the first countries to recognize, and assist, the government in Skopje. Ankara exploited Greece's problems with Albania by establishing close ties and providing aid to the government in Tirana.

When the Bosnian war broke out in April 1992, Turks resented Greek support for Serbia. Greece gave diplomatic support to the Serbians and helped Belgrade skirt international sanctions. In turn, Ankara provided diplomatic and covert military support to the Muslim-led Sarajevo government and was NATO's strongest advocate of lifting the UN arms embargo against Bosnia. A Turkish contingent served with both UN- and NATO-led forces in Bosnia: the UN Protection Force (UNPROFOR) and the Implementation Force-Stabilization Force (IFOR-SFOR). Turkish troops also participated with the multinational protection force in Albania. In the aftermath of the 1995 Dayton Accords, Ankara—with U.S. support—assumed a major role in training the Bosnian-Croat federation's army. Ankara was a keen supporter of and participant in NATO's Kosovo-related military campaign against Yugoslavia in 1999. In the aftermath of NATO's action, the Turkish government argued, albeit to no avail, that Turkey should join the ranks of the big-power Contact Group dealing with Belgrade.[9] The Simitis government in Greece felt obliged as an ally to endorse NATO action in Kosovo, however reluctantly, while coping with widespread domestic opposition to it. Nonetheless, Greece joined Turkey in providing troops for the NATO-led Kosovo force (KFOR); as noted, Ankara and Athens also cooperated in providing humanitarian relief to Kosovars during the war.

In the post-Communist Balkans, Ankara also played the "kinship card" with numerous Turkish or Muslim groups who looked to Turkey for support. These included the Muslims of Sandjak, the Albanians of Kosovo, Bulgarian Turks, the Gagauz of Moldova, and the Turks of Macedonia. The links of these communities with Turkey inflamed Greek worries about the expansion of Turkish influence in the Balkans, particularly given Athens's sensitivities regarding Ankara's support for the Turks of Greek Thrace. However, Turkish leaders generally discouraged these vulnerable groups from developing unrealistic expectations concerning Turkey's capacity to assist them in securing more rights or—as in the case of Kosovar Albanians—secession. While exploiting opportunities to expand its influence, Ankara tried not to stoke historical fears that Turkey is bent on projecting its power and restoring something akin to past Ottoman domination.

On this score Turkish policy-makers were satisfied that their conciliatory policy toward democratically elected governments in neighboring Bulgaria helped the Turkish minority there make impressive progress in the 1990s while also ameliorating Turkish-Bulgarian ties. The governments that succeeded the communist regime of Todor Zhivkov in Bulgaria restored the cultural rights taken from the Turkish minority during the 1980s. As the Cold War thawed in the mid-1980s, the Zhivkov regime had pursued close bilateral ties with Athens based on shared fear of the "Turkish threat." Ankara succeeded in persuading Sofia to pursue a more equidistant policy in the 1990s.

While Turkey acquired new influence in the post-Cold War Balkans, Athens improved its regional standing by revising its policies of the early 1990s. It ended its confrontation with Macedonia, improved its relations with Albania, and even distanced itself from too close an association with Serbia. Turkey used its NATO membership to some diplomatic advantage (as did Greece) with the Balkan countries aspiring to join NATO. But, as an EU insider, Greece could wield even greater influence with those who hoped eventually to join the European community in all its aspects.

Whatever the gains of Ankara's diplomacy in its rivalry with Athens for influence in the Balkans, Turkish leaders have been wary of the dangers that could push their country into costly entanglements in that unstable region. Thus, Turkish leaders have strongly favored multilateral, rather than unilateral, responses to crises such as those in Bosnia and Kosovo.

A series of diplomatic initiatives by Ankara boosted Turkey's profile in every region on its borders, and some of these invited Greek-Turkish interaction and modest cooperation. The Black Sea Economic Cooperation (BSEC) zone, launched on the initiative of the late Turkish president Turgut Özal in 1992, brought together Greece and Turkey as well as nine states in the Black Sea area, the Balkans, and the Caucasus. Another Ankara initiative yielded an agreement for a Balkan peace-keeping force.[10]

Just as Turkey took advantage of Greek setbacks in the Balkans to extend its influence, Greece played the game similarly in the Caucasus and the Black Sea region. In this connection, Ankara resented the warm relations that Greece established with Armenia. It viewed a Greek-Armenian defense cooperation agreement in 1996 as aimed at Turkey. Turkish leaders were even more wary of Athens's attempts to forge closer relations with Russia, in view of the multi-faceted Turkish-Russian rivalry in the region. While Ankara and Moscow competed over oil and gas pipelines from the Caucasus and Central Asia, Greece, Bulgaria, and Russia proposed transporting Caspian oil from Russia's Black Sea port of Novorossiisk through Burgas on Bulgaria's coast to the Greek Aegean port of Alexandroupolis. Turkey, with Washington's support, has vigorously promoted an overland pipeline terminating on its own Mediterranean coast, known as the Baku-Ceyhan pipeline.

Ankara has perceived the most immediate threats to its interests to be from the Middle Eastern states with which it shares a border: Syria, Iraq, and Iran. Syria was the most troublesome for Ankara, providing sanctuary to the PKK from the beginning of its separatist campaign in 1984 until Turkey pressured Damascus to expel Öcalan in 1998. Like Iraq, Syria has an ongoing dispute with Turkey over sharing the waters of the Euphrates River, which originates in eastern Turkey. Given the magnitude of these disputes and long-standing hostility from Damascus, Turkish leaders were deeply concerned about the possibility of Syrian acquisition of chemical and biological weapons and of long-range missiles.

Thus, Ankara was upset by Greek initiatives to enter into what was reported to be a "strategic partnership" with Damascus in 1995.[11] However, in spite of the effusive claims of Greek defense minister Gerasimos Arsenis, it was probably at most only an informal defense accord with Syria, perhaps allowing Greek warplanes to land in Syria in case of emergency, such as Turkish attacks on southern Cyprus.[12] By comparison, Ankara's own far-reaching military cooperation agreement with Israel in February 1996, although not aimed at Greece, promised to enhance Turkey's future military capabilities. Among the benefits of this relationship likely will be the ease of purchase of some types of sophisticated armaments. Ankara hopes that Turkish-Israeli military cooperation will indirectly tip the strategic balance with Greece in its own favor. In addition, Ankara hopes that the U.S. Jewish community will help "ease the problems it encounters in the U.S. Congress from pro-Greek, pro-Armenian, pro-Kurdish, and human rights lobbies."[13]

The EU Factor

Even as Ankara showed remarkable activism in winning new allies and extending its influence in its immediate neighborhood, it has long assigned a higher priority to its relations with Western Europe. In keeping with the Kemalist vision that Turkey's rightful place is within the Western family of nations, the Turkish secular establishment has pursued closer European ties for many years. Turkey's associate EU membership—attained in 1963, a year later than Greece—envisioned eventual full membership. Although Turkish leaders did not apply for membership when Greece did in 1975, they sought and received assurances from the EU that Turkish interests and membership prospects would not be affected by Greece's full membership.[14] Credible or not at the time, these assurances proved hollow. In the eyes of Turks as well as many EU members, Greece for years used its membership to impede progress in EU-Turkish relations.

In the aftermath of the EU's Luxembourg summit of December 12-13, 1997, which rejected Turkey's bid to be included among the countries eligible for EU membership, Ankara vented its anger toward Greece (and Germany) for their active role in the decision. Turkish bitterness was compounded by the EU's decision to bend to Greek pressure and place Cyprus on a fast track for EU accession, in spite of Ankara's insistence on a prior settlement between Greek and Turkish Cypriots. Turkish leaders were additionally upset that, instead of placing the onus for settlement of bilateral problems jointly on Athens and Ankara, EU members called upon Turkey to settle its disputes with Greece "in particular by legal process, including the International Court of Justice."[15]

From the Turkish point of view, the EU's Helsinki summit of December 1999, although overall more pleasing than Luxembourg in its acceptance of Turkey as an EU membership candidate, nevertheless was similarly problematic in endorsing recourse to the ICJ. In the words of the Helsinki communiqué:

> The European Council stresses the principle of peaceful settlement of disputes in accordance with the United Nations Charter and urges candidate states to make every effort to resolve any outstanding border disputes and other related issues. Failing this they should within a reasonable time bring the dispute to the International Court of Justice.

> The European Council will review the situation relating to any outstanding disputes, in particular concerning the repercussions on the accession process and in order to promote their settlement through the International Court of Justice, at the latest by the end of 2004.[16]

Some Turkish officials considered these statements—together with a separate assertion that Cyprus's accession would not be conditional on a political settlement on the island[17]—troublesome enough that they counseled the rejection of the EU's offer of candidate status. However, others in Ankara argued that the benefits of Turkish candidacy and prospective membership in the EU far outweighed the handicaps posed by these statements, and their counsel prevailed.

While tilting toward Greece, the Helsinki summit communiqué also seemed to acknowledge Turkish interests somewhat. Thus, the EU statement called for the resolution of "any outstanding border disputes and other related issues," in seeming acknowledgment of Ankara's position that there are Aegean issues unrelated to maritime boundaries (e.g., the militarization of Greece's eastern Aegean islands) that require resolution. Moreover, the communiqué called on candidate states to make "every effort" to resolve disputes; Ankara will argue that this underscores the necessity for bilateral negotiations in the resolution of its Aegean disputes with Greece prior to any recourse to the ICJ.

As much as Ankara has been upset by EU states' episodic involvement in Greek-Turkish disagreements, it should be recognized that European governments usually have preferred to steer clear of bilateral Greek-Turkish disputes, as well as the Cyprus issue. Most EU countries prefer that Greek Cypriot leaders, who have ardently pursued EU membership, reach a settlement with the Turkish Cypriots before Cyprus becomes an EU member. However, Greece's EU membership has made this very difficult. When its EU partners have disagreed with its policies, Athens has often retaliated by using its veto power, as it did in blocking EU aid earmarked for Turkey under the 1963 association agreement and the 1995 customs union agreement. It has also used the threat of a veto as leverage to boost the Greek Cypriots' cause. For example, Athens lifted its veto against the customs union in 1995, but only as a *quid pro quo* for the EU to begin negotiations with Cyprus for full membership. As noted, Greece secured a similar trade-off concerning Cyprus and Turkey at the December 1999 Helsinki summit, when it lifted its veto to allow the EU's assignment of candidate status to Turkey.

Even though the EU partners defer to Athens in many instances, they also have resisted Greek pressure on several major issues. In an area of paramount concern to Turkish security, the Western European Union (WEU, the EU's security arm) in 1992 "declared Greek-Turkish differences to be beyond its scope."[18] Furthermore, Greece's EU partners rejected its attempts to include a commitment to EU "territorial integrity" in the Amsterdam Treaty of June 1997.[19] That gambit was intended to drag the EU into bilateral Greek-Turkish territorial disputes.

Turkish leaders would like the EU partners to do more in restraining Greece, preventing it from converting Greek-Turkish issues into EU-Turkish problems. Greece's success in getting the EU to begin accession talks with the Republic of Cyprus in 1998 caused great dismay and anger in Ankara. In Turkish eyes, the EU had effectively sided with Greece in a dispute involving Turkish and Greek Cypriots as well as Athens and Ankara. On the Kurdish issue, too, Ankara resented attempts by Greek and European officials to involve the EU. In the aftermath of European appeals that Öcalan be assured of a fair trial in Turkey, the Turkish foreign ministry, as the *New York Times* put it, "accused the European Union of hypocrisy for seeking to protect Öcalan's human rights while failing to condemn Greece for harboring him."[20]

Thanks to the improvement in bilateral relations with Greece in late 1999, officials in Ankara have become more optimistic about Turkey's prospects for achieving EU membership. The desire to overcome a future Greek veto on membership could provide a strong incentive for Turkey to pursue rapprochement with Greece. At the same time, Turkish officials will strive to ensure that Greek-Turkish disputes are tackled bilaterally, without the involvement of the EU.

Perennial Irritant: Greece's Turkish Minority

Other issues compound the problems in Greek-Turkish relations, even though they are not as critical as the Aegean and Cyprus. For Ankara, one of the most important is the poor treatment of the Turkish community in western Thrace, whose number is estimated to be 125,000. Its members have accused the Greek government of neglecting their economic and educational needs, as well as restricting their rights in a number of areas, including the freedom to choose their *muftis* (religious leaders). [21] Until 1999, Athens refused even to call this group "Turks," insisting instead on the terminology of the 1923 Lausanne Treaty, which designates them merely as "Muslims."

The Greek government has generally denied applying a policy of discrimination against its Turkish minority. Moreover, it accuses Turkey, with some justification, of having forced out most of the Greek minority in Istanbul. Whereas the population of the Turkish community in Thrace has been constant, that of the Greek community in Istanbul has diminished drastically over the decades, from roughly 120,000 in 1923 to about 3,500 in 1999. Depopulation was particularly rapid during the 1950s and 1960s when Greek-Turkish relations were at a low point due to the Cyprus issue.

Ankara found that the virtual disappearance of the Istanbul Greeks substantially reduced its leverage vis-à-vis Athens regarding the Thracian Turks. Still, the discriminatory treatment meted out to this community is widely reported in the Turkish media. Ironically, while resisting pressures from several EU countries regarding its own human rights practices, Turkey sought additional leverage against Greece by using European forums such as the Council of Europe to publicize the plight of Thracian Turks. To some extent, this approach has worked. For example, members of the European Parliament in Strasbourg also raised questions on the issue. It was European, rather than Turkish, pressure that prompted Greece to abolish the controversial Article 19 of its constitution on June 11, 1998. This law had effectively deprived many Thracian Turks of their Greek nationality when they traveled to Turkey or to other countries.[22] However, the Greek government rejected an appeal to make the legislation retroactive and would not restore citizenship to those who were affected earlier.

In recent years Athens has taken numerous measures to improve the economy of Greek Thrace, which remains the country's poorest region. With the help of EU funds, investments were made in large projects to boost employment prospects, thus benefiting the Turkish community. The end of official restrictions on assertions of Turkish ethnicity—as of July 1999—was welcomed by members of the Turkish minority in western Thrace. Nevertheless, both the Thracian Turks and Ankara contend that the Greek government should adopt further measures to improve the minority's economic status and educational opportunities and allow it to elect its own *mufti*s.

The Greek–PKK Relationship: A Fading Issue?

The newer issue of alleged Greek support to the PKK seems now to be fading, but it would seriously undermine Greek-Turkish relations if it again comes to the fore. The violent rebellion spearheaded by the PKK has caused great problems for Turkey since it began in 1984. According to most estimates, it has claimed well over 30,000 lives. At an estimated $8 billion dollars annually, the cost to the Turkish treasury is also steep.[23] In 1999 imprisoned PKK leader Öcalan called on his fighters to lay down arms and withdraw from Turkey, suggesting that the insurgency may indeed be coming to an end. Nevertheless, Turkish authorities have been enormously frustrated over the years by the success of PKK guerrillas in keeping the insurgency alive and by the external support the insurgents have enjoyed. They have thus lashed out at those governments that have assisted the PKK. For many years the Syrian government bore the brunt of Turkish criticism for providing a safe haven to PKK fighters in Syria and in the Syrian-controlled Bekaa Valley in Lebanon. But Turkey has accused other neighbors, too, of aiding the PKK, including Iraq, Iran, and Greece, as well as Armenia and the Greek Cypriots.[24]

According to Turkish leaders, Athens assisted the PKK, even before the 1999 Öcalan escapade in Kenya, by allowing PKK fighters unhindered access to Greek territory and by allowing political groups associated with it to have offices and operate freely on Greek soil. Turkey also accused Athens, more significantly, of providing funding and covert training to PKK fighters. In the aftermath of Öcalan's capture by Turkey, Demirel asserted that "there are camps in Greece that extend arms and tactics to the terrorist PKK."[25] He also castigated Greece for "supporting a bloody movement so that Turkey is attacked from within."[26] Turkish officials have periodically reported the testimony of captured Kurdish fighters who "confessed" to the training they received in Greek safe houses and camps, particularly the refugee camp in Lavrion. These "confessions" have been widely publicized in the Turkish media.

Greece has denied all of these charges, while acknowledging that many Greeks are sympathetic to the Kurdish cause. Most Turks consider Öcalan a pitiless terrorist responsible for the deaths of thousands, but in Greece he has been seen as a hero fighting against Turkish oppression.[27] Even Greek officials have made statements in support of the "just struggle" of the Kurdish people.[28] Moreover, groups of Greek legislators have met with members of PKK-associated political groups in Athens as well as in other capitals. And Öcalan's ties to influential Greeks were revealed by his managing to get himself smuggled into Greece and then onward to the Greek embassy in Nairobi in late January 1999. Greek governments nonetheless have denied holding any officially sanctioned meetings with the PKK, although only equivocally so in the case of the Öcalan affair.

Ankara has rejected the distinction Greece makes between government policy and the legitimate political activities and sympathies of the Greek people. It likewise dismisses Greek protestations that Athens has not provided material aid to the Kurdish insurgents. Turkish leaders were disappointed that European governments did not take Greece to task over its alleged PKK ties or, indeed, examine their own policies that Ankara views as sympathetic to the PKK. Nevertheless, Demirel—citing France and Germany—spoke approvingly that "they have seen what the PKK stands for, and they banned it. There are several European countries who are cooperating with us on the terrorism issue."[29] The United States, whose policy on the PKK has been particularly satisfying to Turkish leaders, raised questions with Athens concerning the reported opening of a PKK office in Athens[30] and "condemned what it said was support by some Greek parliamentarians for the group."[31]

It is uncertain whether the Kurdish issue will continue to aggravate future Greek-Turkish relations. If Greek-Turkish rapprochement achieves momentum and the PKK has ended its armed struggle for good, the Kurdish issue likely will fade as a bilateral bone of contention. Turkish threats of retaliation over the Öcalan affair seem to have had a sobering effect on the Simitis government, and future Greek governments may be wary of provoking Ankara on an issue of existential importance to Turkey and only peripheral interest to Greece. Although he declined to condemn the PKK as a terrorist organization, Prime Minister Simitis in March 1999 affirmed Greece's opposition to any form of terrorism and its support for the inviolability of borders, including Turkey's.[32] Nevertheless, even as the PKK insurgency might be ending, Ankara continues to be concerned that Greece, as well as other European countries, will continue to criticize Turkey over Kurdish and other human-rights issues.

Domestic Factors

Turkish officials and commentators habitually claim that, although Greeks are obsessed with Turkey and the "Turkish threat," Greece is not a major preoccupation for the Turks. This is only partially accurate. For years before the August 1999 earthquake, the image of Greece portrayed in most of the Turkish media was usually that of a country whose leaders and people harbor perpetual enmity toward the Turkish nation. The press regularly carried news stories and articles highly critical of Greek policies concerning Cyprus, the Aegean, EU-Turkish relations, and the PKK. Thus the friendship expressed toward Greece and the Greeks in much of the Turkish media after the earthquake was a rare occurrence. Time will tell if this warming trend continues.

For Turkish policy-makers, Greece is one of a number of states, including Syria and Iraq, that pose a direct security threat to Turkey. While the security threats posed by Iraq and Syria do not find much resonance in the Turkish public, Greek threats do. This helps explain the ease with which nationalist feelings were mobilized during the Imia-Kardak episode. When the issue of contested sovereignty over the uninhabited islet first emerged, both Ankara and Athens discussed the matter quietly for weeks. However, once the story was leaked to the Greek press, both countries' media turned it into a *cause célèbre*. Aroused public opinion constrained both governments, making it difficult for the leaders to end the confrontation without losing face.

Policies toward Greece and Cyprus enjoy considerable support across the Turkish political spectrum—unlike more controversial foreign policies such as collaboration with Washington against Iraq in Operation Northern Watch (formerly Operation Provide Comfort), or even EU membership, which is opposed by many Islamists. More importantly, given the vital security issues involved in disputes between Ankara and Athens, key issues relating to Greece are deliberated within

Turkey's National Security Council (NSC). Chaired by the president of Turkey, the NSC consists of five top military officers and five senior civilian leaders, including the prime minister and the defense and foreign ministers. "Although constitutionally merely an advisory body that makes recommendations to the cabinet, its decisions are rarely overruled."[33]

During the 1990s, particularly with short-lived coalitions serially serving in office after 1991, military influence in Turkish decision-making increased. Turkey's senior military establishment is obviously keen to influence the Greek-Turkish military balance. While Middle Eastern adversaries such as Syria and Iraq became weaker, Greece continued to use its diplomatic and military assets, as well the Greek lobby in Washington, to check Turkish power. It was in this light that the Turkish military and civilian leadership worriedly viewed Greek Cypriot plans to deploy S-300 missiles and allow Greece to construct an air base and naval base in south Cyprus. Turkey's threats to destroy the missiles forced Nicosia to cancel the deployment. The missiles ultimately were delivered to Crete for Greek use.

A persistent irritant for the Turkish military has been the ability of the U.S. Greek lobby, in collaboration with the Armenian, Kurdish, and human rights lobbies, to influence Congress to stall arms sales to Turkey. Indeed, this was one of the motives for military cooperation with Israel.[34]

Turkey's military leaders are confident that its land and air forces are superior to those of Greece. In the early 1990s it embarked on a military modernization program that is more extensive than Greece's and is likely to maintain Turkey's military advantage into the foreseeable future.[35] Nevertheless, some Turkish military leaders have charged that Greek leaders contemplate waging a "controlled war" in the expectation that they could make quick gains and that the Western allies would stop such a war within a few days.[36]

Other key Turkish institutions, such as the foreign ministry, share the military's judgment that inimical Greek actions warrant an assertive policy response. At the same time, while a war with Greece is not discounted, both military and civilian leaders recognize the high costs that Turkey would bear. Turkish policy-makers long have favored confidence-building measures to reduce Aegean tensions.

The Imia-Kardak crisis reminded the two neighbors of how quickly and easily they can come to the brink of an unplanned war. Pressures of an aroused public opinion and populist leaders looking for domestic political advantage may be more likely to push Turkey into such a confrontation than the initiatives of the military. Prime Minister Tansu Çiller's inflammatory rhetoric during the Imia-Kardak crisis is a case in point.

During the 1990s, weak coalition governments shuffled in and out of office at the average rate of one per year. Eleven governments, including nine coalitions, and eleven different foreign ministers held office in Ankara during the decade. This made any major policy changes toward Greece most unlikely, since only a strong government could undertake bold policy departures. It is not a coincidence that one recent major effort for rapprochement took place during the leadership of Turgut Özal, whose party enjoyed a solid majority in Parliament during 1983-91. Keen on securing Turkey's accession to the EU, for which his government applied in 1987, Özal initiated the "Davos process" together with Greek prime minister Andreas Papandreou following their meeting in Davos, Switzerland, in early 1988. But the Davos initiative failed to yield any major breakthroughs, and momentum was lost by 1989. The domestic political weakening of both leaders soon afterwards spelled the end of the "Davos spirit."[37]

The Davos initiative failed in part because public opinion in both countries did not appreciate the "top-down" approach of their leaders. By contrast, after the Turkish and Greek earthquakes of August and September 1999, public opinion in both countries displayed a strong desire for improved relations. This augurs well, as do the activities of an impressive number of nongovernmental groups that have sought to promote better bilateral understanding. Even when relations were dismal at the governmental level, contacts between Greek and Turkish businessmen, academics, and even legislators were commonplace. After the earthquakes such contacts proliferated, signaling hope of changing the distorted images that Greeks and Turks have had of each other and of inducing policy-makers to continue to pursue more cooperative relations.

The U.S. Factor and NATO

The United States has long been involved in managing Greek-Turkish differences, particularly since the onset of civil strife on Cyprus in 1963. This has not been an easy task, and U.S. actions at times have caused major strains in Washington's relationship with both countries, sometimes simultaneously. The arms embargo Congress imposed on Turkey in 1975 is a case in point, as is the famous letter from President Lyndon B. Johnson to Turkish prime minister İsmet İnönü in 1964 warning him against a military intervention in Cyprus. Both caused much bitterness in Turkey and strained relations for several years.

Ankara also resented the 7:10 ratio applied by Congress (usually against White House wishes) to foreign aid for Greece and Turkey, respectively, starting in 1980. Turkish leaders contended that their nation, with its larger military and greater strategic assets, deserved far more funding than Greece. The end of the assistance program for both countries in 1998 put that problem to rest, however.

Turkey faces more obstacles in Washington than those posed by lobbies and Congress. Successive U.S. administrations have routinely called upon Ankara to remain committed to solving its problems with Greece and to helping settle the Cyprus issue. In Turkish eyes, Washington's handling of these issues is unwelcome, even if less offensive than that of European governments. Far more than the EU, which is often beholden to Greece, the U.S. has pursued a nuanced policy on Greek-Turkish disputes. U.S. policy on a number of Aegean issues actually lends indirect support to Turkey, such as the U.S. position that the sovereign airspace of a state corresponds to its territorial seas, which is identical to Turkey's. Moreover, by discouraging any unilateral move to alter the territorial status quo in the Aegean, Washington may also be said to bolster indirectly the Turkish position on the six-mile territorial-sea limit.

Washington's close relations with both Ankara and Athens, together with the NATO link, have given the U.S. considerable leverage in stabilizing the Greek-Turkish relationship and in exploiting opportunities to help resolve disputes. There is, after all, a shared general interest between Washington, Ankara, and Athens in avoiding confrontations in the Aegean. But moving beyond crisis prevention to the settlement of disputes has been a daunting task.

Since Ankara and Athens have rejected U.S. involvement in the possible resolution of their Aegean disputes, Washington has expended a good deal more effort in trying to settle the Cyprus issue. Like many Western capitals, Washington hopes a Cyprus breakthrough will pave the way for substantially improved Greek-Turkish relations and enhance prospects for settling Aegean disputes. However, after more than thirty years of intermittent communal talks, a Cyprus settlement remains elusive.

Still, the U.S. regularly has looked for opportunities to foster a better Greek-Turkish bilateral climate. One notable initiative in the aftermath of Imia-Kardak was an agreement by Ankara and Athens to adopt the U.S.-brokered Madrid Communiqué on July 8, 1997. That carefully drafted document addressed both Turkish and Greek sensitivities, calling for "respect for the principles of international law and international agreements" as well as "respect for each other's legitimate, vital interests" and "commitment to refrain from unilateral acts."[38]

However, any expectation that the Madrid Communiqué would usher in more stable and peaceful relations was quickly disappointed. Ankara's anger at the Greek role in its December 1997 EU rejection and growing acrimony over the S-300 crisis led to charges, counter-charges, and threat of war. Given these reverses, Washington's focus again shifted to crisis management rather than inducing Turkey and Greece to address their perennial disputes. Much to its dismay, Washington has had to spend a great deal of diplomatic capital dealing with what it considers to be avoidable crises, such as that surrounding the S-300s. However, in the aftermath of the encouraging "seismic" diplomacy of late 1999, Washington acted to exploit the momentum of warming ties. It focused especially on Cyprus, trying to enlist Ankara's support for a new diplomatic initiative.

A recurring concern for the U.S. and its allies has been the perennial threat that Greek-Turkish tensions pose to NATO cohesion, as well as the potential collapse of the southern flank. Indeed, NATO has been preoccupied with Greek-Turkish quarrels throughout much of its existence. Ankara and Athens have regularly brought their disputes to NATO councils and occasionally used their veto or delaying powers to stall alliance plans.[39]

It is hard to assess the contribution of NATO, especially as distinct from that of the U.S., in moderating Greek-Turkish conflicts over the years. It seems logical to credit NATO with a moderating role. NATO meetings have afforded opportunities for Ankara and Athens to cooperate occasionally and to discuss their problems in a forum where allies encourage them and offer ideas for bridging their differences. Greece and Turkey have reached numerous agreements pertaining to NATO arrangements within alliance councils. Despite occasional setbacks, NATO has persevered in promoting a series of confidence-building measures in the Aegean. As NATO admits new members and seeks to define new roles for itself, it remains well positioned to continue playing its modest role in moderating Greek-Turkish tension, acting together with the U.S. and other leading members of the alliance. On the other hand, it has been argued that their membership in the alliance has unwittingly exacerbated conflicts between Greece and Turkey. According to political scientist Ronald Krebs, NATO membership has allowed Greece and Turkey, in effect, to contract out their national security and thus pursue regional rivalries and interests with reduced vulnerability.[40]

In this connection, questions have been raised concerning the destabilizing effect of allies' arms transfers to Turkey and Greece. Both nations significantly modernized and upgraded their arsenals in the 1990s. As one concerned observer asserted, "Until now, the two could only fight it out in the Aegean, but things are changing rapidly. The emphasis on both sides is on 'force multipliers' such as smart stand-off missiles, avionics, radar, and air-to-air refueling capabilities."[41]

Conclusion

In spite of several past confrontations, Greece and Turkey have maintained the Aegean status quo, without warfare, for many years. In the wake of "seismic" diplomacy, prospects for promoting more stable bilateral relations have improved. Although their positions on settling major Aegean disputes remain far apart, Ankara and Athens could defer resolution to a later date while adopting a series of confidence-building measures to help prevent future confrontations. Turkey and Greece could reach agreement on confidence-building measures in Cyprus, as well, to reduce tensions along the Green Line. However, it is doubtful whether anything short of resolving the island's key issues can bring long-term peace there.

While it has resisted international mediation of its disputes with Greece, Ankara has nonetheless been receptive to U.S. efforts to manage them. Ultimately, however, the impetus for progress on the substance of the disputes will have to come from Turkey and Greece. This is what propelled the Davos initiative, when both countries' leaders made a concerted effort to break the diplomatic logjam.

Indeed, in contemplating possibilities for progress, it is worth recalling some of the essential lessons of Davos. That enterprise was made possible, at least in part, by the strong parliamentary mandate held by the visionary Özal, who was confident enough to provide civilian leadership over Turkey's powerful military establishment. His goal was to secure Turkey's accession to the EU, which remains a major objective of the secular establishment. The domestic political weakening of Özal and Greek prime minister Papandreou, and their failure to achieve any movement on Cyprus, led to the abandonment of the Davos initiative. To revive some variant of Davos and succeed where those two towering political figures failed will test the statesmanship of Turkish and Greek leaders in the years ahead.

Notes

1   *Christian Science Monitor*, February 26, 1999.
2   Tozun Bahcheli, *Greek Turkish Relations since 1955* (Boulder: Westview Press, 1990), p. 142.
3   Andrew Wilson, *The Aegean Dispute* (London: International Institute of Strategic Studies, 1980), p. 27.
4   Ibid.
5   Ibid.
6   Ibid.
7   *Country Report: Turkey,* 1st quarter 1996 (London: Economist Intelligence Unit, 1997), p. 17.
8   "Turkish Prime Minister Interviewed on EU Membership Bid," *El Pais* (Madrid), November 25, 1997, in Foreign Broadcast Information Service Daily Report-West Europe (FBIS-WEU), November 25, 1997.
9   Reuters, April 14, 1999.
10 Alan O. Makovsky, "The New Activism in Turkish Foreign Policy," *SAIS Review* 19, no. 1 (Winter-Spring 1999), p. 105.

11 Malik Mufti, "Daring and Caution in Turkish Foreign Policy," *Middle East Journal* 52, no. 1 (Winter 1998), p. 35; Şükrü Elekdağ "2-1/2 War Strategy" *Perceptions* 1, no. 1 (March-May 1996), p. 37.

12 *Foreign Report*, July 4, 1996.

13 Makovsky, "The New Activism," p. 102.

14 Constantine Stephanou and Charalambos Tsardanides, "The EC Factor in the Greece-Turkey-Cyprus Triangle," in Dimitri Constas (ed.), *The Greek-Turkish Conflict in the 1990s: Domestic and External Influences* (Houndmills and London: Macmillan, 1991), p. 210.

15 Luxembourg European Council, *Presidency Conclusions*, December 12 and 13, 1997, paragraphs 31-36: http://www. europarl.eu.int/dg7/summits/en/lux1.htm

16 Helsinki European Council, *Presidency Conclusions*, December 10 and 11, 1999: http://www.europa.eu.int/council/off/conclu/dec99/dec99/_en.pdf

17 "The European Council underlines that a political settlement will facilitate the accession of Cyprus to the European Union. If no settlement has been reached by the completion of accession negotiations, the Council's decision on accession will be made without the above being a precondition. In this the Council will take account of all relevant factors." See http://www.europa.eu.int/council/off/conclu/dec99dec99_en.htm#enlargement. Even as these statements allowed for the possibility of Greek Cyprus's accession to the EU prior to a political settlement on the island, the EU Presidency took note of Turkish sensibilities by promising to take "account of all relevant factors."

18 Monteagle Stearns, "Greek Security Issues," in Graham T. Allison and Kalypso Nicolaidis (eds.), *The Greek Paradox: Promise vs. Performance* (Cambridge and London: MIT Press, 1997), p. 71.

19 Philip H. Gordon, "Storms in the Med Blow towards Europe," *World Today* 54, no. 2 (February 1998), p. 43.

20 *New York Times*, March 6, 1999.

21 *Destroying Ethnic Identity: The Turks of Greece*, Helsinki Watch Report (New York: Human Rights Watch, 1990).

22 Bahcheli, *Greek-Turkish Relations*, p. 182.

23 Christopher de Bellaigue, "Turkey: Into the Abyss?" *Washington Quarterly* 21, no. 3 (Summer 1998), p. 143.

24 A forged Greek Cypriot passport was found in Öcalan's possession when he was captured in February 1999.

25 Reported by Turkey's Anatolia News Agency, February 28, 1999.

26 Ibid.

27 "Former Greek Official on Öcalan, Issues," *To Vima Tis Kiriakis* (Athens), March 21, 1999, in FBIS-WEU, 99-322, March 22, 1999. The article is a March 16, 1999, interview with former Greek foreign minister Theodore Pangalos.

28 Athens News Agency, February 3, 1999.

29 "Exclusive TDN Anniversary Interview with President Demirel: 'The civilized world should act on Greek support for terrorism,'" *Turkish Daily News (TDN)*, March 15, 1999.

30 U.S. Department of State, *Daily Press Briefing*, May 6, 1998.

31 Reuters, May 6, 1998.

32 *Kathimerini* (Athens), March 9, 1999, in FBIS-WEU, March 10, 1999.

33   Alan O. Makovsky, "Turkey," in Robert Chase, Emily Hill, and Paul Kennedy (eds.), *The Pivotal States: A New Framework for U.S. Policy in the Developing World* (New York and London: W.W. Norton, 1999), p. 104.

34   Makovsky, "The New Activism," p. 102.

35   Ibid., p. 98.

36   This assessment is supported by U.S. officials whom the author interviewed during the spring of 1996 in Washington, D.C., on a nonattribution basis. See also *TDN*, November 16, 1997; and Wes Jonasson, "Greece and the U.S. Fall Out," *Middle East International*, August 21, 1998, p. 14.

37   Geoffrey Pridham, "Linkage Politics Theory and the Greek-Turkish Rapprochement," in Constas (ed.), *The Greek-Turkish Conflict*, pp. 84-86.

38   The document generally known as the Madrid Communiqué, citing elements of a Greek-Turkish "convergence of views," was issued as a statement by the U.S. Department of State under the title, "Meeting of Secretary of State Madeleine K. Albright with Greek Foreign Minister Pangalos and Turkish Foreign Minister Cem," July 8, 1997: http://secretary.state.gov/www/briefings/statements/970708b.html

39   Lowell Bezanis, "Diplomatic Initiative to Solve Greek-Turkish Rift within NATO," *Open Media Research Institute (OMRI) Daily Digest*, May 18, 1995: www.hri.org/news/agencies/omri

40   Ronald R. Krebs, "Perverse Institutionalism: NATO and the Greco-Turkish Conflict," *International Organization* 53, no. 2 (Spring 1999), p. 369.

41   Tassos Kokkinides, "Turkey-Greece: Two Nations Arming for Peace," InterPress Service, October 10, 1997.

Clement H. Dodd

Turkey and the Cyprus Question

Before examining Cyprus in the framework of Turkish foreign policy, we should clarify the nature of the Cyprus issue. The gap between its simple appearance and its complex reality is large and filled with a history that each party to the conflict interprets diffently. These varying historical constructs are an inescapable part of the present problem.

Greek Cypriot Attitudes and Demands

The Greek Cypriots' predicament lies in how to return to an approximation of the situation that existed in 1974, before the Turkish military "invasion" (as the Greeks and Greek Cypriots call it), or "intervention" (as the Turks and Turkish Cypriots say). Foremost is the need to ensure that the 150,000-200,000 Greek Cypriot refugees from the northern part of the island have the opportunity to return home, or at least that their families may do so. The Greek Cypriots regard this as a human right that has to be recognized, even if in some cases it entails only monetary compensation instead of actual return. They also demand the rights to move freely about the island, live where they choose, and buy property. Likewise, they demand that the Turkish Cypriot zone be reduced in size to encompass some 25 percent of the island at most. In particular, they want the return of the coastal town Varosha-Maraş and all—or, at least, most—of the agriculturally productive Morphou-Güzelyurt region.[1]

The Greek Cypriots reluctantly accept that a resolution of the Cyprus dispute holds out the prospect, at best, of a bizonal, bicommunal federation with the Turkish Cypriots, based broadly on the principle of equality.[2] (By virtue of their greater population, however, the Greek Cypriots expect to be "more equal" than the Turkish Cypriots in at least some instances—for example, in the manning of the institutions of state.) Essentially, the Greek Cypriots seem to envision the continuation of the present-day, Greek Cypriot-controlled Republic of Cyprus, with the Turkish Cypriots readmitted into a federation in which the most significant state functions are located in the central government. They stress the need for a single sovereignty, international personality, citizenship, and territorial unit (viz., the whole island). Also important to the Greek Cypriots is security, to be achieved by the island's demilitarization. They fear the military power of Turkey, with its population of 63 million, one-hundred-fold their own population of some 630,000. They also fear the presence of some 35,000 Turkish and Turkish Cypriot troops in the north against their 11,500 in the south. The Greek Cypriots are deeply perturbed by the inflow of Turkish immigrants ("settlers," in Greek Cypriot parlance) to the north since 1975, which they see as altering the demographic structure of the island. They want these people returned to the Turkish mainland.[3]

Many Greek Cypriots are deeply passionate about these demands. This is where their view of history is important. They attach importance to the fact that the island was Greek in language and culture already centuries before Christ. Many invaders appeared in subsequent years, but they all went away in the end—save the descendants of the Ottoman Turks, who conquered the island in 1571. By 1960 Turkish Cypriots comprised some 18 percent of the population, otherwise predominantly Greek. Greek Cypriots thought that the Turkish Cypriots should be treated as a minority, with appropriate minority rights. Instead, by virtue of "imposed" 1959 and 1960 treaties, Turkish Cypriots were raised to the level of a community and given a veto and other rights in a constitutional arrangement that soon proved to be unworkable. The Greek Cypriots claim that the Turkish Cypriots, aiming at a division of the island (*taksim* in Turkish), behaved uncooperatively in a conscious effort to undermine the constitutional arrangement after it went into effect.

As a result, violence arose in 1963. The Turkish Cypriots abandoned their governmental posts and showed their true intent of setting up a state within the state. By 1974, after long negotiations, a new agreement was near conclusion according the Turkish Cypriots a less powerful status. At that point, however, Greek Cypriot military officers favoring union with Greece (*enosis* in Greek) and backed by the junta ruling in Athens staged a coup, providing a "pretext" for Turkey to invade the island, ostensibly to protect the Turkish Cypriots from *enosis*. The coup leaders had acted against the will of the Greek Cypriot people, most whom opposed *enosis*. The Turkish Cypriots then set up their illegal state, which exists only with the financial help of Turkey and is recognized only by that country.

This version of history seems to have wide acceptance in the south and is therefore a factor in the present. It engenders Greek Cypriot outrage at the injustice and deprivation they have suffered.[4] Schemes devised by the ingenious intelligentsia of international organizations—often stressing other-cultural concepts like bargaining or horse-trading—tend to bounce off the protagonists of such deeply felt disputes, who usually see compromise as abandonment of principles.

Turkish Cypriot Attitudes and Demands

On the Turkish Cypriot side, the problem is seen differently, and the priorities consequently differ. Turkish Cypriots see themselves as a community, not as a minority. For them, the Hellenic, or "Hellenistic," claims of the Greek Cypriots are romantic and historicist. The two communities have always been different in language, religion, and culture and have rarely intermarried. Majority-minority criteria cannot apply to such a long-established cultural difference. It is recognized everywhere, the Turkish Cypriots say, that communities cannot be dismissed as mere minorities.

Always afraid of *enosis* and aware that *taksim* would have been difficult to implement, most Turkish Cypriots welcomed the 1959-60 treaties and the arrangements arising out of them. Nevertheless, Greek Cypriots really believed that their rights as a majority should have been recognized, hence the violence directed against the Turkish Cypriots in 1963 and afterwards. This violence made it physically impossible, the Turkish Cypriots claim, for them to work in joint institutions; they did not withdraw from their positions but feared for their lives if they presented themselves for work. The reality of Greek Cypriot intentions was apparent when they refused in 1965 to allow Turkish Cypriot deputies to resume their seats in the House of Representatives unless they accepted constitutional changes that would have turned them into a minority. Worst of all, however, was the recognition by the United Nations (UN) in 1964 of the Greek Cypriot administration as the legitimate government. Turkish Cypriots see themselves as having been deprived thereafter of their rights, largely for considerations of international politics.[5] In 1974 they were rescued from Greek Cypriot violence and from the *enosis* that the Sampson coup intended, thanks to a Turkish military intervention staged in accordance with the 1960 Treaty of Guarantee. They had no recourse but to establish their own state, they say. Their lack of international recognition and the embargo placed upon them by the international community amounts to a great injustice in their eyes. By preventing the development of international tourism, the embargo has crippled their economy.

As seen in post-1975 negotiations, this view of history made the Turkish Cypriots determined to obtain recognition of their equality in a new bizonal, bicommunal federation with federal powers very limited or offset by Turkish Cypriot veto rights and with residual powers left to each federated state. They also insisted on the maintenance of the Turkish guarantee and the physical presence of Turkish troops in the north. At one point they accepted limitation of their territory to some 29 percent of the island, but they do not intend to give up Famagusta-Gazi Mağosa or the Morphou-Güzelyurt region. They want the Greek Cypriots to accept monetary compensation for former Greek Cypriot property—not large-scale return—and they, in turn, would be satisfied with monetary compensation for their property in the south. They would like to join the European Union (EU), but not without a settlement on the island first.[6] They deeply distrust Greek Cypriots as a result of the treatment they received in the 1960s. It has aptly been said that Turkish Cypriots cannot forget the violence they suffered between 1963 and 1974 and that the Greek Cypriots cannot remember.

In recent years there has been a gradual but important change in the Turkish Cypriot approach to a settlement. With full Turkish support, they now insist that their independent statehood must first be recognized. Moreover, any union with the south has to be on the basis of a confederation, not a federation.[7] Why this changed approach? First, UN-led negotiations have always assumed that an agreement was being sought between two *communities*, whereas the blunt truth was that, outside the negotiating room, the south continued to be internationally recognized as the Republic of Cyprus with jurisdiction over the whole island and therefore as a *state*. The EU is now holding accession negotiations with the government of the south as if for the whole island. Second, Turkish Cypriots feel they must avoid joining a federation so long as the UN—adopting the Greek Cypriot approach—insists that a federation must have a single sovereignty with one territory and one citizenship. This denies the Turkish Cypriot view that in the last resort sovereignty lies with the constituent states that make a federation, save for those aspects that are transferred to a federal center. Moreover, in a federation there are normally strong pressures from business, labor, and other groups that tend to unite across state boundaries to create general federal policies. On Cyprus this could lead to domination of the federal structure by the numerically stronger Greek Cypriot component, which in turn would disturb the more nationalist elements among the Turkish Cypriots.[8]

Turkish Support of the Turkish Cypriots

Contrary to widespread views, the Cyprus issue has not always engendered enthusiastic support in Turkey for the Turkish Cypriots. Until Britain showed unmistakable signs of retiring from Cyprus in the 1950s, Turkey was quite content to see British rule continue there. Ankara was alerted to strategic dangers when the possibility arose that Cyprus could become a Greek island, but there was in those days little desire to help Turkish Cypriots simply because they were Turks. The Atatürkist doctrine that Turkey should focus only on Turks in Anatolia and what was left of Rumelia—that is, Turks within its own borders—was still strong. The only "outside Turks" of real interest to Atatürkists were the original Turks in the Central Asian heartland, because their language and culture had not been much subject to Arab or Persian influences. However, to avoid conflict with the Soviet Union, they were put firmly out of political bounds by Atatürk. Nor did Atatürk encourage Turkish nationalism among the Turkish Cypriots; he was eager for good relations with Britain. Besides, Turkish Cypriots were seen as much less Turkish than Central Asians are, the former having been so influenced by British colonialism[9] and by the propinquity of the Greeks.

Between 1955 and 1960, the Turkish government under prime minister Adnan Menderes became sensitive to the strategic implications of a Greek-dominated Cyprus and thus gave full diplomatic support to the Turkish Cypriots, even demanding *taksim* on their behalf. After 1960, however, there was some equivocation. In 1964 Turkish prime minister İsmet İnönü, relying on the U.S. and Britain, was seemingly persuaded that UN Security Council Resolution 186 would not accord international legitimacy to the Cypriot government fully and solely in the hands of the Greek Cypriots. He was also cautious about intervening militarily in 1964 and gave U.S. president Lyndon B. Johnson, in effect, the chance to warn him against it—in the most forthright and offensive terms, as it turned out. In 1967, Prime Minister Süleyman Demirel was, only with some difficulty, persuaded by the military and Turkish public pressure into demanding an end to Greek Cypriot attacks on Turkish Cypriots, who were penned into tiny enclaves and suffering a blockade that prevented the importation of all but sheer necessities. A Turkish ultimatum achieved some results, including the withdrawal to Greece of the Cyprus-based Greek National Guard, but Turkey did not go so far as to insist on the right of the Turkish Cypriots to return to their seats in government.

Between 1967 and 1974, Ankara was in close touch with Athens in a desire to settle the Cyprus question. Advisers were appointed by both Greece and Turkey to help the two leaders, Rauf Denktaş and Glafcos Clerides, in their negotiations for a settlement, but it was clear that, in order to strike a deal, the Turkish Cypriots would have to give away a good deal and reduce their status relative to what they had achieved in the 1960 constitution. With eyes fixed firmly on the West and preoccupied with economic development, Ankara did not want Cyprus to muddy relations with Europe or the U.S. Foreign Minister İhsan Sabri Çağlayangil once stated that Cyprus "should continue to be independent, and a unitary form of state could be adopted." Demirel was reported to be ready to consent to minority status for the Turkish Cypriots.[10]

In November 1983 Turkey supported the declaration of independence made by the newly named Turkish Republic of Northern Cyprus (TRNC), which was timed to occur just between the relinquishing of power by the military in Turkey and the assumption of power by the newly elected civilian prime minister, Turgut Özal. Upon taking office, Özal had no option but to accept the *fait accompli*, though, it was said, he did so with little grace. İlter Türkmen, the outgoing foreign minister of the military government, said the government would have "undoubtedly preferred it if a just and lasting solution could have been reached through the intercommunal negotiations without arriving at the present state of affairs."[11] Özal was as eager for good relations with Greece as Demirel had been, and, with U.S. support, he tried in 1991 to involve both Cypriot sides in quadripartite talks with Greece and Turkey. Özal did not expect the Turkish Cypriots to make major concessions—he had come to accept the need for a bicommunal, bizonal solution that included a Turkish security guarantee for the Turkish Cypriots—but he felt frustrated by Denktaş:

> The Turkish Cypriots can prefer what they like, but we have made great sacrifices and are continuing to do so. They should appreciate the value of this. More than $200 million [is] spent on Cyprus each year. And to a large extent this will go on. One way or another a solution must be found. This issue is standing in Turkey's way. It really is a major obstacle to Turkey's growth. I say this without hesitation. I have told Denktaş to his face.[12]

In 1993 anti-Denktaş articles appeared in *Sabah*, a major daily newspaper in Turkey, on the occasion of Denktaş's address to the Turkish parliament. The articles reflected the views of the business community and other middle-class groups that believed Cyprus was a serious hindrance to Turkey's European ambitions. Denktaş, in the view of detractors, was but an opportunist and master manipulator of Turkish public opinion. But nobody disputed his oratorical skills, one of his most effective tools in winning Turkish public support; few, if any, Turkish politicians are his equal in public speaking. His 1993 speech to the Turkish parliament, in which he explained his rejection of UN-proposed confidence-building measures, evoked a tumultuously positive response.

The strength of Turkish forces cautious about support for Turkish Cypriot ambitions was evident in early March 1995, when Tansu Çiller was prime minister. Responding to pressures in her own *Doğru Yol* (True Path) Party (DYP) and in line with Turkey's aspiration for full membership in the Western community of nations, Çiller's government made what has come to be regarded as a damaging concession on Cyprus. In order to elicit a positive response from the EU on a proposed EU-Turkish customs union agreement, Turkey seemed implicitly to give a boost to Greek Cyprus's efforts to join the EU. The Greek government had indicated that it would veto the projected customs union agreement if the EU did not also decide to establish a firm date for the commencement of membership negotiations with the Greek Cypriot-controlled Republic of Cyprus. In response, the Çiller government's attitude was to look the other way—to say, in effect, that if the EU chose to make such an agreement with Greece, that agreement had nothing to do with Turkey. This was much criticized by *Anavatan* (Motherland) Party (ANAP) leader Mesut Yılmaz, as well as by the far left and the Islamic and nationalist right. EU-Greek Cypriot membership negotiations, they insisted, contradicted the 1959-60 treaties, which made Turkey a guarantor power in Cyprus and forbade a Cypriot application to join an organization like the EU, to which not all the guarantor powers (Greece and the United Kingdom, as well as Turkey) belonged. In addition, no decision on such an important matter could legally be made without Turkish Cypriot participation, they said. Turkish foreign minister Murat Karayalçın immediately made it clear in Brussels that Turkey would continue to oppose EU membership for Cyprus before Turkey's own accession as a full member. He went on to state that the opening of negotiations with the Greek Cypriots before a settlement of the Cyprus dispute would leave Turkey with no option but to take steps towards integrating northern Cyprus with Turkey. However, the Çiller government's approach, critics contended, still meant that Turkey had allowed its customs union bid to go through by abetting a major EU concession regarding Cyprus.

The Çiller government's ambivalent attitude toward Cyprus showed itself again in late March 1995, when the Turkish sports minister allowed the national handball team to play in southern (Greek) Cyprus and agreed to its traveling via Israel, since the Greek Cypriot government would not allow access from what it calls the "pseudo-state" in the (Turkish) north. This raised a storm of criticism in the press, echoing outrage also expressed by Yılmaz, *Demokratik Sol* (Democratic Left) Party (DSP) leader Bülent Ecevit, and prominent intellectual and politician Mümtaz Soysal.

Less noticed by the press was the continuing use of Turkish ports by Greek Cypriot shipping, formally prohibited in 1987, and the exclusion of Turkish Cypriots from attending in their own right Turkey-based international meetings where Greek Cypriots represented the Republic of Cyprus, such as the UN Habitat Conference held in Istanbul in May 1996.[13] The ban on Greek Cypriot shipping, reportedly more breached than observed, is a matter of considerable concern to Greek Cypriot shipping interests, as often revealed in the Greek Cypriot press. From September to November 1998 the ban was discussed, on reference from the European Council, in the Organization for Economic Cooperation and Development (OECD) Maritime Transportation Committee, where Turkey has a voice. The issue is difficult for Ankara because, although Turkey does not recognize the Greek Cypriot-controlled Republic of Cyprus, both it and Turkey have customs union agreements with the EU.[14]

The Turkish Press, 1995-97

The rather personal attacks on Denktaş by well-known columnist and political analyst Hasan Cemal, which appeared in 1993 in *Sabah*, suggested that an examination of leading columnists at Turkish newspapers might be revealing.[15] What is the general opinion of the Turkish press regarding Cyprus and Turkish policy? The findings presented below reflect the results of a survey of columns in major dailies and private interviews with seven leading columnists between 1995 and 1997.

Increased interest in Cyprus, intensified by its connections with the customs union issue, has led to more press coverage in recent years. Not all of it is opinionated. Most columnists' articles on Cyprus provide good factual information without much interpretation. As they reveal themselves, attitudes vary a good deal not just among newspapers, but among journalists at a particular paper. One may be sympathetic with the Greeks, another inclined toward the left in northern Cyprus, another rather starry-eyed about the possibilities of a solution. All are usually informative, though some are better informed than others. The columns are nearly always on inside pages, though when politicians like Bülent Ecevit or Mümtaz Soysal make contributions they usually appear on the front page. For that matter, news articles about Cyprus also rarely make the front page.

On the whole, columnists in *Sabah* tended to be the most critical of northern Cyprus, with one columnist, Cemal, critical of Denktaş himself, as noted. The well-known writer Mehmet Ali Birand—with *Sabah* at the time of this study—is critical in a different way, inclined to try to restrain the enthusiastic support for northern Cyprus shown by politicians and others like Ecevit. For instance, the announcement by the Greek Cypriots in January 1997 that they were importing Russian S-300 missiles prompted hasty condemnations in various Turkish quarters, not least from Çiller. Birand visited Clerides and others in southern Cyprus and put their point of view across in *Sabah*. He and Sami Kohen in *Milliyet* are clearly well informed, the latter certainly closely aware of movements of opinion in the Foreign Ministry. Many *Sabah* reports contained frank and pertinent criticism of the Turkish Republic of Northern Cyprus, its large and expensive bureaucracy with salaries higher than those in Turkey, and its draining effect on the Turkish economy. Others have been critical of Turkish or Turkish Cypriot actions like the shooting of the Greek Cypriot who in 1996 tried to climb up a flagpole on the Green Line to bring down a Turkish flag. Çiller's aggressive response to these events was much deplored. Articles in *Sabah* tend, it is said, to reflect the anxieties of the business community that Cyprus should not stand in the way of Turkey's European ambitions.

Journalists critical of Denktaş felt he was independent-minded and difficult to handle, as Özal had found, but that he would bow to Ankara in the end. Nevertheless, they admitted he was a force in Turkey, adept at playing shifts and turns in Turkish politics. They also recognized that "the cause" was of supreme importance to him and acknowledged that, in this way, he rose above the sometimes sleazy level of Turkish politics and merited respect therefore.

Leading journalists have close relations with the Turkish Foreign Ministry in some instances. But they claim that, unlike Greek journalists, they do not have to follow their foreign ministry's line closely. They acknowledge, however, that they sometimes take the ministry's advice not to respond to Greek government (or Greek government-inspired) assertions. They say the Turkish Foreign Ministry does not seem to have well-thought-out policies with regard to Cyprus. On the issue of federation, for example, they claim the ministry followed UN formulations, then simply turned to Denktaş for his views. By contrast, the press questioned the very applicability of federation to Cyprus.[16]

On the whole, the journalists revealed in writings and conversation with this author that they believed Cyprus should enter the EU, though only after a settlement. There was much sympathy for the view that northern Cyprus could join the EU as part of a new federal Cyprus without waiting for Turkey to qualify. One columnist in *Hürriyet* believed quite fervently in the need for a settlement and the need to trust the Greeks and the EU more. One *Milliyet* writer showed in conversation a marked understanding of Greece and the Greek position and was very sensitive to the dangers of conflict, but articles by this journalist did not reveal this "radicalism."

Overall, Turkish columnists are reasonably well informed about the Cyprus problem and moderate, if somewhat varied, in their views. They try not to overplay Greek and Cypriot issues but point out that there is strong nationalist feeling in Turkey to which newspapers respond as issues arise on their front pages. There exists latent Turkish sentiment that can express itself in hostility to any number of countries or international organizations, but it is not a specifically anti-Greek nationalism.[17]

Political Parties' Attitudes toward Cyprus

From interviews with leading members of Turkish political parties conducted in the mid-1990s, it is clear that the rank and file generally follow their leaders in policy matters, especially foreign policy. As might be expected, however, the parties are all very sensitive to expressions of nationalist fervor in the media. They can tolerate more easily denunciations of, say, corruption than accusations that they are betraying the national interest by concessions to foreign powers.[18]

The political parties all support the Turkish Cypriots. Politically, they cannot afford not to, but some are more supportive than others. Members of the now-defunct *Refah* (Welfare) Party (RP) expressed themselves in the interviews as very supportive of northern Cyprus in principle but deplored the lack of religion there and the size and extravagance of its administration. The Turkish Cypriots were also seen as insufficiently entrepreneurial, expecting everything from Turkey. RP members seemed to believe there was no point in trying to reunite Cyprus, which they felt would lead to endless trouble. They deplored the tendency in some parties—including its coalition partner, the DYP—to make concessions on Cyprus to get closer to the EU. In fact, despite its self-proclaimed full support for northern Cyprus, the RP's attempts when in power to promote Islam there did not go down well in the Turkish Cypriots' highly educated and secularized society, which has strong European connections. There is hardly a Turkish Cypriot who does not have close connections with family and friends in the West, especially in London.

The Turkish political parties most favored in the north in recent years are ANAP and the DSP. The firmly pro-Turkish Cypriot *Milliyetçi Hareket* (Nationalist Movement) Party (MHP) was not important in Turkish politics until recently, but its success in the April 1999 elections was no doubt welcomed by most Turkish Cypriots. The DSP-MHP-ANAP coalition government those elections produced is as solidly pro-Turkish Cypriot as any imaginable in Turkey.

ANAP under Yılmaz has been much less ambivalent about Cyprus than it was under Özal. It also has in one of its leading members, Kamran İnan, a recognized authority on foreign policy who is a firm supporter of northern Cyprus. ANAP interviewees were very suspicious of the Greek Cypriots. For example, they believed the Greek Cypriots would swallow up the whole island if they could and that the Turkish guarantee for the north is thus vital for Turkish Cypriot security. For strategic reasons, they said, Greeks must not be allowed to dominate the whole island. Many of them saw permanent division of the island as the best solution. The ANAP members believed that the Greek Cypriots would have cynically exploited a package of confidence-building measures the UN proposed in 1994 that foresaw the reopening of Nicosia airport for both Turkish Cypriot and Greek Cypriot use, as well as the return of the town of Varosha-Maraş to Greek Cypriot control. (Denktaş rejected the package.) The Greek Cypriots would have trumped up environmental reasons as a pretext to close a reopened Nicosia airport, the interviewees said. They also felt that allowing Varosha-Maraş to be settled by the Greek Cypriots would have been a mistake, putting a bomb on the doorstep of nearby Famagusta-Gazi Mağosa, the only real port under Turkish Cypriot control. The ANAP members deplored the link Greece made between Cyprus and the Turkey-EU customs union and insisted on the necessity of a settlement of the Cyprus problem before the Republic of Cyprus accedes to EU membership. They claimed Europe does not want Turkey among its ranks, mainly for religious reasons. Britain is friendly, they said, but it now has little political or economic strength and will do nothing to offend the Greek Cypriots, since it does not want to risk its bases in Cyprus or the safety of the large British community in southern Cyprus. Turkey's hopes for support lie more with the U.S., according to the ANAP members.

Ecevit's DSP shared these views but was more rigid. Interviewees from the DSP were simply opposed to Turkey's joining the EU and regretted the Çiller government's decision to recognize the jurisdiction of the European Court, which they feared might try to undermine Turkey's position in Cyprus. Ecevit often says—for example, during a May 1999 visit to northern Cyprus—that the present solution in Cyprus is the best solution, that the Cyprus file should be closed, and that the role of Turkish troops in Cyprus is vital. DSP interviewees supported these views. ANAP and the DSP have much in common regarding Cyprus, but there was some feeling among ANAP members that Ecevit's views are a little too severe.

Some members of the much-weakened DYP also apparently accepted that the customs union "concession" was a political mistake, while insisting that the economic benefits of customs union should not be underrated. DYP interviewees indicated that many of their party colleagues regretted Denktaş's success in forging a special relationship with Ankara, which, they said, hurt Turkey's relations with the EU.

Members of the *Cumhuriyet Halk* (Republican People's) Party (CHP), then under Deniz Baykal and also pro-European and secularist, came across in interviews to be the least pro-Turkish Cypriot of the parties. The CHP suffered a grievous defeat in the April 1999 elections, not winning a single seat.[19]

From these discussions with leading politicians it is clear that, despite some suspicion of Denktaş and impatience with the Cyprus problem, there is very wide support for a Turkish policy strongly supportive of northern Cyprus. The 1999 general elections and the resulting coalition government suggest this support will become even stronger.

The Military and the Ministry of Foreign Affairs

The military's views are not easy to assess, but it may be said with certainty that it favors a solid Turkish presence in Cyprus for strategic reasons.[20] The military is alert to the dangers created by Greek Cypriot rearmament. Whereas in 1991 the Greek Cypriots spent 25 percent of their budget on arms, by 1995 it had reached 31 percent and the purchase of more heavy tanks from Russia was in the offing. The military's view, as expressed in interviews in 1995, was that Greece wants to control the Aegean—as the fortification of the Aegean islands showed—and that its defense arrangements with Cyprus are part of this policy. The military did not favor reuniting Cyprus; as in Bosnia, there would be trouble that would be very difficult to control without bloodshed, they suggested. Nor would the military like the Greek Cypriots to have freedom of movement in northern Cyprus if it meant having Greek Cypriots close to Turkish military installations. In the military's view, Cyprus is an aircraft carrier that has to be in safe hands. A divided island presents no great defense problems for the military, the interviewed officers indicated, and it is not more expensive to keep Turkish troops in Cyprus than in Turkey.

The foreign ministry must bear these military views in mind, but it has always supported UN efforts to end the dispute and bring about a federation. In 1992 Turkish officials helped the UN draft proposals for solving the Cyprus problem, the so-called "Set of Ideas."

The ministry also believes Turkey should have a European destiny. This was expressed recently by a senior diplomat:

> In recent years Turkish foreign policy has systematically tried to extend [its] model of democratic political stability, international cooperation, and economic prosperity to the region around us. This thinking lies behind our formidable trade and investment volume with the Russian Federation, the countries of the Caucasus, and Central Asia, and our joint energy projects with them, and also behind our support for the Middle East peace initiative. But we recognize that these are essentially sideshows. The central story—the one which will confirm the success of our endeavors—lies in our relations with the countries to our west and northwest.[21]

This sentiment also shapes the ministry's approach to Cyprus.

Aware of the difficulties that would ensue if the Greek Cypriot-controlled Republic of Cyprus accedes to EU membership without the north, the foreign ministry strongly desires a settlement of the Cyprus problem first. Had Ankara received early positive signals from the EU regarding its own membership bid, it would have favored EU membership for a post-settlement, reunited Cyprus that included the Turkish Cypriots. In this respect, the Turks actually differed from the view of Denktaş and the Turkish Cypriot government, which would not contemplate accession for a federated Cyprus without the protection in Europe that Turkey's simultaneous entry would provide. However, this matter has become moot since Turkey was disabused of hopes for early entry into the EU in December 1997. Turkey, too, now insists that Cyprus, reunited or not, should not precede it in joining the EU. It has held to this position, notwithstanding the EU's December 1999 decision to designate Turkey a candidate for membership.

Otherwise, the Turkish foreign ministry supports northern Cyprus and does all it can to follow the lead of Lefkoşa in its Cyprus policies. Usually, the greatest determinant of foreign policy is the attitude of the government in power, but there were so many changes in the mid-1990s that Turkish foreign policy was in some turmoil. Under Foreign Minister İsmail Cem, a greater sense of direction was discernible. Moreover, the recruitment of Şükrü Gürel as minister of state with special responsibility for Cyprus was greatly welcomed in Lefkoşa. An academic by training and a member of Ecevit's DSP, Gürel was a keen student of Cypriot affairs and sympathetic to the Turkish Cypriot cause. There is very little direct pressure from domestic advocacy groups regarding Turkey's Cyprus policy, save for an intermittent Turkish Cypriot lobby in Ankara. Groups that may be influential in the press in urging a less rigid policy do not, it appears, act as formal or semi-formal pressure groups directly on the ministry itself.

Turkey's Legal Offensive

The foreign ministry has in the past challenged the legality of the Greek Cypriot administration as the government of the Republic of Cyprus. Ankara rejected the Greek Cypriots' claim to govern under the "Doctrine of Necessity," pointing out that the Turkish Cypriots were, in fact, compelled by the violence engendered by the Greek Cypriots in 1963 to leave their government posts and were later refused readmission.[22] Turkish claims were rejected by the Commission of Human Rights of the European Council, which based its ruling on the fact of UN recognition—the position also taken by other courts, including the European Court of Human Rights and the European Court of Justice. These judgments, by not questioning the process leading to UN recognition, are often seen by Turkey as begging the question. They ignore an eminent authority's legal opinion that the "basic structure and the Constitution [of the Republic] had been inoperative . . . since the time (in 1963-64) when the Greek Cypriot community had effectively excluded the Turkish Cypriot community from the scheme of power-sharing established by the Basic Structure and the Constitution."[23]

In recent years, the Turkish government has been intent on explaining its reasoning that the Republic of Cyprus may not legally enter the EU. In 1997 it took legal advice from Professor M. H. Mendelson, Q.C., who argued that, since Cyprus is forbidden by Articles 1 and 11 of the 1960 Treaty of Guarantee from participating in political or economic union with any other state, it cannot legally join the EU. Further, Article 1 "prohibits any activity likely to promote, directly or indirectly, either union with any other state, or partition of the island." Mendelson asserts that in the EU Cyprus would be far more closely connected to Greece, "politically, militarily, ethnically, and geographically [than it would be] to any other member state," thus promoting union with Greece. [24]

This line of argument was rejected in a counter-opinion submitted to the UN on behalf of the Republic of Cyprus.[25] The counter-opinion claimed that the treaty text clearly means union with another state, in the singular, not with organizations of states or a supranational organization. As to EU membership indirectly promoting union with Greece, the counter-opinion asserted that "Cyprus as a member of an organization such as the EU, with between 15 and 21 members, would be less dependent on any single state."[26]

Recent Developments in Turkey's Cyprus Policy

The major determinants of Turkish foreign policy with regard to Cyprus are the policies of the political parties and their leaders (particularly those in power), the basically West-leaning inclination of the foreign ministry, the strategic concerns of the military, the influence of Denktaş, and a public opinion in Turkey in which national pride plays an important part. These are, however, the somewhat static features of the situation. The importance of the various players involved can be altered by the specific nature of events. Recent developments in the Cyprus dispute forced Turkey to react and thus imparted a new dynamic to its Cyprus policy.

After the failure of the UN "Set of Ideas" initiative in 1992, the Cyprus problem began to develop new urgency. By 1994 the Greek Cypriots had clearly decided to concentrate on their EU application, hoping to obtain by this route an EU endorsement of their major desiderata: the so-called "three freedoms" of movement, residence, and land purchase, as well as the right of returning refugees to their former homes. Resort to the EU was an important new departure. The EU is an organization in many ways more solid and effective than the UN, one that Turkey could not so easily ignore. At the same time, the Greek Cypriots began an arms buildup that they described as a defensive response to potential Turkish aggression.

By 1995 tension began to mount significantly. The EU decision in March 1995 to set a date for accession talks with the Republic of Cyprus was hopefully dubbed a "catalyst" that would force the parties to reach a solution to the Cyprus problem. The premise of this contention was that the prospect of EU membership would persuade both Cypriot parties, particularly the Turkish Cypriots, to reach a settlement. Although the promise of a customs union was welcome news in Turkey to many businessmen and to Europeanists generally, the manner of its achievement was an affront to nationalist and pro-Turkish-Cypriot elites. In addition, the military was distinctly worried by Greek Cypriot rearmament, which included heavy Russian tanks. Turkish public opinion was inflamed against Greece in January 1996 when a dangerous dispute broke out over ownership of a tiny island (Kardak in Turkish, Imia in Greek) off the Turkish coast. It took the expert help of Richard Holbrooke, U.S. assistant secretary of state for European affairs, to bring the sides back from the brink. Greek Cypriot aggressiveness on the "green line" in August 1996, leading to an incident in which Turkish Cypriot troops shot dead a Greek Cypriot demonstrator climbing a flagpole to remove a Turkish flag, further raised hackles on both sides. Foreign Minister Çiller voiced a popular Turkish sentiment when she justified the shooting on the basis of how dear the flag is to Turks.

The January 1997 Greek Cypriot announcement of plans to import Russian-made S-300 missiles again raised the temperature of the Cyprus conflict. From Ankara, deployment of S-300s in southern Cyprus was seen not just as a matter of security for northern Cyprus but for Turkey itself. Çiller again proved provocative, declaring that Turkey would not hesitate to make a preemptive strike if the missiles were delivered. Russia immediately responded that it could not accept such threats to the sovereign Republic of Cyprus. There followed vague suggestions that Turkey might intercept the missiles in the Turkish Straits. The Turkish military hinted that there might have to be a proper Turkish military base in the north. The issue was heightened by existence of the 1993 Greek-Greek Cypriot "Joint Defense Doctrine" and by plans to establish a Greek air base in Paphos-Baf. A reported intention to involve Syria in defense arrangements with Greece and the Republic of Cyprus also perturbed the military. Was Turkey being surrounded by a ring of fire? There were now new dimensions to the conflict.

Yet some members of the Turkish press did not accept this gloomy thesis. The influential Birand tried to convince readers that Greek Cypriots regarded the missiles and the air base as simply for self-defense. They could not see why Turkey was so worried. How could they start a war against giant Turkey? The reason for the missiles, as Birand reported Clerides' words, was great insecurity in the face of a hostile Turkey.[27] Other Turkish commentators thought the rearmament drive was but the latest of several attempts to internationalize the issue in the Greek Cypriots' favor, now with the aim of bringing in Russia. It was also seen as a bargaining chip and as a passport for Clerides' reelection in February 1998. Prompted by public opinion, official reaction in Turkey was not so sanguine. Prime Minister Yılmaz stated, "For the sake of our security there cannot be anything we cannot do. . . . If hiding behind the European Union's back, they bring in Russia to obtain their ends and [try to] force us to respond . . . the existing situation [on the island] will be the final one."[28]

These mounting pressures were met not only with general expressions of defiance, but also with a series of formal agreements between Turkey and the TRNC. The Turkish-Turkish Cypriot "joint declaration" of December 1995 confirmed the validity of the Turkish guarantee and asserted that the Turkey-EU customs union soon to begin would not affect relations between the two states. The "declaration of solidarity" of January 1997 incorporated a defense agreement for the first time.[29] The "joint statement" of July 1997 essentially added that Turkey would take a measure of formal responsibility for Turkish Cypriot foreign policy and would include Turkish Cypriot representatives in its own delegations, and that Turkey and the TRNC would form an economic and financial union. This last set of pledges was seen as an important step toward Turkish-Turkish Cypriot integration, alarming Nicosia.[30]

Tension increased throughout 1997. The two Cypriot leaders held UN-sponsored meetings in Troutbeck, New York, in July and in Montreux, Switzerland, in August. At these meetings UN assistant secretary-general Diego Cordovez repeated the attempt made in the 1992 Set of Ideas to obtain agreement on a set of principles for a reunified Cyprus, again with little success. During the Troutbeck meetings, media reports claimed the EU had resolved to proceed with accession negotiations with the Greek Cypriots. This almost convinced Denktaş not to attend Montreux, but Turkey persuaded him to do so anyway. Denktaş later declared that if the EU persisted, northern Cyprus would integrate with Turkey and there would be no point in future UN-sponsored talks. Ankara supported Turkish Cypriot insistence that talks on a federal solution could only take place between equals, intimating that there must be two internationally recognized states. Cem, on a visit to Lefkoşa, stated:

> How can you talk about a federation if you accept one side as a community and the other side as a state? . . . We have tried to explain this fact for years. We have insisted on the political equality of the two communities for years. We won't take any steps until this equality is achieved.[31]

Ankara also associated itself with an August 31, 1998 Turkish Cypriot proposal for confederation, including the statement that "by participating in these negotiations the parties will acknowledge that the . . . sides are two sovereign and equal states." The proposals were announced at a press conference at which Cem was present.

Intensification of the dispute by the Greek Cypriots in the 1990s clearly resulted in considerable hardening of Turkey's Cyprus policy and propelled northern Cyprus into an even closer relationship with

Turkey, making the possibility of Cypriot reunification seem even more remote. The Greek Cypriot approach clearly played into the hands of Denktaş, for whom integration with Turkey seems now to be more attractive than federation, though a recent poll in northern Cyprus showed that integration was anything but popular.[32] The August 1998 federation proposal suggests, however, that Denktaş prefers independence to integration. It is not clear that Athens and Nicosia always appreciate that raising tension plays into the hands of those Turks and Turkish Cypriots who are determined that northern Cyprus be recognized as a separate, independent state.

The U.S. Connection

It is impossible for the U.S. to exert influence over Turkey to anything like the extent demanded by the Greek Cypriots and their allies in the Greek lobby in Washington. This is because the U.S. and Turkey have mutual interests. The U.S. needs Turkey as a gateway to, and to an extent as a barrier against, the Middle East and Central Asia. Turkey is a potential ally against any further attempts to threaten U.S. oil interests in the Persian Gulf and is also close to the Caspian Sea, another vast energy reserve. An oil pipeline through Turkey would be more reliable for the West than one through Iran. For its part, Turkey needs U.S. cooperation and support to realize its ambitions with regard to the transportation of Caspian oil and is keenly aware of the strong U.S. position in international finance and commerce. Many members of Turkey's elite were educated in the United States and understand American ways. Spurned to a degree by the EU, those elites who feel the need to assert the Western character of their culture find an opportunity through American connections. Europe, too, needs Turkey, as Turkey needs Europe, but Europe does not have the global concerns of the U.S. and is historically accustomed to regard Turkey as part of a different and seemingly hostile culture situated right on its doorstep.

Washington is aware of Greek Cypriot goals and eager to prevent conflict between North Atlantic Treaty Organization (NATO) partners Turkey and Greece. In addition, it has to be careful not to jeopardize in any way the British bases in Cyprus, which serve NATO purposes in a number of quite significant ways. The U.S. cannot come down on one side or the other in the Cyprus dispute—hence the inability of successive U.S. "special Cyprus negotiators," including Clinton administration trouble-shooter Richard Holbrooke, to bring real pressure to bear on the antagonists.

Conclusion

In Turkey, foreign policy—including Cyprus policy—is mainly the concern of the state, that is, the government and the military. Large businesses favor a policy that will keep Europe open to them. Yet they are not inclined to distance themselves from state policy. Educated elites do not concern themselves much with Cyprus and its problems, which many see as creating difficulties for Turkey elsewhere. Turks do not harbor strong animosity toward Greeks or Greek Cypriots. There is, however, a strong nationalist sentiment in Turkish society generally that reacts quickly to outside aggression or hostility, as the Imia-Kardak crisis and S-300 flap clearly demonstrated. At such times, this nationalist impulse is exacerbated by the Turkish press and electronic media. The nationalist MHP's new prominence, if anything, seems bound to intensify Turkish support for northern Cyprus.

A major influence on Turkey's Cyprus policy is the impressive leadership of Rauf Denktaş. Forthright in his views, he is politically very experienced and knows how to wait to advance his aims until the time is ripe. Any escalation of the Cyprus conflict only provides him with an opportunity for greater influence over Turkish policy. The Turkish Cypriots' antagonists would do well to remember that.

Notes

1 Every city, town, and village in Cyprus has two names, one Greek and one Turkish. In this paper, both names are presented in hyphenated form with the Greek name first; hence, "Varosha-Maraş" and "Famagusta-Gazi Mağosa." One exception: "Nicosia," the Greek form of the city that is the capital of both parts of the island, will refer only to the southern, Greek Cypriot portion of the city or to the Greek Cypriot government. "Lefkoşa," the Turkish form, will refer to the northern, Turkish Cypriot portion of the city or to the Turkish Cypriot government.

2 The United Nations secretary-general stated on August 9, 1990, that "both sides have reaffirmed their support for a federal solution, and a bizonal solution of the Cyprus problem." UN Document A/35/385-S/14100.

3 According to the December 1996 census, confirmed November 27, 1997, the total population of the Turkish Cypriot zone was 200,587. Of this number, 164,460 were of Turkish Cypriot nationality, 30,702 of Turkish nationality, and 5,425 of other nationalities. The figure of 164,460 included 23,924 former Turkish nationals and 3,138 born elsewhere who adopted Turkish Cypriot nationality. The 30,702 Turkish nationals in the north included 8,287 students, with the remainder likely to include a number of occasional workers. Out of the northern zone's total population, 137,398, or 68.5 percent, were native Turkish Cypriots according to these figures, although some would have been the children of post-1974 immigrants from Turkey.

4 Zenon Stavrinides, "Greek Cypriot Perceptions," in Clement H. Dodd (ed.), *Cyprus: The Need for New Perspectives* (Huntingdon: Eothen Press, 1999).

5 Clement H. Dodd, *The Cyprus Issue*, 2nd. rev. ed. (Huntingdon, England: Eothen Press, 1995); Michael Moran (ed.), *Rauf Denktaş at the United Nations: Speeches on Cyprus* (Huntingdon: Eothen Press, 1997), pp. 1-34.

6 A well-conducted poll in the north in November 1997 revealed that some 95 percent of the population wished to join the EU, but not without a settle-

ment first, and in the case of some 42 percent, not unless Turkey was also a member. Reported in *Kıbrıs*, November 23, 1997.

7   The proposal for a confederation was made on August 31, 1998.

8   Clement H. Dodd, *The Cyprus Imbroglio* (Huntingdon: Eothen Press, 1998), pp. 47-49.

9   A common enough observation about Turkish Cypriots by Turkish students in north Cyprus is that they are "too British."

10 Süha Bölükbaşı, *The Superpowers and the Third World: Turkish-American Relations and Cyprus* (Lanham, New York, London: University Press of America, co-published with the Miller Center, University of Virginia, 1988), p. 147. Çağlayangil's remarks are as quoted by Bölükbaşı, who reports that it was agreed upon (presumably by the Turkish government) that the Cyprus state should be unitary, not federal, and that the requirement for separate majorities for major legislation and the use of the veto were to be abandoned.

11 *Keesing's Contemporary Archives*, January 1984, p. 32639.

12 *Briefing*, no. 854 (September 16, 1991), p. 14.

13 The Turkish government intervened to allow the Turkish Cypriots to attend as part of the Turkish delegation, not the ideal solution from their point of view.

14 At the OECD committee session, Turkey argued that it imposed an embargo not exclusively on Greek Cypriot shipping, but on all ships transporting goods from Greek Cypriot ports to Turkey. It also declared that no Turkish vessel would be permitted to visit Greek Cypriot ports. Ankara insisted that these measures were based strictly on foreign policy and national security concerns and thus were not an appropriate subject of discussion for the OECD.

15 Columnists' articles on Cyprus from March 1995 to August 1997 were examined in *Sabah, Milliyet, Hürriyet, Cumhuriyet*, and *Türkiye*. Seven leading journalists were also interviewed in 1996 primarily in İstanbul and also London.

16 By Mehmet Ali Birand, for instance, in *Sabah*, December 30, 1996.

17 Yılmaz Esmer shows that the countries considered most harmful to Turkey by its own public are, in order of importance, the Muslim countries, the U.S., and Greece. "Turkish Public Opinion and Europe," *Cambridge Review of International Affairs* 10, no. 1 (1996), p. 83.

18 These and the following observations derive mainly from interviews with a number of leading politicians from the major political parties in 1995 and 1996. The politicians do not wish to be named.

19 The current distribution of major-party seats in the Turkish Grand National Assembly (parliament) after the 1999 election is as follows: DSP, 136; MHP, 130; *Fazilet* (Virtue) Party (FP), the successor to the RP, 111; ANAP, 86; and DYP, 85.

20 From interviews with senior officers in 1995.

21 Özdem Sanberk (Turkish ambassador to London), "Turkey and the EU: Where Do We Go After *Agenda 2000* and the Amsterdam Summit?" address to Wilton Park Conference, October 7, 1997. Sanberk was formerly undersecretary in the Foreign Ministry.

22 For the Doctrine of Necessity and its refutation, see Zaim Necatigil, "The Cyprus Conflict in International Law," in Clement H. Dodd (ed.), *The Political, Social, and Economic Development of Northern Cyprus* (Huntingdon, England: Eothen Press, 1993), pp. 59-60.

23 *Opinion of E. Lauterpacht, CBE, QC, on the Status of the Two Communities in Cyprus* (UN Doc. A/44/968 S/21463 (1990)), para. 37.

24 Professor M. H. Mendelson, QC, "The Application of the Republic of Cyprus" to Join the European Community, June 6, 1997 (UN Doc. A/51/951 S/1997/585, July 25, 1990).

25 *Opinion of J. Crawford, Gerhard Hafner, and Alain Pellet, on Republic of Cyprus Eligibility for EU Membership* (UN Doc.17/52/81, S/1997/805, October 17, 1997).

26 Ibid., para. 16.

27 Mehmet Ali Birand in *Sabah*, September 29, 1997. Clerides adduced the following evidence for Turkish aggressiveness: constant Turkish warnings to him, the mapping of all Greek Cypriot military positions by Turkish aircraft, and the retention of 30,000 Turkish troops on the island.

28 Reported in *Kıbrıs*, September 12, 1997.

29 This declaration was confirmed unanimously by Turkish legislators, who added that any direct or indirect modification of the 1960 treaties would upset the existing Turkish-Greek balance in the region and would not be tolerated.

30 These documents are appended to Dodd, *The Cyprus Imbroglio.*

31 *Cyprus Today*, November 22, 1997.

32 *Kıbrıs*, October 21, 1998.

Atila Eralp

Turkey and the European Union in the Post–Cold War Era

The relationship between Turkey and the European Community (EC)—known since 1992 as the European Union (EU)—was born and shaped within a Cold War context in which security considerations were paramount.[1] EC-Turkish links were intended to reinforce Turkey's strategically based ties with the West. When East-West tensions relaxed somewhat in the 1970s, however, the EC started to treat Turkey not only in accordance with security imperatives but economic and political considerations as well. Economic problems in EC-Turkish relations, centered around the terms and timetable of a planned customs union, came to the fore during this period. Political problems followed in the 1980s, focused on Turkey's human-rights and democratization record.

Turkey, however, continued to view its relations with the EC throughout this period as fundamentally based on security considerations. As a result, the real requirements of European integration were increasingly diverging from Turkey's approach to that process. This trend accelerated with the end of the Cold War, creating rancor in EU-Turkish relations and disaffection from Europe among the Turkish elite. However, the December 1999 EU summit in Helsinki, which acknowledged Turkey as a candidate for EU membership, produced the possibility of a new, positive turn in EU-Turkish relations.

The Cold War and After

For the Turkish governing elite during the Cold War, "the West" largely meant Western Europe and the United States, undifferentiated as "the Western alliance." At the end of the Cold War, Turkish elites belatedly realized that the West was no longer an undifferentiated entity and that cooperation with the U.S. no longer ensured a smooth relationship with the European Community (EU). Turkey's relations with the U.S. were relatively smooth, but relations with the EC were increasingly strained.

Europe had been the central focus of Turkey's Cold War foreign policy, and, until the mid-1970s, all other regional policies were seen strictly within the context of the East-West conflict. The dramatic changes brought about by the end of the Cold War prompted Turkish

173

policy-makers to develop new options for integration into the emerging international system. They directed their efforts toward emphasizing Turkey's strategic importance in its immediate region. In particular they believed that the dissolution of the Soviet Union and the ensuing independence of the Central Asian republics created a viable option for a new regional foreign policy orientation. Ankara undertook an unprecedented drive to increase economic, political, and cultural links with the new Central Asian states.

The coincidence of this new Turkish orientation with the EC's negative attitude toward Turkey's EC membership bid both increased anti-European tendencies in Turkey and led many Turks to feel that their country no longer needed Europe. As a result, between 1989 and 1992, Turkey distanced itself from its traditional policy of Europeanization. The Gulf crisis reinforced this tendency, as Turkish policy-makers began to speak of "strategic cooperation" with the U.S. based on Turkey's regionally pivotal role. Then-President Turgut Özal increasingly asserted that Turkey provided a model for countries in the region. Özal believed that the Turkish model, wedding Islamic identity and Western-style modernity, could be emulated by other countries in the Middle East and Central Asia and thus deserved the support of the West, especially the United States.

The euphoria of regionalism did not last long, however. Expectations were too high, and Turkey did not have adequate resources or expertise to meet them. As Turkey established more economic, political, and cultural links with Caucasian and Central Asian peoples from whom it had been cut off for decades, it came to realize that it needed more time to develop this new regional orientation. Turkey also had crucial links with European countries that could not easily be forsaken. Turkish policy-makers began to think of relations with the former Soviet states not as an alternative to the traditional policy of Europeanization, but as a potentially valuable asset in Turkey's relations with the EC. A Turkey influential in its region would have a greater role in Europe as well, went this line of thinking, which increasingly took hold after 1992. At the same time, the EU saw a need to pursue new patterns of cooperation with Turkey, even if these fell short of full membership.

Attempts to establish a revamped working relationship with the EU began after 1992. The long-dormant EU-Turkish Association Council—a grouping of the Turkish and EU foreign ministers—convened again after a long hiatus. The Association Council sought to normalize EU-Turkish relations on the basis of two documents: the 1964 EU-Turkey Association Agreement, the umbrella document and legal basis for EU-Turkish relations;[2] and a newer "cooperation package," a set of proposals for improving EU-Turkish relations put forward by the EC's executive arm, the European Commission, in 1990. For both Turkey and the EU, the prospect of a customs union arrangement, as first foreseen by the 1964 Association Agreement, emerged as the lowest common denominator among realistic possibilities for developing relations. Thus the Association Council focused its attention on reactivating and completing the customs union.[3]

Many Turks initially thought the council's decision on March 6, 1995, to approve a customs union arrangement would be a turning point in EU-Turkish relations. However, major differences remained over its interpretation. While the EU viewed the customs union as a mechanism to improve its relationship with Turkey without linking it to the issue of full membership, the Turkish side viewed customs union as part of a tacit comprehensive package that would eventually lead to full membership. These differing views undermined prospects for developing an effective working relationship.

Post-Cold War changes in Europe also made Turkish aspirations for full EU membership more difficult to realize. Now the EU had to focus simultaneously on both "widening" and "deepening"—that is, planning for more members, particularly from among European neutral and nonaligned states and former Warsaw Pact states, and increasing the integration of all its members, old and new. While not abandoning the ideal of deeper integration, the EU aspired to be inclusive and to become an institution of the whole of Europe, that is, a truly European union. But it faced a major challenge in incorporating Central and Eastern European countries that had never previously been part of its half-century-old integration process. As a result, the EU gave less attention to the issue of Turkey's membership.

In fact, the Turkish case is one of the most controversial in the enlargement process. As the EU contemplated enlargement, four possibilities emerged for Turkey's relationship with it. One approach, which held the upper hand in the beginning, would have definitively excluded Turkey from the membership process. EU officials felt that Turkey's long-standing economic and political problems, its size, and its need for considerable financial support if it were to approach EU living standards all militated against its inclusion in the enlargement process. This attitude was quite apparent not only in Greece and Germany, but also within the European Commission. Its reflection was clearly visible in the Commission's summer 1997 *Agenda 2000* report on enlargement, which focused on eleven applicant countries and left Turkey out.

Another possible approach foresaw giving Turkey special status in its ties with the EU but without any link to membership. This line of thinking emerged particularly after Ankara's heated reaction to *Agenda 2000*, which demonstrated that complete exclusion of Turkey—the EU's longest-standing applicant—would aggravate tension between the EU and the Turkish government and increase anti-European feeling among Turks. As the December 1997 Luxembourg summit approached, discussions on the nature of such a special status grew more intense. But Turkey's traditional policy of Europeanization made it extremely difficult for Ankara to give up the idea of full membership. The Turkish side also believed that granting the possibility of full membership to eleven other countries while putting Turkey in a special category would be unjust. Moreover, some EU members—such as France and Italy—were naturally more favorably inclined toward Turkey as a fellow Mediterranean state and sympathized with Turkey's viewpoint. There was also mounting U.S. pressure on the EU to include Turkey in its membership plans.

A third approach would grant Turkey special status as well as a road map or "perspective" toward full membership. Turkey would be included in the enlargement process albeit without a "pre-accession strategy," the package of financial support and close mentoring offered to the other eleven candidates to facilitate progress toward full membership. The questions of "when" and "how" for Turkey's membership would be left open. This strategy was seen by its proponents as the most feasible way to solve the Turkish problem. On the one hand, it would send a message to Turkey that it was included in the enlargement process. On the other, it would not over-commit the EU financially. The pressure would be on Turkey to reform its political and economic structures and to prove itself worthy of an accession strategy.

A fourth approach, which had almost no chance to succeed, was to make Turkey a candidate for membership like all other applicants. Turkish officials supported this strategy—indeed, they considered it the only acceptable alternative. But within the EU, Greece and Germany argued against it. Their arguments met general acquiescence in the EU due to the long history of problematic EU-Turkish relations, and more importantly because no EU countries were strongly supporting the Turkish case.

The December 1997 Luxembourg summit chose the third option, giving Turkey a special status with a long perspective toward full membership. Turkey was included in the enlargement process but not given a pre-accession strategy. The EU promised a "European strategy" that would prepare Turkey for accession by bringing it closer to the union in unspecified ways. This decision was a clear improvement over *Agenda 2000*, and EU officials felt that they had handled the Turkish case fairly. However, the Turks believed otherwise. They reacted strongly against the decision, which they considered unfair. The attitudes of the Turkish elite shaping this reaction can be best understood if we clarify Turkey's attitude toward the EC after it applied for full membership in 1987.

Domestic Attitudes toward Full Membership

Support for Westernization at home has always been a dominant factor in the way the Turkish elite perceives its relations with Europe. In the view of the Turkish elite, closer association with Europe is above all a "civilizing mission" that brings an increasingly larger section of the population into contact with Western lifestyles, behavior, and methods. But this goal was shaped by political and economic considerations. Efforts toward Westernization would bring economic development and greater political stability, Turkish leaders believed. Europe and the West also were seen as the main sources of economic support as well as models for social change. Finally, the governing elite viewed security as a force for binding Turkey with the West. Post-World War II Turkish elites defined membership in the main Western security structure—the North Atlantic Treaty Organization (NATO)—as integral to Westernization policy. Seeking closer relations with Europe's economic bloc was a logical extension of this approach. Turkey regarded the EC as the economic axis of the Western alliance, supplementing and cementing its unity.

This broad consensus among the Turkish elites started to crack during the 1970s with the emergence of tension between the two major Turkish national projects—Westernization (at least in the sense of integration with the EC) and economic development—which had hitherto seemed mutually reinforcing. This tension was particularly pronounced among those key societal actors and government agencies that viewed association with Europe as important primarily in terms of economic development.[4] Problems began to emerge after Ankara and the EC signed the 1973 "Additional Protocol," which foresaw a twenty-two-year transition period to establishment of a Turkey-EU customs union. As economic difficulties increased—particularly balance-of-payments problems after the 1973 oil crisis—industrialists started to complain that the envisioned transition period was too short for achievement of the necessary restructuring of Turkish industry. Even in usually pro-European institutions like the Istanbul Chamber of Industry, strong opposition to the terms of the customs unions began to mount. Some industrialists went so far as to ask the government to abandon efforts at achieving customs union altogether and seek different forms of association with the EC. These demands were welcomed by the government's powerful State Planning Organization (SPO), which also emphasized the likely detrimental effects of a customs union on Turkey's industrialization efforts and on the SPO's preferred development strategy of import substitution. Meanwhile, the Turkish foreign ministry maintained its traditional support for accession to the EC based on foreign policy considerations.

Within the EC itself, political concerns were acquiring increasing weight. Belief that membership would strengthen democratic regimes guided EC responses to Greek, Portuguese, and Spanish membership applications. These countries' policy-makers captured this shift in EC emphasis in their decision to forge ahead with their bids. In contrast, Turkish policy-makers' emphasis on independent economic development, widened the gulf between Turkey and the other southern European countries that actively sought closer economic and political ties with the rest of Europe. Notions of economic self-reliance reflected the conditions under which the Turkish Republic was established in 1923 and over time had hardened into core state values. A staunch advocate of self-reliance was prime minister Bülent Ecevit, who led three governments in the 1970s and defied the international community in defending the Turkish Cypriots in 1974. In 1978 Ecevit's government decided to "freeze" the customs union timetable for five years.

With issues of democracy increasingly important to the EC, the 1980 military intervention in Turkey exacerbated EC-Turkish divergence and ushered in a new tense phase in EC-Turkish relations, one increasingly dominated by human-rights issues. The 1980-83 military government and later the government of civilian Prime Minister Turgut Özal rejected European human rights criticism as unwarranted interference in a sovereign country's internal affairs.

The EC regarded democracy as a *sine qua non* for inclusion in its ranks and saw Turkey as falling well below the required democratic threshold. For their part, Turkish leaders seemed to see democracy in relative rather than absolute terms. The military, in particular, insisted that each nation had a right to its own form of democracy and that Turkish democracy, as reflected in Turkey's 1982 constitution, should be seen as the equal of any other. The 1980-83 military government believed that relations with Europe would resume a smooth course once Turkey was able to announce a timetable for transition to democracy. Later, Özal believed all would be well once the Turkish economy achieved greater integration into world markets as a result of his radical economic reforms.

Relations with Europe no longer depended on the economy alone—a fact completely overlooked by Turkish policy-makers, who seemingly continued to believe that issues of democracy and human rights were but a secondary concern for the EC. While normalization of EC-Turkish relations was still being debated, Özal abruptly decided to apply for full EC membership on April 14, 1987. This decision surprised many, particularly EC officials. In hindsight, one could say there were serious problems with the timing of the application. It came at a time when the EC was facing serious problems of consolidation and had turned inward.

Within Turkey, the Istanbul-based big-business community was once again the strongest supporter of full EC membership.[5] Özal's export-oriented free-market reforms had reduced the importance of the customs union as a concern for the industrialists and instead raised the possibility of new links with European investors. Attraction of foreign investment to Turkey was an integral part of Özal's economic policy. Full EC membership, it was thought, would attract foreign technology and capital, which had been limited despite progressively more favorable regulations. The private sector believed Turkey as an EC member could expand into world markets in partnership with foreign companies.

Economic factors alone do not sufficiently explain the significance of the EC for much of the private sector. Full EC membership appeared to the mainly secularist Istanbul-based industrialists as a bulwark against the growing strength of political Islamic movements in Turkey. In contrast, small-capital traders and industrialists in central Anatolia generally supported more nationalist and political-religious tendencies themselves and thus regarded membership in the EC suspiciously.

Political parties represented in parliament unanimously supported Turkey's 1987 application for full membership.[6] Although opposition parties had some reservations about the timing of the application and emphasized the need for prior political and economic reforms, they were still in favor of integration with Europe and the EC. However, crucial differences existed between the ruling *Anavatan* (Motherland) Party (ANAP) and the main opposition party, the *Sosyal Demokrat Halk* (Social Democratic Populist) Party (SHP) regarding EC membership. In line with private-sector views, ANAP saw the EC mainly as a stable market for Turkish exports as well as a source of funds and technology. ANAP was apprehensive of European definitions of democracy and human rights, however. The SHP took the opposite approach, viewing the EC question in political rather than economic terms. It supported EC views on democracy and human rights but equivocated regarding the economic consequences of membership. As heir to Kemal Atatürk's and Ecevit's *Cumhuriyet Halk* (Republican People's) Party (CHP), the SHP stressed the need for a largely indigenous industrialization capacity and fretted that integration with the EC would undermine Turkish industries, which were comparatively weaker than their European counterparts. The religious *Refah* (Welfare) Party (RP)—which did not pass the 10-percent barrier in the 1987 election and remained outside parliament—vigorously opposed Turkey's accession to the EC. Party leader Necmettin Erbakan depicted the EC as a Christian community organized to undermine the Islamic world and denounced the pro-EC lobby in Turkey as part of a Zionist plot to sow dissent among Islamic countries.

The EC's long-delayed February 1990 response[7] to the Turkish application was negative in tone, mainly confining itself to a list of Turkey's shortcomings, without any words of encouragement, and implying that Turkey should stay on the membership sidelines for an indefinite period. Turkish officials and private-sector representatives had hoped the EC at least would indicate a date for starting membership negotiations. The mere announcement of a date—any date—would have been regarded as an important symbolic statement of EC support for ultimate Turkish membership. Although the EC formulated a "cooperation package" of economic aid and other benefits to Turkey at this time in order to re-energize the Association Agreement, each side interpreted the package differently. Turkish officials saw the proposals as a step toward full membership, but EC officials viewed them simply as measures to increase cooperation with Turkey without any commitment regarding membership.

The EC response to Turkey's membership application prompted an unprecedented domestic debate on Turkey's "Europeanness." For most in Turkey's center-right and center-left, as well as for the governing economic and political elites, this decision carried the message that Europe did not consider Turkey one of its own and that Turkey's Westernization goals had not been accomplished as they had hitherto believed. The religious right, however, saw the EC decision as a welcome slap in the face to Turkey's rulers—a slap that it hoped would demonstrate once and for all that the EC is nothing more than a Christian club and that Turkey should not seek to emulate an identity it would never share. The RP stepped up its anti-EC rhetoric and proposed an Islamic common market as an alternative. Overall, the EC's response to Turkey's application increased anti-European feelings among Turks in a way that nationalist and Islamist politicians could easily exploit.

Customs Union Debate and Political Fragmentation

Turkey's 1987 membership application, although dismissed by the EC, at least succeeded in goading the EC (and then the EU) to work with Turkey in completing customs union arrangements. Efforts began in earnest after 1992, and by early 1995 Turkey and the EU had reached agreement on the terms.

Most Turks at first thought the Turkey-EU Association Council's decision on March 6, 1995, to implement the customs union—ratified by the European Parliament on December 13, 1995—would be a positive turning point for EU-Turkish ties. Tense relations of some twenty years' duration were expected to improve quickly. However, almost immediately, major, if familiar, differences of view emerged. Turkish officials believed the customs union was intended to lead to full membership and supported it at least partly for that reason. EU officials viewed it solely as a mechanism to improve cooperation and did not link it to full membership.

Once clearly perceived, the EU's attitude created resentment toward the customs union in Turkey. Many Turks derided the value of a customs union that did not foresee eventual full membership and that thus forced Turkey to obey economic rules it never would be able to influence. Turks increasingly viewed the customs union merely as an EU effort to compensate Turkey for nonparticipation in the membership process. This view took root more deeply as the EU institutionally focused its membership consideration on Central and Eastern European countries and Cyprus.

The broad consensus that existed among political and economic elites during the 1987 membership application effort came apart during customs union negotiations.[8] Division of opinion between the parties in government and the opposition was clearly visible. The governing coalition parties, center-right *Doğru Yol* (True Path) Party (DYP) and center-left SHP, naturally supported the move toward the customs union, but all opposition parties, including center-right ANAP—which originally had led the drive for full EC membership—were against it. Prime Minister and DYP leader Tansu Çiller presented the customs union as an important victory and a major step toward becoming part of the European family—and as an arrangement that would lead to full membership. The opposition parties questioned the value of customs union without full membership. They cited the examples of Greece, Spain, and Portugal, who had all understood this and thus had pushed for full membership without the intermediate step of customs union. They also stressed the traditional concern about the likely adverse effect customs union would have on Turkish industry, that it might harm sectors not ready to compete with Europe. Asserting that the EU should have been more forthcoming on funding to help Turkey overcome the short-term adverse effects of customs union, they claimed the government had failed to negotiate firmly and had conceded too much.

The customs union also became politically contentious because of the sensitive Cyprus issue. The EU's resolution on customs union and its decision to start membership negotiations with the Greek Cypriot-controlled Republic of Cyprus on a "date certain"—specifically, six months after the EU's planned Intergovernmental Conference—were issued on the same day. In Turkey, opposition parties asked if the government, to achieve the customs union, had made concessions related to the Greek Cypriots' full-membership application. The governing coalition insisted that it had not, that Turkey had in no way linked the customs union with the Cyprus issue. Foreign Minister Murat Karayalçın said he had warned the EU that, if it started negotiations with the Greek Cypriots, Turkey would begin a process of "integration" with the Turkish Republic of Northern Cyprus (TRNC), the state declared by the Turkish Cypriots in 1983 and recognized only by Turkey. He insisted Turkey had not made concessions on Cyprus. Nevertheless, widespread suspicion and resentment on this point persisted among Turks.

Luxembourg Summit and Its Aftermath

After the 1997 Luxembourg summit, the Turkish government for the first time assumed a distant, if not negative, attitude toward the EU. Virtually all elements of Turkish society—political and economic elites, government and opposition parties—coalesced around this more skeptical view of the EU.

The government regarded the Luxembourg decision as discriminatory and taken primarily under Greek influence. Government officials also felt the so-called "Copenhagen criteria"—broad political and economic criteria for membership established at a 1993 EU summit in Copenhagen and purportedly the basis of the Luxembourg summit's decisions on candidacies for EU membership—had been applied subjectively. Turkey considered itself more advanced than some of the countries chosen as candidates, both in fulfilling the requisite economic and political criteria and in adapting to the *acquis communitaire*, the EU's set of laws and regulations. The EU's placement of those countries ahead of Turkey in the membership queue was unfair, in Ankara's view.

The EU decision to put the Republic of Cyprus in the first wave of applicant countries and to implement its earlier decision to open membership negotiations with it reinforced Turkish resentment. Ankara saw the Cyprus decision as a clear sign that the EU was taking sides with Greece and acting under Greek influence. Ankara also thought the decision would result in a *de facto* partition of the island, as the Greek Cypriot government would no longer have a serious incentive to negotiate a settlement. Ankara hardened its own position on the Cyprus problem, emphasizing that Cyprus is a primary security concern and re-emphasizing its threat to take steps toward further integration between Turkey and the TRNC. Ecevit, then deputy prime minister and known for his strongly pro-Turkish Cypriot views, was quite influential in shaping Turkey's Cyprus policy in the aftermath of the Luxembourg summit.

Despite its disappointment, the Turkish government opted to continue relations with the EU based on existing legal arrangements, primarily the 1964 Association Agreement. But Ankara also decided to suspend political dialogue with the EU and not to participate in the newly established European Conference, an envisioned grouping of EU members and candidates, plus Turkey, that the EU designed specifically to mollify Turkey. Ankara felt the EU had set out discriminatory "preconditions" in its requirements for participation in the European

Conference. These "preconditions" included the establishment of stable relations between Greece and Turkey, seemingly putting the onus for achieving this on Turkey; commitment to the settlement of disputes by legal process, including the International Court of Justice, as desired by Athens and rejected by Ankara in their dispute over continental-shelf rights in the Aegean Sea; respect for and protection of minorities and human rights; and support for negotiations toward a Cyprus settlement under the aegis of the United Nations.

A Turkish parliamentary committee established to assess relations between Turkey and the EU backed the government's position.[9] Composed of all political parties represented in parliament, this committee listened to all influential Turkish political and economic decision-makers during its hearings. Its report stressed the discriminatory and unjust attitude of the EU toward Turkey and asserted that Turkey had lost its confidence in the EU as a result of the Luxembourg summit. The report recommended that Turkish-European relations proceed according to the Association Agreement for the short term but warned that longer-term relations would depend on the EU's attitude toward Turkey's quest for full membership. It reiterated Turkey's commitment to be part of the EU while acknowledging that that goal would take longer than Turkey had expected.

Noting that representatives of the private sector who testified during the hearings remained supportive of customs union, the report also affirmed Turkey's commitment to that arrangement. Following the Luxembourg summit, some Turks had advocated revision of the customs union, suggesting that Ankara downgrade it into a free-trade arrangement or scrap it altogether. The parliamentary report urged against such an approach, saying that Turkish efforts to alter the customs union agreement would raise doubts about Turkey's commitment not only to customs union but to EU membership as well. It recommended that Turkey fulfill its customs union obligations and pass the necessary implementing legislation while pressing the EU to fulfill its unfulfilled commitments, primarily financial obligations vetoed by Greece. The customs union approach outlined in the report carried the day with the Turkish government and helped provide the government with political cover to pursue a moderate and pragmatic course, notwithstanding the angry tone of its public rhetoric regarding the EU.

The June 1998 EU summit, held in Cardiff, Wales—the first summit since Luxembourg—was unable to break the stalemate in the EU-Turkish relationship. The Turkish foreign ministry declared after the summit that it saw no major change in the EU's discriminatory attitude toward Turkey. It acknowledged, however, some slight improvements relative to the results of the Luxembourg summit. For example, the summit did accept the need for funding to implement the so-called "European Strategy"—a set of proposals put forward by the European Commission to deepen EU-Turkish relations—and it asked the commission "to reflect on ways and means of underpinning the implementation of the European Strategy and to table appropriate proposals to this effect." Also, the summit communiqué did not mention sensitive political issues, such as Cyprus and human rights. Finally, the communiqué affirmed that Turkey's progress toward EU accession should be based not only on the conclusions of the EU summits but also on Article 28 of the Association Agreement, which clearly envisages Turkey's full membership once conditions are met. These developments pointed toward an evolution in the EU's approach that would pave the way for a Turkish success eighteen months later at the EU's final summit of the 1990s.

The Helsinki Summit and EU–Turkish Prospects

Following the Luxembourg summit, there were two possible options for EU-Turkish relations. The first was Turkey's exclusion from the emerging European project. Increasing marginalization of Turkey in post-Cold War Europe and growing anti-European feeling among Turks both pointed to this as a possibility. The second option was to establish a working arrangement that goes beyond customs union, incorporating political and security dimensions and keeping open the prospect of Turkish membership. With the December 1999 Helsinki summiwhich acknowledged Turkey, at last, as a "candidate State destined to join the Union on the basis of the same criteria as applied to the other candidate States"—the EU and Turkey seem definitively to have chosen the second option.

There were many reasons for this choice. Both the EU and Turkey came to realize that exclusion benefited neither. Had Turkey not received candidacy and the prospect of membership, the customs union itself may have been in jeopardy. The notion that Turkey would forever be linked in a customs union arrangement, without any influence over its rules, was becoming increasingly politically unsustainable among Turks.

But the post-Luxembourg change in EU-Turkish relations emanated mainly from the EU. One important factor was the 1998 change in government in Germany from a Christian Democrat-dominated coalition to a Social Democrat-Greens coalition. The new government projected a more open, inclusive attitude toward the EU enlargement process, rejecting narrow geographical interpretations and religious-cultural criteria. Another important factor was the Greek-Turkish rapprochement that followed tragic earthquakes both countries suffered in late summer 1999. This led to a surprising Greek decision not to veto Turkey's bid for candidacy.

From the EU's standpoint, geopolitical and security considerations were probably among the most important factors in its decision to affirm Turkey's candidacy. The 1999 Kosovo crisis made EU states more aware of the need for security in its surrounding regions. Indeed, Greek-Turkish cooperation in providing humanitarian assistance to Kosovar refugees was one of the first signs of a bilateral thaw. It is reasonable to speculate that the EU may have encouraged Greek-Turkish rapprochement as a means of enhancing Balkan stability.

Moreover, it is no coincidence that the EU offered Turkey candidacy for membership in the same summit in which it made important decisions to consolidate so-called "European Security and Defense Identity (ESDI)." At the Helsinki summit, the EU decided to create a military force of 50,000-60,000 troops capable of conducting autonomous operations in response to international crises. This decision went beyond the 1999 NATO "strategic concept," which foresaw that ESDI-based operations would be carried out strictly in coordination with NATO, and is a measure of the EU's new-found determination to increase its focus on security-related issues.

Europe's political and economic success partly depends on stability in its surrounding regions, the Mediterranean, the Middle East, and Eurasia. Turkey is one of the few countries in these regions that is relatively stable and long tied to Western security. Turkey also has crucial roles to play in establishing trade, transport, and energy routes linking Europe with the Middle East, Transcaucasia, and Central Asia. An unstable Turkey would be a force for instability in its neighboring regions, unsettling Europe's links with those areas, particularly in an era of transregionalization of security issues like terrorism and drugs. By the time of Helsinki, the EU apparently had come to realize that closer links with Europe, via the EU, would reinforce Turkish stability and, therefore, European stability as well. The results of the Helsinki summit suggest that an EU more attentive to geopolitical concerns is also more attentive to Turkey.

Of course, the benefits of closer EU-Turkish ties are hardly one-sided in the EU's favor. For Turkey the link is essential, and not only for economic reasons. First, it strengthens Turkey's "civilizational project"—the policy of Westernization pursued since the founding of the Turkish republic in 1923. Second, strong links to the EU increase Turkey's prestige and influence in its various neighboring regions.

Before Turkey can begin formal "accession talks" toward achieving membership, it must meet the political requirements of the "Copenhagen criteria," including full democratization and protection of minority rights. To meet those requirements, Turkey will have to undertake numerous reforms, and it is not clear how rapidly that will occur. Even before talks begin, however, there are a number of steps the EU could consider to improve EU-Turkish relations.

First, Turkey's links with emerging EU security institutions need to be strengthened. Turkey's functions in the Western European Union, scheduled to be dissolved by 2001, should be transferred to the EU. Regarding ESDI, it is essential that Turkey participate in both the formulation and implementation of policies.

Second, the EU should find a way to overcome the Greek veto on Turkey-related issues, should that problem persist despite recent improvements in Greek-Turkish relations. Since virtually all EU decisions require unanimity, Greece over the years has been able persistently to use its veto power to block EU financial aid to Turkey. After the earthquake, the EU lifted its veto on some of the funds owed to Turkey, with Greek consent, but hundreds of millions of dollars of funding pledged by the EU, including structural adjustment funds under the customs union agreement, remain bottled up. EU action on internal proposals to move away from consensus decision-making toward some form of majority rule could greatly benefit EU-Turkish relations.

Third, the EU should come up with a means to handle Greek Cyprus's membership application without aggravating the Cyprus problem or alienating Turkey from the EU. The EU took a potentially fateful step with its decision at the Luxembourg summit to include Greek Cypriots in the first wave of enlargement negotiations. Including Greek Cyprus, while excluding Turkey, effectively drew the EU into the Cyprus dispute on the Greek side. This decision harmed EU-Turkish ties and escalated tension between the Greek and Turkish Cypriot communities and between Greece and Turkey, thus hardening the political status quo and *de facto* partition of the island. The decision also contravened the basic goal of European integration, which is to enhance stability.

The EU should make Greek Cyprus's accession to the EU conditional on a solution to the Cyprus problem and on the participation of Turkish Cypriots in the accession negotiations. This remains possible, at least on a *de facto* basis, even after the Helsinki summit. Although the summit declared that settlement of the Cyprus problem is not a "precondition" for Cyprus's EU membership, it fudged the issue in a subsequent statement strongly implying that a settlement or lack thereof would be one among "all relevant factors" considered in deciding on Cyprus's accession.

As the EU is drawn into the Cyprus issue and Greek-Turkish disputes, any politically feasible solution to these problems must include incorporation of Turkey into the EU. With Greece and the Greek Cypriots inside the EU and Turkey and the Turkish Cypriots outside, it would be extremely difficult to solve these problems.[10]

In the wake of the Helsinki summit, it seems likely that Turkey and the EU will be able to discuss these issues without the tension that characterized their relations for two years after Luxembourg. EU-Turkish relations had reached a historical crossroads on the eve of Helsinki. The EU could have chosen to further marginalize or exclude Turkey from the emerging European project, or it could have chosen improved ties and a fair prospect of Turkish membership. Fortunately for both sides, it chose the latter.

Notes

1   Canan Balkır and Allan M. Williams (eds.), *Turkey and Europe* (London: Pinter, 1993). The fifteen-nation European Union has been commonly known by other names over the years. The 1957 Treaty of Rome, which went into effect that year, transformed the "European Coal and Steel Community" into the "European Economic Community" (EEC). In 1965, the "European Community" (EC) was set up to integrate the EEC with some other European institutions and to establish an integrated common market and eventually a European federation. "EEC" nevertheless remained a commonly used, if informal, designation until roughly the mid-1980s. In February 1992, member states signed the Treaty on European Union (the "Maastricht Treaty"), formally christening the group the "European Union" (EU). The treaty did not go into effect until 1993, but "EU" became a commonly used designation once the treaty was signed. In time-specific references in this paper, the organization is designated as the EEC before 1965, the EC from 1965 through 1991, and the EU from 1992 to the present. In non-time-specific references, it will be designated EC or EU, as deemed appropriate. (Technically, the European Community continues to exist as a legal entity, co-terminously with the European Union.)

2   The "Agreement Creating an Association between the Republic of Turkey and the European Economic Community," also known as the "Ankara agreement," was signed in Ankara on September 12, 1963. It entered into force on December 1, 1964.

3   İktisadi Kalkınma Vakfı (Economic Development Foundation), "Avrupa Birliği Bütünleşmesinin Vardığı Nokta: 1996 Hükümetlerarası Konferans ve Türkiye'nin Bu Gelişimdeki Yeri" (The point reached by European Integration: the 1996 Intergovernmental Conference and Turkey's role in this development), İstanbul, no. 137 (1996), pp. 45-48.

4   Mehmet Ali Birand, *Türkiye'nin Ortak Pazar Macerası 1959-1985* (Turkey's European Union adventure, 1959-1985) (İstanbul: Milliyet Yayınları, 1985); Atila Eralp, "The Politics of Turkish Development Strategies," in Andrew Finkel and Nükhet Sirman (eds.), *Turkish State, Turkish Society* (London: Routledge, 1990); İlhan Tekeli and Selim İlkin, *Türkiye ve Avrupa Topluluğu* (Turkey and the European Union) (Ankara: Ümit Yayıncılık, 1991).

5   Vehbi Koç, "25.Yılında Türkiye-AT Ortaklık İlişkileri" (On the 25th anniversary of Turkey-EU relations), *İktisadi Kalkınma Vakfı Dergisi*, no. 59 (September 1988), pp. 24-26.

6   İlter Turan, "Turkish Political Parties and the European Community," *Yapı Kredi Economic Review* 3, no. 1 (1998), pp. 73-88.

7   The European Commission actually issued its "opinion" on the Turkish application on December 18, 1989. The EC's Council of Ministers formally endorsed the Commission's "opinion" on February 5, 1990.

8   Esra Cayhan, *Dünden Bugüne Türkiye-Avrupa Birliği İlişkileri ve Siyasal Partilerin Konuya Bakışı* (Turkey-European Union relations from yesterday to today and the views of the political parties on this issue) (İstanbul: Boyut Kitapları, 1997); Canan Balkır, "The Customs Union and Beyond" in Libby Rittenberg (ed.), *The Political Economy of Turkey in the Post-Soviet Era* (Westport, Conn.: Praeger, 1998).

9   *Türkiye Büyük Millet Meclisi (10/21) Esas Numaralı Meclis Araştırma Komisyonu Raporu* (Report of the Parliamentary Investigation Commission no. 10/21 of the Turkish Grand National Assembly), 1998.

10   F. Stephen Larrabee, "The EU Needs to Rethink Its Cyprus Policy (in Response)," *Survival* 40, no. 3 (Autumn 1998), pp. 25-29.

George S. Harris

U.S.–Turkish Relations

Turkey and the United States are facing a challenging time in their relations. Originally conceived in the post-World War II era's focus on containing the Soviet Union, Turkey's alliance with the U.S. lost this sustaining rationale after the USSR collapsed. More recently, another venerable pillar of the relationship fell, as U.S. military aid to Turkey ended in 1998. That means a number of challenging decisions and issues inevitably will test the alliance. It is therefore an appropriate time—even a highly desirable one—to reinspect this important relationship. This essay will seek to identify the sinews that keep the relationship strong and to suggest possible ways in which bilateral relations may develop. It will also advance some modest policy suggestions that could attenuate the most vexatious of the problems confronting the allies in the near future.

The past has left a complex set of problems and possibilities that will inevitably influence the course of U.S.-Turkish relations. Turkey is no longer the inward-looking, economically weak state that it was for many decades after coming into alliance with the U.S. Economic and military aid were commanding imperatives when Turkey joined the North Atlantic Treaty Organization (NATO) in 1952. Industrial activity needed a jump-start, which it got with a massive inflow of resources from Turkey's Western allies, principally the U.S. Much of the early aid went to infrastructure projects whose benefits were realized only in successive generations.[1]

U.S. military assistance to Turkey in its early years played an essential role in revitalizing the Turkish armed forces, which until then had developed little more than a World War I-era fighting capability. The appetite for military modernization fed by U.S. liberality also ensured that the armed forces would demand a significant share of available Turkish resources to keep Turkish equipment up to date.[2]

Contact with NATO allies and the stimulation of new operating procedures also created a new dynamism and self-esteem in the rapidly improving Turkish officer corps. This dynamism, plus the military's deepened stake in Turkey's links with the West, ultimately led to one unintended result: It stimulated Turkish officers to intervene in domestic politics when they considered their constitutional regime or its Westernizing and pro-Western principles under assault. Nevertheless, most

Turkish officers, like their Western counterparts, continued to regard democracy as the only legitimate form of governance over the long term.

Turkish demand soon exceeded U.S. willingness to provide ever newer generations of military systems, especially those which could be used against Cyprus (landing craft) or against domestic insurgents (helicopters). Indeed, Congress regularly manipulated military aid as a tool to try, however unsuccessfully, to force political decisions on Turkey. By the late 1990s U.S. military aid had declined to the point that it was viewed by many Turks as too onerous in its political implications. Also, although the Turkish government saw aid as an important vote of confidence from the U.S., the robust development of the Turkish economy after 1980 rendered the assistance steadily less important in material terms. Hence, the end of military aid in 1998 occasioned no great furor in Turkey.[3]

Turkey's New Environment

Like its economic status, Turkey's internal political environment has changed dramatically over the past half-century of alliance with the U.S. A basically two-party, simple-plurality electoral system has given way to a multiparty arrangement with a complex system of proportional representation. The latter feature in particular encouraged fissiparous tendencies to the point that, on the eve of 1999 elections, ten parties and groups were represented in the parliament. This generated considerable instability in government policy. The need for parliament to approve arrangements with the U.S., often ignored in the early days of the relationship, imposed an increasing strain on the alliance. Nevertheless, attachment to the alliance with the U.S. remained a constant, despite sharp disappointments at critical junctures.

Domestic ethnic problems have arisen to threaten the unity of the Turkish polity. The Kurdistan Workers Party (known by its Kurdish initials PKK) attacked Turkish authorities and targeted Kurdish tribal structure in eastern Turkey starting in the mid-1980s, provoking extensive military operations against small hit-and-run guerrilla bands. This conflict was expensive for the Turkish state and led to military excesses. Because it was difficult for the Turkish authorities to distinguish PKK terrorists from the rest of the population, these military engagements saw numerous villages destroyed. Huge numbers of Kurds fled their traditional homes for Turkey's larger cities. The authorities conducted indiscriminate arrests; as a result, human-rights violations intruded on Turkey's dealings with NATO allies and impeded its quest to join the European Union (EU). The U.S. administration, however, proved more understanding of the terrorist provocation that lay behind the conflict. Turkish authorities have been grateful for this measure of tolerance.[4]

As Turkey evolved, new institutions grew that have to be taken into consideration in the elaboration of foreign policy. That has had both positive and negative implications for Turkey's relationship with the U.S. On the positive side, for example, the emergence of the Istanbul stock market in the past decade created the need for Ankara to calculate the impact of its decisions on the market. The Istanbul market, in turn, is linked to other international markets, especially those in the U.S. Thus it becomes a force for continuing alliance and is taken into consideration by politicians. Businessmen's associations, which are increasingly active and well funded, also share this bias for Western relationships and have even begun to lobby in the U.S. for stronger ties.

On the negative side, the media have broadened their impact as well. The press remains often sensationalist, and journalists are all too frequently predisposed to see conspiracy in U.S. dealings with Turkey. The conspicuous role of the media in inflating the dispute with Greece over the Imia-Kardak rocks in the Aegean in 1996 illustrates their ability to exacerbate a crisis and complicate U.S.-Turkish relations. One thing is certain: Any serious bilateral difference is likely to be made more difficult by the treatment it receives from major media organs, including hundreds of local TV stations, representing almost every shade of opinion in Turkey, that have been established in the past few years.[5]

The Turkish foreign policy environment has also shifted radically during the years of NATO membership. In the Stalinist era of active Soviet pressure on Turkey, the Atlantic alliance provided reassurance. Even after the mid-1960s, when many Turks actually had lost their fear that Moscow would attack, Ankara used the Soviet bogeyman to bolster arguments for additional aid. Indeed, as the years went on, aid rather than defense became the prime value of the alliance to senior Turkish military leaders as well as many top civilian politicians.

The demise of the Soviet Union ushered in an era in which Turkey's justification for receiving military equipment from its NATO allies naturally had to be argued on grounds other than preparing for attack from Moscow. The Turkish general staff got nowhere with Washington in claiming that Russian violations of weaponry limits in the Caucasus (required by the 1990 Conventional Armed Forces in Europe treaty, or CFE) presented a danger to NATO. President Turgut Özal tried another tack in portraying Turkey as the West's "bridge" to the Turkic states on Russia's southern border—rhetoric that also proved inadequate.

The Gulf War offered more promising possibilities, such as casting Turkey as an essential base for NATO "out-of-area operations" and an "island of stability in a turbulent Middle East."[6] Turkey's İncirlik air base served as the key installation for policing the "no-fly zone" in north-

ern Iraq and supporting the security zone for Iraqi Kurds—key political requirements for U.S. foreign policy toward Iraq after the Gulf War.
That policy, however, was questioned by Turkey's Islamists as well as
by many in Bülent Ecevit's Demokratik Sol (Democratic Left) Party
(DSP) and even at times by some influential military figures. Opposition from these political circles eventually led to restrictions on U.S.
activity on the ground in northern Iraq.[7]

Turkey's international environment was marked by poor relations
with neighboring countries. NATO partner Greece was intensely hostile to Turkey as a result of the Cyprus and Aegean issues. This bitterness fed on historical animosities. Long-standing difficulties with Syria
worsened in the 1970s after Turkey began to construct dams on the
Euphrates River without reaching prior accord with Damascus. The
Syrian regime, for its part, provided a safe haven and base for the PKK.
Ties with Central Treaty Organization (CENTO) ally Iran were disrupted
by Khomeini's revolution, though Mohammad Khatami's election as
president in 1997 seems to have moderated Tehran's campaign to export its brand of religious fanaticism. These problematic relations convinced a succession of Turkish governments that they "live in a bad
neighborhood." This type of thinking provided Turkey with justification for seeking ever more modern military systems and detracted from
its commitment to the Universal Declaration on Human Rights.

Bilateral Problems

Changing circumstances in the world and the rise of new domestic imperatives in both countries have led both the U.S. and Turkey to load
new elements onto their alliance that were never envisaged at its incep-
tion. The attempt to make these new preoccupations the touchstone of
the alliance has at times caused considerable friction.[8]

The Cyprus dispute imparted the greatest stress. U.S. mishandling
of the issue left a legacy of Turkish unhappiness, beginning with the
1964 "Johnson letter" to Turkish prime minister İsmet İnönü—a
comunication infamous in Turkey for President Lyndon B. Johnson's
threat that NATO would not defend Turkey if the Soviet Union attacked
it during a Turkish intervention on the island. The rise of a Greek lobby
in Washington, especially after the 1974 intervention, heavily influenced
congressional attitudes toward Turkey. The Greek case was abetted by
an increasingly effective Armenian lobby primarily bent on gaining
world recognition of the mass killings of Armenians in the Ottoman
Empire in 1915 and 1916.

In this atmosphere, a congressionally imposed embargo on military weapons transfers to Turkey badly shook bilateral relations from
1975 to 1978, when the Carter administration was able to get it lifted.
Importantly, the embargo did not make Turkey change policy. Instead

the Turks froze negotiations with Greece and closed U.S. intelligence collection facilities during the embargo period.

Cyprus has remained a sore point ever since, with the U.S. (and the rest of the world) refusing to join Turkey in accepting the declaration of northern Cyprus as an independent state in 1983. Moreover, Congress has periodically withheld aid and prevented shipment of weapons already purchased to persuade Turkey to remove its forces from the island. Even attempted mediation in 1998 by the Clinton administration's star diplomat Richard Holbrooke abraded rather than soothed Turkish feelings as Holbrooke publicly blamed Turkish Cypriots for the failure of his initiatives. He also stirred Turkish passions by characterizing the 1974 Turkish intervention as a violation of the 1959 London-Zurich accords, which established the basis for an independent Cyprus and to which Turkey was a party. Turks saw Holbrooke's position as hostile to Turkey and noted that it was inconsistent with previous U.S. stands. Statements by the U.S. ambassador to Greece, Nicholas Burns, in June 1998 deprecating the Turkish Cypriot administration only reinforced the long-standing Turkish impression that the U.S. is not a reliable ally on the Cyprus issue.[9]

Fortunately for the cause of good U.S.-Turkish relations, the crisis over the Greek Cypriot purchase of S-300 anti-aircraft missiles from Russia was attenuated at the end of 1998, as Republic of Cyprus president Glafcos Clerides decided to have the weapons delivered to the island of Crete—part of Greece—instead. The Turks had threatened to prevent their deployment by force. Washington successfully maneuvered through this minefield, urging that the S-300s not be delivered to Cyprus but insisting on a peaceful resolution. Although Ankara continues to complain about the Crete solution, this matter is now largely quiescent.[10]

The Balkans also proved to be a tricky area for the U.S.-Turkish alliance. Sympathy for the Muslim population of the former Yugoslavia runs high in Turkey, where a significant part of the population traces its ancestry to the Balkans. Consequently, Ankara has at times wanted a more prominent role in peacekeeping than the U.S. deemed appropriate. After early reports of clandestine Turkish assistance to the Bosnian Muslims emerged, Ankara fell into line with NATO. The Kosovo conflict created additional pressures in Turkey for a more activist policy.[11]

The propensity of both countries to put unforeseen burdens on the alliance did not end with international issues. Human rights became a major concern during the Carter administration and has strained relations ever since. The annual human-rights report issued by the State Department was gentle at first in regard to Turkish transgressions. By the late 1990s, however, it was criticizing Turkish practices rather strongly, objecting to torture, administrative detention, restrictions on free speech, and the like.[12] Turkish governments listened to the Americans and, rhetorically at least, agreed to move in the direction of resolving problems. Nonetheless, it is generally recognized in Turkey that U.S. interest in human rights reflects the attitude of the world at large, which Ankara must take into consideration.

In 1998 a similar concern over religious policy was raised by enactment of a law to restrict U.S. relationships with countries that practice religious intolerance toward groups within their borders. The International Religious Freedom Act, passed in October 1998, established an ambassador-at-large in the State Department to report annually on the state of religion around the world. While the final version of the act eliminated provisions aimed specifically at Turkey's treatment of its Greek Christian minority, the prominence it gives to religious tolerance eventually could raise problems for Turkey, as the Armenian and Greek diasporas have never been content with Turkish treatment of their co-religionists. The act provides for sanctions of varying degrees of severity for "violation of the internationally recognized right to freedom of religion."[13] The first U.S. State Department Annual Report on International Religious Freedom, issued in September 1999, gave Turkey generally high marks for freedom of religion, however.[14]

In the early 1970s, the issue of illicit drugs was an acrimonious bilateral issue. But after an Ecevit coalition government in 1974 changed the method of opium harvesting to prevent large-scale diversions of raw opium, cooperation rather than conflict became the order of the day for the allies. The Turkish government has been willing to work closely with the U.S. Drug Enforcement Administration. At the same time, Ankara tried to ensure U.S. cooperation against the PKK by continually asserting that the Kurdish terrorist organization supports itself with drug trafficking, a claim that may have some basis in fact. Generally the U.S. government has been satisfied with bilateral collaboration in trying to shut off the drug transit trade from Afghanistan and the Middle East through Turkey.[15] Nevertheless, scandals that emerged in Turkey in the latter half of the 1990s suggested that some Turkish officials may have cooperated with drug traffickers as part of an underground war against the PKK.

Another difficult issue for the allies flowed from Turkey's conclusion in the mid-1970s that it needed to move toward self-sufficiency in the manufacture of weaponry. As a result of the U.S. arms embargo and continuing congressional efforts to place conditions on military aid, the Turkish general staff determined that Turkey should position itself—through technology transfer and co-production agreements—to manufacture a larger proportion of the weapons systems used by its

military. Implementation of that decision entailed finding foreign pur-
chasers for enough equipment to make these manufacturing concerns
economical. The U.S. has been quite helpful in that regard, persuading
Egypt, for example, to purchase F-16s co-produced in Turkey. But the
requirement for U.S. congressional approval for such sales carries an
inherent risk of friction.[16]

After Turkey established an export-oriented economy in 1980, Özal
raised the slogan of "trade, not aid," a formula embraced by the U.S.
The main feature of this campaign was an effort radically to expand
the Turkish textile industry. Ankara pressed for greater access to the
U.S. market, seeking to overcome quotas that favored long-established
producers. This has proven far more difficult to achieve than Ankara
anticipated, but the U.S. has occasionally increased some textile quotas
for Turkey, most recently in April 1998.[17]

The newly created Armenian state has also had an impact on U.S.-
Turkish relations. Turkey's leadership recognized U.S. interest in helping the new state and for a time in 1992 and 1993 facilitated humanitarian
aid through Turkey. Groundless suspicions in the Turkish media that
these shipments contained arms led the government to stop this traffic,
however. U.S. pressure on Ankara to open a land corridor to Armenia
and the U.S. embargo on assistance to Azerbaijan rankle the Turks. And
the enthusiasm of the Armenian lobby in the U.S. over the advent of
Robert Kocharian as president of the lobby in place of the much more
pragmatic Levon Ter-Petrossian forms an additional thorn in the Turkish side, though Ankara took some comfort in the U.S. administration's
condemnation of Armenian threats to annex Nagorno-Karabakh.[18]

The need to deal with Islamic politics has bedeviled the alliance in
recent years. The U.S. has not handled this issue well. Already deeply
suspicious of Necmettin Erbakan after his deputy prime ministership
in the 1970s, Washington was not happy with his tours of Islamic countries, including Iran and Libya, as his first order of business as prime
minister in 1996. The U.S. administration's unhappiness with Erbakan's
Refah (Welfare) Party (RP) was evident in the State Department
spokesman's refusal to condemn the Turkish military's transparent efforts, ultimately successful, to bring down Erbakan's government in
1997. That stand potentially could create problems. It might encourage
the Turkish military again to take an active role to prevent a religiously
oriented party from heading a future government. Moreover, Washington might find it harder to work with such a party if one should
again come to power.[19]

Turkey's efforts to deal with its energy deficiency also have complicated bilateral relations. This issue has several dimensions. The Turkish government was under heavy domestic pressure to build a pipeline

to receive Iranian natural gas, badly needed by Turkey's growing industry. Doing so, however, could violate the Iran and Libya Sanctions Act (ILSA) of 1996, risking sanctions against the Turkish pipeline firm BOTAŞ. In terms of oil, Ankara exerted constant pressure on Washington to ease restrictions on the petroleum pipeline from northern Iraq, closed in accordance with United Nations (UN) resolutions after the Gulf War. Washington has generally winked at overland border trade with Iraq, a trade principally in diesel fuel that makes an important contribution to the economy of southeastern Turkey. On the question of building the Baku-Ceyhan pipeline through Turkey to bring oil from the Caspian basin, however, Turkey and the U.S. are in agreement, each wanting to foster the independence of the Caucasus states and to discourage Russian and Iranian dominance of the area.[20]

Schools of Thought in Ankara

How this complex agenda of issues plays out will partly depend on the amount of support the U.S. enjoys in the Turkish polity. Over the years, Turkish politicians have become increasingly sophisticated in their understanding of American politics and in how to deal with the U.S. generally. That represents a significant change. For many decades, most Turkish officials felt it was sufficient to deal with the executive branch alone, then let it deal with Congress. That attitude was especially evident in the critical months in 1974 and 1975 when Congress was shaping the terms of its arms embargo. The Turkish embassy in Washington was left in the hands of a chargé who expected the State Department to argue the Turkish case.

In the past two decades, however, Turkish politicians have begun to differentiate between the administration and Congress. The sympathy shown by the executive branch for Turkey's point of view was too marked to miss, while the skepticism of the legislators in Washington and their responsiveness to domestic lobbies was equally self-evident. But while it is still common for Turkish officials and politicians to appeal to the White House or State Department to intervene with Congress, they now see the need to put their best foot forward with the legislative branch as well. The recognition that Congress has its own agenda, often in conflict with that of the administration, softens the reaction in Turkey when aid is withheld or when members of Congress try to put pressure on Turkey in order to please some of their domestic constituents.

All Turkish politicians recognize the importance of the U.S. in the world, and most do not want to appear to harm bilateral relations. A few important voices, however, seem to accept the "conspiracy theory of politics" that accuses the U.S. of seeking to control small countries behind the scenes. Politicians like Bülent Ecevit, particularly in the 1970s and when he was out of office in the 1980s and 1990s, and former foreign minister Mümtaz Soysal firmly maintain this point of view. They constantly worry that the U.S. may try to create a Kurdish state in eastern Turkey or at the least will pursue policies that inadvertently produce such an outcome. But fortunately, some left-of-center figures have healthier views of the United States. Foreign minister İsmail Cem, of Ecevit's DSP, has emerged as a supporter of close ties with the U.S., somewhat balancing off Ecevit-Soysal–type views in the DSP.[21]

Yet even parties and politicians who have expressed suspicion about U.S. intentions have, when in power, attempted to maintain cooperative relations. Ecevit, who on a number of occasions served as prime minister in the 1970s, reopened U.S. joint intelligence installations once the arms embargo was lifted. As prime minister in 1999 and beyond, he continued to work cooperatively with Washington—even with regard to the northern Iraq "no-fly" zone, which he criticized upon taking office but professed to understand better, and implicitly accept, after a lengthy conversation with U.S. ambassador Mark Parris. Soysal, in his brief tenure as foreign minister in 1994, did not use that office to interrupt relations. As head of the RP in opposition, Erbakan expressed strong reservations about U.S. activities in northern Iraq after the Gulf War. Once in power, however, he accepted continuation of the U.S. Turkey-based operation enforcing a "no-fly" zone in northern Iraq. He also sent representatives to Washington to keep relations on an even keel and to dispel the impression that he was opposed to the West.[22]

Why the Alliance Continues

Ties to the United States form the basis of the Turkish foreign policy construct. Along with NATO membership, they are the visible link and justification for Turkey's claiming a European vocation. This is of major psychological importance to the majority of the Turkish political elite, who follow the precepts of the modernizing founder of the Turkish Republic, Kemal Atatürk. It is also of cardinal importance to the current Turkish military leadership, which has always had intimate relations with U.S. counterparts and to a large extent identifies with U.S. culture. Having a European link is also highly important to businessmen, who form an ever more important pressure group and are increasingly internationalist in outlook. This by now deeply ingrained orientation imparts institutional inertia to relations with the U.S., ensuring that radicals cannot easily sunder the alliance.

Reinforcing this attachment is the fact that Turks respectfully regard the United States as the world's only superpower; hence, to have it at Turkey's side has obvious benefits. This is particularly so as Washington could damage Ankara's position on Cyprus and in other respects if it became hostile to Turkey—an unlikely eventuality, of course, given U.S.-Turkish NATO links. On a more positive note, the success of Turkish diplomacy in many areas of the world depends heavily on how much it can influence U.S. policy. For example, Washington's support for the Baku-Ceyhan pipeline route is of major importance in making that project possible, if still uncertain. On a continuing basis, U.S. support for Turkish membership in the EU is highly valued in Turkey. Moreover, Ankara was highly pleased with U.S. support for its effort to extradite PKK leader Abdullah Öcalan from Italy in 1998 and apparent, if not officially confirmed, U.S. help in Turkey's capture of Öcalan in Nairobi, Kenya, in February 1999. Economic and informational links to the United States grow every day in importance.

Despite the end of military aid, U.S. arms remain the mainstay of Turkey's military might. Occasional internal prohibitions on arms purchases from countries that offend Turkey regarding the PKK or the 1915-16 Armenian genocide issue have restricted European efforts to enter the Turkish arms market, leaving the U.S. and Israel positioned as favored sources. General İsmail Hakkı Karadayı's July 1998 trip to Washington focused on regional cooperation Turkey can offer in return for being able to purchase air-defense systems.[23] At the same time, Turkey's actions in dropping European companies from the defense bidders list leave it more vulnerable to the whims of Congress. Of course, the EU's December 1999 decision formally to name Turkey a candidate for membership may help restore Ankara's interest in European arms.

The U.S. administration's recognition of the need to ease difficult problems could be helpful to the alliance. However, the assignment of Holbrooke, the Clinton administration's best negotiator, to push for a Cyprus solution had little effect. He was unable to overcome deep Turkish suspicions. The Turkish Foreign Ministry spurned his efforts to promote informal dialogue between Greek Cypriot and Turkish Cypriot businessmen. Holbrooke's practice of going to Nicosia and Athens before presenting proposals to the Turks fed suspicion that Washington was unduly influenced by the Greek side.[24] On a more positive note, periodic visits by the State Department's assistant secretary for democracy, human rights, and labor helped convince Turkish military leaders, in particular, to become more conscientious about avoiding human-rights violations.

The Turks are counting on their newly established military cooperation with Israel to help reduce problems in relations with the U.S. Many politicians in Ankara believe that the rapidly deepening link with Israel will incline the U.S. pro-Israel lobby to lend its support. That may set them up for disappointment, as they seem to ascribe more weight to the Israel lobby than it actually enjoys. But in a general sense the growing Turkish relationship with Israel can reinforce U.S.-Turkish relations.[25]

Prospects

As the calculus of benefits and liabilities for U.S.-Turkish relations has changed over the years, it is not sufficient to assume that close ties in the past will assure smooth relations in the future. The alliance now faces greater challenges than at any time in the recent past. The U.S. seems to have few ideas about how to head off major problems, and the Turks seem largely unprepared and oblivious to the danger bilateral ties face. It will be a considerable accomplishment if U.S.-Turkish relations can be kept fully on track over the medium term.

In the case of Cyprus, it is important to continue to work for a settlement, however far off one now appears. As long as Cyprus is on the agenda, the U.S. Congress will use it as a lever on Turkey in ways that will roil relations. All that can realistically be done in the near to medium term is to promote confidence-building measures, such as the reopening of the Nicosia airport. The U.S. must be willing to advance such proposals vigorously, making sure that its pattern of consultations appears objective and non-partisan. It should also discourage provocative military acts on both sides, such as flying military aircraft into Greek Cypriot and Turkish Cypriot airfields as the Greeks and Turks, respectively, did during the S-300 crisis.[26]

A more immediate concern is the question of policy toward Iraq. Ecevit, upon taking office in January 1999, wasted no time in making clear his unhappiness with Washington's military strikes. His successors may be less inclined than previous leaders to go along with U.S. policy. U.S. proposals to let Iraq sell all the oil it wishes as long as the proceeds are kept under UN control may dampen Turkish concern about penalizing the Iraqi people in the effort to control Saddam Husayn. Yet continued U.S. airstrikes against Iraqi radar and missile sites are increasingly hard for Turkey to accept. More extensive bombing, similar to that in December 1998, would only reinforce Turkish doubts. The 1999 U.S. decision to supply Patriot missiles to Turkey, probably on loan, will help assuage objections from the Turkish military. Support from top Turkish military leaders is essential to keeping Turkey cooperative with U.S. policy toward Iraq.[27]

Unfortunately for the alliance, U.S. human-rights concerns are moving into higher gear. With the addition of religious persecution as a possible topic of dispute, the human-rights agenda important to the U.S. has become more intrusive. Moreover, the U.S. foreign policy community is increasingly convinced that Turkey's military plays an outsized role in its fragmented political scene. The continuing confrontation between the generals and the Islamists exacerbates fears that no Ankara government will carry out undertakings to decriminalize "thought crimes." Washington and Ankara appeared at odds over the jailing of İstanbul's pro-Islamist mayor, Recep Tayyip Erdoğan, whom the U.S. consul general in Istanbul visited publicly after his pending arrest was announced.[28]

If the *Fazilet* (Virtue) Party, the banned RP's *de facto* successor, ever should be kept out of government as a result of machinations by the military, the resulting black eye to Turkish democracy will make congressional approval of military sales to Turkey less likely. Hopes that General Kıvrıkoğlu, who became chief of the general staff in August 1998, might in the long run prove somewhat less active in combating Islamic trends than his predecessor now seem unrealistic. Unfortunately, there seems little that the U.S. can do to reduce the political role of the Turkish military.[29]

Turkey's energy supply problem has elicited active U.S. engagement. Richard Morningstar, former chief of U.S. Caspian Sea energy diplomacy, and his successor John Wolf have been frequent visitors in the quest to promote the Baku-Ceyhan pipeline. But disappointing exploration results in the Caspian and the U.S. administration's unwillingness to put public money into developing the line make it unlikely that cooperation in pushing this alternative will succeed.[30]

Although the Turkish government is satisfied with U.S. efforts on the oil pipeline thus far, other energy concerns hold the prospect of souring relations. The proposed "Blue Stream" line under the Black Sea to augment current supply from Russia is regarded unfavorably by the United States. Washington instead supports a trans-Caspian line that would bring Turkmenistani gas to Azerbaijan and then run along the proposed Baku-Ceyhan route through Georgia to Turkey. The decision by the companies on the trans-Caspian line will be heavily influenced by the fate of Baku-Ceyhan, as the two would follow roughly the same route. That means no early decision is likely.

Meanwhile, the Turks seem to be proceeding cautiously with plans for obtaining natural gas from Iran, having persuaded Tehran to delay delivery until mid-2001, eighteen months after it was originally scheduled to begin. Ankara told the Iranians it would take that much longer for Turkey to complete its portion of the pipeline. Washington would do well to invoke a national security waiver to avoid ILSA sanctions on the Turkish pipeline company involved should the Iranian line be built. Otherwise Turkish disappointment could disturb the larger relationship with the U.S.

The most serious challenge ahead, however, looms in the field of security cooperation, since congressional approval is needed for production and export licenses for big-ticket military sales to Turkey. Congress has reservations about Turkey's human rights record, and, as long as Turkey does not implement fundamental human-rights reforms, approval for those licenses will be an uncertain prospect. Nevertheless, Washington has an interest in demonstrating that the end of aid does not mean an end to U.S. support for a strong Turkey. If the U.S. fails to deliver on key arms sales, it would alienate the powerful Turkish military establishment, perhaps scuttling cooperation on the "no-fly" zone in northern Iraq and decreasing U.S. leverage to secure Turkish cooperation in other arenas. As this book goes to press, an important test case may be looming, with Ankara in the process of deciding whether to grant a U.S. firm the contract for a major purchase of attack helicopters.[31]

With these numerous problems likely to affect relations, the years ahead loom as difficult ones for U.S.-Turkish cooperation. Ankara and Washington will need considerable luck and inventiveness if bilateral ties are to emerge unharmed. Yet it would be a mistake to see the alliance as likely to sunder in the years ahead. However contentious the relationship may become, it is too important to both parties for either to allow a major break.

Notes

1 George S. Harris, *Troubled Alliance: Turkish-American Problems in Historical Perspective, 1945-1971* (Washington, D.C.: American Enterprise Institute, 1972) pp. 71-75.

2 George S. Harris, "The Causes of the 1960 Revolution in Turkey," *Middle East Journal*, Autumn 1970, p. 441.

3 William Hale, *Turkish Politics and the Military* (London: Routledge, 1995), passim.

4 Henri J. Barkey and Graham E. Fuller, *Turkey's Kurdish Question* (New York: Carnegie Commission on Preventing Deadly Conflict, 1998), pp. 133-134.

5 "The Kardak Rocks Problem between Greece and Turkey," SocRates *Turkey's Scope*, January 1996, pp. 23-25.

6 George S. Harris, "The Russian Federation and Turkey," in Alvin Z. Rubinstein and Oles M. Smolansky (eds.), *Regional Power Rivalries in the New Eurasia: Russia, Turkey, and Iran* (Armonk, N.Y.: M.E. Sharpe, 1995), pp. 16-20.

7 Taha Kıvanç, "Talk of the Town," *Turkish Daily News (TDN)*, December 7, 1998; Turkish News Hour broadcast, December 21, 1996, internet edition.

8 Harris, *Troubled Alliance*, passim.

9 "Ambassador Burns Says that U.S. Will Not Recognize Denktaş as Head of State," *TDN*, June 16, 1998.

10 "S-300s Hit Greek Cypriot Government," *TDN*, January 1, 1999.

11 "Ankara: Turks Should Be Included in Kosovo Talks," Turkish Press Review in English (TPR) (an internet service of the Turkish Embassy in Washington), May 15, 1998.

12 *Country Reports on Human Rights Practices* (Washington, D.C.: Government Printing Office, 1991 to 1998).

13   *Congressional Record*, October 10, 1998, H10434-H10442; David S. Broder, "Sanctions Addicts," *Washington Post*, June 24, 1998, p. A17.

14   U.S. Department of State, *Annual Report on International Religious Freedom for 1999: Turkey*; see U.S. State Department website: www.state.gov

15   Harris, *Troubled Alliance*, pp. 191-198, 209-210; "State Gangs Are Being Cleaned Out," *TDN*, August 24, 1998.

16   "TAI to Train Egyptian Technicians on F-16s," *TDN*, June 16, 1998.

17   "U.S. Expands Textiles Quota Implementation," TPR, April 30, 1998 (quoting *Cumhuriyet*).

18   "Turkey Criticizes Armenian Threat," TPR, June 24, 1998.

19   "Praise for Yılmaz Government Stability," *TDN*, July 24, 1997.

20   Uğur Akıncı, "Cem: 'A New Beginning Is Upon U.S.-Turkish Relations'," *TDN*, December 6, 1997; Saadet Oruç, "Intensive Talks on Baku-Ceyhan Underway," *TDN*, May 11, 1998.

21   *Cumhuriyet*, Sept. 5, 1998; *Milliyet*, July 24, 1994; "Talk of the Town," *TDN*, December 7, 1998.

22   "Parliament to Decide on OPC Replacement," *TPR*, December 20, 1996; "Turkey Extends Cooperation with Washington over Iraqi Affairs," *TDN*, January 26, 1999.

23   "Karadayı Going to U.S.," TPR, June 18, 1998.

24   Sibel Utku, "Holbrooke to Come to Istanbul for Cyprus Civil Initiative," *TDN*, December 8, 1998.

25   *TDN*, August 22, 1997.

26   Harun Kazaz, "Is This a Case of the Blind Leading the Blind, or Just Cheap Heroism?" *TDN*, June 20, 1998.

27   R. Jeffrey Smith, "Turkish Premier Criticizes U.S. Iraq Policy," *Washington Post*, January 15, 1999, p. A24; "More Patriot Batteries Are Expected to Arrive," *TDN*, January 22, 1999; Çlnur Cevik, "Ankara Remembers the Iraqi Reality at Last," *TDN*, September 28, 1998.

28   İlnur Çevik, "The American Reaction Was Inevitable," *TDN*, October 2, 1998.

29   İlnur Çevik, "Will Anything Change after Karadayi?" *TDN*, July 7, 1998.

30   Saadet Oruç, "Turkey to Lose Second Round of 'Great Game'," *TDN*, October 28, 1998; Harun Kazaz, "Baku-Ceyhan Pipeline Project Needs to Be Expedited," *TDN*, January 23, 1999; "Negotiations Continue on Caspian Pipeline," *TDN*, January 23, 1999.

31   "Busy Agenda Awaits Cohen in Turkey," *TDN*, April 17, 1998; *Washington Post*, December 31, 1998.

Ian O. Lesser

Beyond 'Bridge or Barrier': Turkey's Evolving Security Relations with the West

I n 1990, RAND launched a study aimed at examining Turkey's role in a changed strategic environment. One part of that study—partially titled "Bridge or Barrier?"—explored the outlook for Turkey and the West after the Cold War.[1] Since that time, the pace of change, both within Turkey and on its borders, has been remarkable. However, the question of whether Turkey serves as a bridge or a barrier in strategic terms remains relevant. Indeed, recent developments have placed this issue in sharper focus and stirred active debate in Turkey and on both sides of the Atlantic. But new directions in Turkey's own evolution, especially in light of growing nationalist sentiment and a more assertive Turkish posture in regional security affairs, complicate the analysis. The question might now be better formulated as "Turkey: Bridge, barrier, or important actor in its own right?"

Political turmoil in Ankara for the better part of the 1990s focused an unusual amount of attention on Turkey and its region. Strategic-minded observers came to regard Turkey as a "pivotal" state, with all that this term implies.[2] The problem facing Turkey today is not the strategic neglect many Turks feared after the demise of the Soviet Union, but conflicting visions of the country's future character and external role. This analysis explores the outlook for Turkish-Western relations in security terms, taking into account changing concerns in Ankara and changing images of Turkey in the U.S. and Europe.

Expanded Policy Horizons

The Turkish policy-making process is not the focus of this paper, but three trends in this sphere are worth noting as they have exerted a growing influence on security relations with the West. First, the Turkish foreign and security policy agenda has expanded enormously since the Cold War. Turks now face a range of regional and functional concerns that would have been unimaginable in the period when deterring Moscow and frictions with Greece were the overwhelming issues. Those issues have not gone away, but Ankara's interests now stretch from the Balkans to western China and include such questions as treatment of

Turks abroad, energy routes, terrorism, and the proliferation of weapons of mass destruction (WMD) on Turkey's borders. This expanded agenda is significant because it provides Turks with substantive measures of cooperation and conflict with the U.S. and Europe. It also suggests that Western engagement with Turkey has not kept pace with changes in the security environment.

Second, foreign and security policies are no longer the province only of a small, Western-oriented elite. To be sure, the fall of the Islamist-led coalition in 1997 and reassertion of the national security establishment's influence on policy-making in many areas, not least foreign policy, has marked a return to a more traditional approach. But important changes have taken place over the past decade, and these may now be regarded as permanently operating factors in Turkish external behavior. Most significant have been the growing role of the media and public opinion and the emergence of special interest groups, including what might be termed "ethnic lobbies." One can point to the central role of the media—not just as reporters and opinion shapers, but actually as actors in crises such as Imia-Kardak and even the hijacking of a Black Sea ferry by Chechen sympathizers. The rediscovery of ethnic and "biographical" identities among the Turkish public, including within some elites, has been an important element in shaping attitudes toward crises in Bosnia, Kosovo, Chechnya, Azerbaijan, and elsewhere.

Third, with heightened importance in light of recent challenges to Turkish secularism and the authority of the state, foreign policy has emerged as a vehicle for furthering competing visions of Turkey's future as a society. Arguably, the key variable today is not Islamism or secularism, but Turkish nationalism—a common denominator across the political spectrum and a reality strongly reinforced by the performance of nationalist parties on the left and right in the April 1999 elections. Turkish national interests are being promoted more assertively, and sovereignty concerns are at the forefront of key relationships, not least with the U.S. Notwithstanding the approval of Turkey's European Union (EU) candidacy at the 1999 Helsinki Summit, there is now a far more critical and measured attitude toward security relations with the West.

The Changing Logic of Strategic Interest

The West has long been interested in Turkey as a barrier in strategic terms. For much of the last two centuries, European policy toward Turkey involved some notion of that country as a vehicle for containing first Russian, then Soviet power in areas of concern: the eastern Mediterranean, the Caucasus, and the Middle East. To this extent, Turkey has always been a part of the European security system, even if its European identity was less clear to Europeans. During the Cold War, Turkey was arguably the most important ally along a southern flank that was, on the whole, marginal to North Atlantic Treaty Organization (NATO) concerns. Ankara did face Soviet military power directly in Thrace and the Caucasus, but the locus of strategic concern for the alliance remained the risk of aggression along the central front. NATO's "Article 5" commitments aside, the defense of Frankfurt and the defense of Ankara were never fully equivalent concerns during the Cold War.

Post-Cold War developments fundamentally altered the position of the five member states (Hungary being a more recent sixth) in NATO's south. The European security debate on both sides of the Atlantic now recognizes that the most likely security challenges have shifted from the center of Europe to the periphery, above all southeastern Europe and the Mediterranean. NATO's southern region was always highly diverse, but even among this group Turkey grew increasingly distinctive. Mediterranean Europe became more European in almost every sense, including defense policy. Turkey was not part of this trend, however, with the result that its strategic position became more unique and more complex.

From Ankara's point of view, the challenge is not only to keep the U.S. engaged in defense of its security interests—a challenge shared by Europe as a whole—but also to preserve links between its security concerns and those of the West more generally, without compromising its regional interests. This "double coupling" problem, simultaneously maintaining strong security bonds with the U.S. specifically and the West generally, is reminiscent of the environment facing Mediterranean Europe during the Cold War, but is now faced in stark terms only by Turkey.

With the collapse of the Soviet Union, many in Ankara and the West anticipated a decline in attention to Turkey and began to redefine its significance along new, functional lines. "Rediscovery" of Turkish links to the Turkic republics, as well as movement in the Middle East peace process, kindled interest in Turkey's potential as an economic, political, and cultural actor far from its immediate borders, in ways that underlined its image as a geopolitical "bridge." Turkey is not alone in its tendency to describe itself as a "bridge" between regions, but the image has special significance in the Turkish context since it implies a positive external role while helping to resolve certain tensions in the country's own identity.[3] Turkey, it was argued, could serve as a conduit for trade and finance—as well as political discourse—between the West and the newly independent states of Central Asia and the Caucasus. Movement in the peace process might also allow a similar role in the Middle East. Beyond the idea of a bridge was the thought that Turkey might also serve as a model for political and economic development in the former Soviet Union and in the Muslim world.

In retrospect this view, as many Turks will admit, was too optimistic. Turkey indeed played an active role in the Turkic republics, although more modest than envisioned in the early 1990s. The most striking growth in economic relations was actually with Russia itself. With the emergence of instability in the Caucasus, it became clear that a larger Turkish role in the former Soviet Union brought with it the potential for more direct and provocative competition with Moscow. In the Middle East, it was long clear that Turkey faced important limitations as a bridge in political and economic terms.[4] Even the *Refah*-led coalition had difficulty in developing closer relations with Arab neighbors. For Arab nationalists, relations with Ankara are clouded by the Ottoman experience and Turkey's NATO membership. In Islamist circles, Turkish secularism is viewed with distaste. The burgeoning Turkish relationship with Israel contributed to the basic ambivalence about Turkey in both Arab nationalist and Islamist camps, although Turkey's good relations with Jordan are an exception. Finally, political instability in Turkey itself made it difficult to portray Turkey as a model for secular, democratic development, although the potential for such a role may still exist. Taken together, these developments wreaked havoc on the image Turkey wished to project as an important post-Cold War "bridge" to its neighbors.

In the security arena, confusion was equally pronounced in the wake of the Gulf War. On the Turkish side, the Gulf experience left a continuing and disturbing legacy. President Turgut Özal led Turkey into an active role in the coalition against Iraq, apparently against the wishes of some in the military who preferred a more cautious stance. The reluctance of some European NATO allies, especially Germany, to reinforce Turkey during the crisis raised concerns about the predictability of the NATO security guarantee that continue to affect Turkish attitudes almost a decade later. The post-Gulf situation in northern Iraq and the opportunities this provided to the Kurdistan Workers Party (known by its Kurdish acronym PKK), together with the large economic cost of the sanctions on Baghdad, led many Turks to conclude that they are less, rather than more, secure as a result of their forward-leaning, pro-Western stance.[5] More broadly, the improvement in EU-Turkish relations some envisioned as a reward for cooperation certainly did not materialize.

For the U.S., and especially for Europe, Ankara's role in the Gulf crisis promoted awareness of Turkey's strategic significance, but in a way sharply at variance with Turkish preferences. Far from reinforcing the idea of Turkey as a key European security partner, the Gulf War caused Western policy-makers and observers to recast its role in a Middle Eastern light. From the perspective of Turkey's foreign and security policy elite, this was an unfortunate development. It reduced the predictability of Turkey's Western security connections precisely as key European security institutions began debating their own post-Cold War role, and at a time when Turkey sought to place itself firmly on the path to integration with Europe. Talk of "new strategic relationships" and "windows of opportunity," common in the wake of Desert Storm, suggested that Turkey was being asked to play a more active role in defense of Western interests outside Europe—as a barrier to Middle Eastern instability and a logistical bridge—while its core security connections with the West were becoming less reliable in Turkish perceptions.

Turkey as a Transregional Actor

As Turkey's European vocation came under growing strain and as developments on the European periphery gained prominence in Western discussions, its policy-makers appeared more comfortable with portraying their country's importance in extra-European terms. Fashionable interest in Caspian energy and in routes for the transportation of oil and gas to world markets has contributed substantially to the new debate on Turkey's external role. This may reflect a growing tendency among Turkish strategists to discuss Turkey's importance in terms aligned with what they consider a U.S. rather than European world view.[6] The emerging conception of Turkey's new geopolitics is inherently transregional, an approach that reflects concrete changes in the strategic environment and avoids the somewhat artificial tension between the country's role as a bridge or a barrier.

Turkey is most directly affected by a key trend shaping Western security: the erosion of traditional distinctions between the European, Middle Eastern, and Eurasian theaters. This trend poses important intellectual and policy challenges and has distinct political, economic, and security dimensions. Turkey is at the center of this phenomenon and the country's future role will be strongly influenced by it.

In political terms, there is a growing interrelationship between events in Europe, the Middle East, and Eurasia. Ankara is unique among NATO members in the degree of its concerns about Russian aims in the Balkans, the eastern Mediterranean, and the Gulf. These concerns have ranged from arms transfers and military assistance for Cyprus (for example, the planned deployment of S-300 surface-to-air missiles, diverted to Crete under pressure from Ankara) to technology transfers to Iran to alleged support for PKK terrorism. Moscow has also been seen as a leading opponent of Turkish routes for Caspian energy exports. Whether or not these problems are part of a concerted Russian strategy or simply a product of opportunism against a background of anti-Turkish experience, they strike many Turks as evidence of a revived security challenge from Russia—a challenge Ankara might be left to face without adequate reassurance from its allies. The most elaborate Turkish arguments along these lines envision an emerging "Orthodox axis" stretching from the Balkans to Eurasia. Although Turkish affinities are clearly engaged on issues such as Kosovo, Bosnia, and the Azeri-Armenian conflict, the notion of a clash along civilizational lines in adjacent regions clearly disturbs Turkey's secular elites. This may provide one explanation of Turkey's more measured reaction to the Kosovo crisis when compared with the Turkish public outcry over the fate of Bosnia's Muslims.

The burgeoning relationship between Turkey and Israel provides another example of this new, transregional security environment. Strategically, the relationship pressures Syria and deters risks emanating from Iraq and Iran, while diversifying and strengthening Turkey's defense relations. Economically, it opens new opportunities for trade, tourism, and joint regional projects. But it also offers political benefits by raising the possibility of a Turkish-Israeli-U.S. (and perhaps Jordanian) alignment in support of "Western" objectives in the region. The result is another way of describing Turkey's strategic role that cuts across traditional Atlantic, European, and Middle Eastern security arrangements. For similar reasons, Turkish strategists express growing interest in NATO's outreach and cooperation efforts in North Africa and the Middle East.[7]

In the economic sphere, two transregional developments hold special meaning for Turkey. First, Turkey is perhaps the most important component of the EU's evolving policy toward the European periphery. Turks have understandably focused on the issue of EU membership. But seen from Brussels, Turkey with its customs union is the most advanced example of a functioning association agreement with a nonmember Mediterranean state. This is very far from the circumstance most Turks would prefer, especially given the EU's failure to transfer funds through the custom union agreement and the Euro-Mediterranean "Barcelona" process and in light of the importance Turks place on a European vocation. But regardless of perspective, there can be little question that the future of relations with Turkey is among the most pressing and critical dimensions of the EU's emerging relationship with its Mediterranean periphery. Ultimately the Euro-Mediterranean partnership is only partly about economic development. The real thrust of the initiative, and the core EU interest, lie in promoting stability along the southern and eastern shores of the Mediterranean—areas increasingly seen as affecting the security and prosperity of Europe itself.

Second, the West is rediscovering the energy security—more properly, "energy geopolitics"—questions that were a key part of the strategic landscape in the 1970s and early 1980s. Turkey is at the center of this new debate, which is more about the politics of alternative transport routes than about supply and demand per se. Existing pipelines across Turkey from the Gulf, together with the still-uncertain prospect of the Baku-Ceyhan route for Caspian oil, suggest a key place for Turkey in the future oil-supply system. Taking into account the likely increase in oil tanker traffic through the Black Sea and the Turkish Straits, Turkey's role appears even more prominent. Future routes for Caspian oil have received considerable attention, but the infrastructure for gas supply is also undergoing rapid expansion. Turkey's own energy security will be strongly affected by new arrangements (for example, with Iran or Turkmenistan) and by additional imports from Russia. Turkey's emerging role as a major distributor as well as consumer of natural gas will likely be an additional factor binding together the longer-term energy security interests of Europe and Turkey.

Beyond new energy routes, the revival of overland lines of communication between Europe and the newly independent states of Eurasia—in many cases, bypassing Russia—has the potential to alter political and economic relationships across a wide region. Movement in the Arab-Israeli peace process could place Turkey at the center of similarly expanded overland commerce between Europe and the Middle East. These very traditional issues hark back to concerns at the turn of the twentieth century, when the Ottoman Empire was seen as the strategic link between continental Europe and the resource-rich Caucasus and Middle East.[8] Future discussion of Turkey's strategic importance to the West is likely to focus heavily on these inherently transregional issues, especially Ankara's influence on the security environment within the "strategic energy ellipse" of the Caspian and the Gulf.[9]

Finally, many of the most prominent security challenges facing Turkey and the West cut across traditional definitions of "European," "Middle Eastern," and "Eurasian" security. Turkey is, again, at the center of this phenomenon. At one end of the spectrum, Turkey is the Western ally most directly exposed to the proliferation of WMD and the means for their delivery at longer ranges. Some of the world's leading proliferators—Iran, Iraq, and Syria—are on Turkey's borders. The potential for conflict with each, while varied, is high enough to create a tangible concern about WMD. For the moment this exposure weighs more heavily on the southern members of NATO. But the steadily increasing range of missile technology available on the world market suggests that all of NATO Europe will eventually be exposed. Turkish attention to WMD and missile risks has increased significantly since the Gulf War, when potential Scud attacks on Turkish territory caused concern. Turkey, along with the U.S., is among the NATO countries most interested in deploying effective theater ballistic missile defenses. Cooperation with Israel could be an important vehicle for acquiring missile defense technology, as well as early warning data and intelligence related to WMD. Further cooperation with Jordan and the U.S. could provide the basis for a regional missile defense architecture.

Proliferation trends are the most dramatic aspect of Europe's growing exposure to Middle Eastern instability and the possible consequences of Western action, including intervention, outside Europe. Issues concerning proliferation and counter-proliferation are certain to occupy a prominent place on the agenda in future security relations between Turkey and its Western partners.[10] Turkey's preference likely will be to address proliferation risks through multilateral regimes and through NATO's deterrent posture. If, however, Ankara loses confidence in its NATO link, a decision to acquire a national deterrent capability (e.g., medium-range missiles) cannot be ruled out. Obviously this would have implications for security perceptions and the military balance beyond the Middle East—in the Aegean, the Balkans, and the Caucasus. WMD and proliferation issues emerged as a key facet of NATO's April 1999 Washington Summit.[11] Turkey will be a leading beneficiary of any further allied initiatives in this area.

At the low-intensity end of the spectrum, Turkey is exposed to cross-border spillovers of terrorism, political violence, and other unconventional security problems. Many of these emanate from the Middle East or Eurasia and also affect the security of Europe. The struggle against PKK terrorism claimed perhaps 30,000-40,000 lives on all sides during the years 1984-99, and was immensely costly to Turkey's economy, political evolution, and international standing. Insurgency in the southeast would likely have evolved in very different ways without the active sponsorship of Syria and the political vacuum in northern Iraq. The consequences of the PKK campaign, as well as the wider Kurdish question, were felt across Western Europe, and the entire issue had a negative effect on Turkey's image in the West. For many Europeans, spillovers of Kurdish refugees and political violence are emblematic of the sort of "Middle Eastern" problems Europe would like to keep at arm's length.

At the same time Ankara looks to Europe and Washington for cooperation in containing PKK operations, and it thus has a strong stake in counterterrorism becoming a feature of U.S.-Turkish bilateral security cooperation and a higher-priority mission for NATO. The capture and trial of PKK leader Abdullah Öcalan placed all of these concerns in sharper relief. Syria's apparent abandonment of direct support for the PKK will need to be tested over time (and some aspects of this support may persist, especially in Lebanon). The Iranian and Russian roles in relation to the PKK may well replace Syrian support as a focus for Turkis criticism. The position of European governments in relation to Kurdish issues will be measured even more closely in Ankara. In the near term, the confluence of Öcalan's capture, the nationalists' strong electoral performance in April 1999, and the potential that residual PKK activists will pursue urban terrorism outside the southeast suggest even greater attention to Kurdish separatism and terrorism in the perception of Turkish policy-makers. Over the longer term, Turkey may have a wider range of political choices in addressing the Kurdish issue, with implications for relations with the West.

From a European perspective, it often appears that Turkey is part of the problem in relation to unconventional security challenges.[12] European officials in particular have been very clear in blaming Turkish traffickers for much of the drug trade in Western Europe and identifying Turkey itself as an important trans-shipment link to the Middle East and Central Asia. In the opinion of some well-informed observers, the Turkish "drug economy" is worth billions of dollars per year, exclusive of other illegal activities with a transnational dimension such as money laundering and non-narcotics smuggling. Over the past few years, European officials were explicit in calling attention to the role of Turkish and Kurdish drug traffickers and were candid in airing their suspicions of official complicity in some aspects of this trade. The Susurluk scandal reinforced concerns about links between terrorism, counterterrorism, and narcotics trafficking. As the EU becomes more actively engaged in addressing "third pillar" issues, including transnational crime, this aspect of relations with Ankara will likely increase in importance.

Between the specter of proliferation risks and low-intensity spillovers lies a set of conventional security problems on Turkey's borders. Although a direct military confrontation between Turkey and Russia is very unlikely, the prominence of this relationship in the security perceptions of both countries and the high degree of suspicion on each side suggests that a confrontation cannot be ruled out. Although Turkey and Russia no longer share a border, turmoil in the Caucasus—where interests and affinities of both countries are engaged—could lead Ankara and Moscow into conflict via proxies or through direct intervention. Russian arms sales and the presence of Russian advisers and technicians in Cyprus or elsewhere could provide another flashpoint. The growing significance of nuclear weapons in Russian military doctrine is also a source of concern and will bear on Turkish attitudes toward NATO and the Western security guarantee. Indeed, Turkish strategists now worry about the possibility that Moscow will compensate for NATO enlargement by pursuing a more assertive strategy on Europe's periphery—that is, on or near Turkey's borders. The evolution of Russia's policy vis-à-vis Serbia and the situation in Kosovo may also strongly influence Turkish security perceptions, already sensitive to the possibility of an "Orthodox axis."

The potential for conflict with Syria—reduced but not eliminated by Öcalan's departure from Damascus and by agreements aimed at improving bilateral relations—suggests the possibility that European security institutions may be engaged in countering a direct territorial threat from the Middle East. Concern about Syria has grown in Turkish security perceptions since the Gulf War and now features more prominently in Western analyses of Turkish security. Turkish concerns were fourfold: Syrian claims on the border province of Hatay, friction over Tigris and Euphrates waters, Syrian WMD and missile programs, and Syrian support for the PKK. Of these concerns, the last has been by far the most consistently dangerous. Öcalan was based in Damascus, and the regime facilitated PKK infiltrations into southeastern Turkey. Turkish officials warned Syria repeatedly on this issue and on occasion have considered the use of air power to attack PKK training camps in the Syrian-controlled Bekaa Valley. A "hot pursuit" incident across the Turkish-Syrian border or a more serious confrontation between forces has at times seemed a very real possibility. Indeed, the credible threat of force against Damascus is widely credited with Syria's expulsion of Öcalan and its sudden withdrawal of overt support for the PKK in late 1998. Any conflict along these lines could easily have been regarded as a "gray area" crisis by some European members of the NATO alliance. NATO's response would have been a major test of post-Cold War security relations between Turkey and the West.

Emerging trends in Western strategy also encourage the portrayal of Turkey as a key actor in a transregional security environment. As Western military establishments continue to restructure themselves for power projection and crisis management rather than territorial defense, and as states such as Germany overcome their reluctance to engage in military operations outside Europe, security relations with Turkey will loom larger for the simple reason that Turkey is the best way to reach key areas of concern. A striking number of post-Cold War flashpoints are on Turkey's borders or in the immediate neighborhood, and access to Turkish facilities and airspace will be important for the projection of Western military power to the Caspian and the Gulf. Moreover, as Turkey pursues an ambitious military modernization program and improves its capacity for mobile operations, its own ability to contribute to Western operations on the European periphery will increase.[13] But against the background of growing urkish sovereignty concerns, and in the absence of a substantial redefinition of the Turkish-Western security relationship, the precise role Turkey will play along these lines is not easily predicted.

Convergence or Divergence in Security Policies?

At the broadest level, Turkey, Europe, and the U.S. share a stake in regional stability and a status-quo-oriented, rather than revolutionary, outlook in international affairs. Much of the rhetoric surrounding security relations is couched in these terms. Yet at the level of regional policies and approaches, the picture is less straightforward. Are Turkish and Western security policies bound to converge in key areas? A brief *tour d'horizon* of regional security challenges suggests important points of divergence. In many instances these are part of broader policy divisions between the U.S. and Europe. In other instances, Turkey has unique interests at play.

Despite some Westerners' fears of unilateral Turkish involvement in the Balkans, Ankara shows every indication of preferring a coordinated, multilateral approach to crisis management in the region. Turkish participation in the Implementation Force (IFOR), Stabilization Force (SFOR), and the air and humanitarian operations in Kosovo are evidence of this preference. Europe's role in the Bosnia crisis was severely criticized in Turkey, but U.S. policy on Bosnia—at least in the final phase of the crisis—and allied policy on Kosovo were very much in line with perceptions in Ankara. The risk of a serious policy divergence over the Balkans is probably low.

On Russia, Turkish and Western interests in long-term Russian stability and integration with the West are congruent, but assessments of present Russian behavior and longer-term risks are divergent, possibly increasingly so. Ankara's concern about Russia is growing, and it is unclear whether this concern is shared with even nearly the same intensity elsewhere in the West. So far there has not been a sharp divergence in Turkish and Western policies toward Moscow (and indeed there are elements of cooperation as well as friction in Ankara's own policy toward Russia), but it might arise, particularly if Turkish policymakers perceive that their interests are ignored by Western partners. In the Caucasus, Ankara could well find itself under pressure to adopt a more forward-leaning policy than do its Western partners toward the conflict between Armenia and Azerbaijan or toward separatist movements in the region, such as Chechnya's. In the Caspian, the U.S.-led policy favoring "multiple pipelines" supports, but does not entirely match, Turkish interests in promoting Baku-Ceyhan while restricting Russian influence.[14]

In the Middle East, policy differences are more pronounced but are part of more generalized trans-Atlantic differences. On Iraq, Ankara is more tolerant of the reassertion of Iraqi sovereignty in the north, provided that this results in additional pressure on the PKK. Certainly, Turkish opinion favors an early end to the costly economic sanctions on Iraq and the resumption of full Iraqi oil exports through Turkish pipelines—a view increasingly in line with much European opinion but unattractive to Washington. Ankara will most likely remain uncomfortable with the idea of placing Turkish facilities at the disposal of a U.S.-led coalition in a renewed confrontation with Saddam Husayn, unless the operation convincingly aims at permanently altering the regional order—in which case Turkey will wish to secure a seat at the post-conflict table. With regard to Iran—concerns about the export of Islamic revolution aside—Turkish policy is essentially in the European mainstream and favorably disposed toward political and economic engagement. In this respect it is at variance with Washington's continued attachment to "dual containment" in the Gulf. Any increase in Iranian tolerance for the PKK could, however, bring Turkish policy closer to the U.S. position.

Turkey shares an interest in the Middle East peace process but has concerns about the containment of Syria. Turkey's strategic relationship with Israel is viewed very favorably by the U.S., although Turkish observers may overstate its effect on congressional attitudes toward Ankara. European governments are generally less enthusiastic about Turkish-Israeli ties, and many tend to view the relationship as a complicating factor in the Middle East equation—one inclined to reinforce a U.S.-centered approach to regional security. Meanwhile, Ankara would prefer a much tougher Western stance toward Syria on the PKK issue and on proliferation.

In the Aegean and on Cyprus, Turkish (and Greek) policy is clearly at variance with broader U.S. and European interests. The West as a whole has an overwhelming stake in crisis prevention and management in the eastern Mediterranean. For Turkey, the various points of friction with Greece are important tests of sovereignty and national interest and, in practice, are primary impediments to a closer relationship with Europe.

Beyond current conflicts in the southern Balkans, relations between Greece and Turkey may well be the most dangerous flashpoint in the contemporary European security environment, if efforts at rapprochement begun in 1999 prove ephemeral. The consequences of a Greek-Turkish clash would not be limited to the immediate region. At a time of profound change in the scope and mission of the Atlantic alliance, a conflict between two NATO allies could severely complicate the process of NATO enlargement and adaptation. However, the risk of Balkan crises "drawing in" Greece and Turkey—a factor often cited by U.S.

policy-makers in explaining Western interests in the Balkans—is in all likelihood rather low.

Turkey and Europe—The Security Dimension

The character of relations between Turkey and the EU could have important implications for Turkish-Western security ties. The traditional European preference for holding Turkey at arm's length is the product of an unsurprising combination of judgments about its economic and political situation, sheer size, cultural "differences," and strategic role. Developments surrounding the EU's 1997 Luxembourg summit made clear what objective observers had long concluded about popular and elite attitudes toward Turkey in Europe. The post-Cold War process of European integration, and the reintegration of Eastern and Central Europe, placed the question of Turkish "otherness" in sharper relief.[15] The 1999 Helsinki summit decision to consider Turkey as a candidate for eventual EU membership, while very positive from the perspective of Turkey's Western vocation and, in particular, relations with Greece, does not necessarily remove these sources of European reservation. In strategic terms the real tensions began earlier and were highlighted by the experience of the Gulf War, in which Turkey's cooperation paradoxically reinforced the notion of Turkey as an extra-European ally. More recently, Turkey's internal and regional travails (and some "successes", e.g. the Öcalan capture and Syria's retreat from active PKK support) have appeared all too "Middle Eastern" to European observers.

The views of traditionally European-oriented foreign and security policy elites in Turkey have become more critical of Europe, and even echo some of the views long held by Islamists and radical nationalists. It is difficult to imagine that these sentiments can be easily reversed by anything other than clearly demonstrated EU openness to Turkish membership. Turkey's security relations with the West already are troubled by its exclusion from full participation in European defense initiatives conducted under Western European Union (WEU) or other auspices. Moreover, as suggested by the outcome of NATO's Washington summit and subsequent EU summits, developments in relation to the European Security and Defense Identity (ESDI) (or European Security and Defense Policy (ESDP), as the EU calls it), make it more likely that WEU functions will be absorbed by the EU itself. But Turkish alienation from Europe creates additional stresses. First, uncertainties about the EU will naturally place greater pressure on Turkey to fortify its bilateral relationship with the U.S. and its relations within NATO. Second, as noted earlier, lack of full Turkish integration in European security arrangements could complicate the outlook for Western crisis management in key areas, including the Balkans, Cyprus, and the Aegean. Third, it is quite possible that Turkish disenchantment with Europe will spill over into Ankara's broader management of security relations with partners on both sides of the Atlantic. It will bolster already potent nationalist sentiment and inspire a more critical approach to regional security cooperation, especially in northern Iraq. Statements by European officials—including an extraordinary one by British foreign secretary Robin Cook that Turkey's eastern border "is not one that is very clear, even perhaps to the Turkish government at times"—cannot help but strengthen Turkish doubts about the aims of Western policy in Turkey's region.[16]

Finally, the flux in relations with Europe comes at a time when Turkey's security establishment has chosen to emphasize the primacy of internal security concerns—in particular, the preservation of the secular state and the struggle against separatism. Given the growing emphasis on human rights in European attitudes toward foreign policy, the outlook for EU-Turkish relations may face further challenges as Ankara's fight against the PKK continues, and as Turkey comes under increasing scrutiny as an EU candidate. Europe's human rights stance could prove counter-productive by strengthening arguments against foreign interference made by Turkey's anti-Western Islamists and, above all, nationalists. Turkish resentment of solutions that appear to be imposed from the outside thus may actually impede Ankara's development of a "liberal" political approach to the issue of Kurdish identity.[17]

Turkish Stakes in a Changing NATO

The flux in EU-Turkish relations serves to emphasize the fact that NATO remains Ankara's paramount link to the Western club and is an overwhelmingly important security connection for Turkey in relation to old (i.e., Russian) as well as new risks. But NATO, like the EU, is changing in ways that complicate Turkey's role.[18] The twin processes of NATO enlargement and adaptation, in particular, raise issues of concern to Ankara. Apart from their worries over dilution of available attention and resources, Turkish strategists are concerned about more troubling implications for the future of Article 5 security guarantees.[19] A larger alliance with more diverse missions might neglect the central commitment to territorial defense. With tangible threats to its interests and territory on virtually all borders, Ankara is concerned that it will fall prey to "selective solidarity" in future crises, with NATO's European allies (Washington is less of a worry) treating threats to Turkey as "gray areas" or, worse, "out-of-area" contingencies. In short, there is considerable and not unreasonable concern that in a changing NATO, security guarantees will become less automatic and more conditional, with potentially negative consequences for Turkish interests.

It was never realistic to imagine that Turkish reservations could have prevented or even altered the NATO enlargement process. To the extent that Turks accept the notion of enlargement as vital to stability in the east, however, they also argue for early extension of the process southward to the Balkans, where Turkish security is directly engaged. From a Turkish perspective, a wider purview for enlargement would also help preserve a political balance of influence within the alliance—that is, to balance what might otherwise be an unhealthy expansion of German weight.

The articulation of a new NATO Strategic Concept in 1999 had special significance for Turkey. Overall, the new document places greater emphasis on defense of common interests, power projection, and crisis management on the European periphery. The bulk of NATO's canonical planning contingencies are already focused on the south, with the majority of these involving Turkey in some fashion. At the same time, it leaves traditional Article 5 commitments intact, a point of considerable importance for Turkey. The new missions are defined largely in functional rather than regional terms. But these new missions, from peacekeeping and crisis management to countering WMD risks, are far more likely to be performed on or near Turkey's borders than elsewhere in the European security space.

The April 1999 Washington NATO summit highlighted Turkey's stake in the future evolution of ESDI. Negotiations among Turkey and NATO allies on this issue were reportedly among the most difficult experienced prior to and during the summit. Ankara is understandably anxious to preserve the position it obtained through associate WEU membership. The prospect of a more active and independent European role in security matters could leave Turkey—as a nonmember of the EU—outside important decision-making circles, unless ESDI is firmly tied to NATO structures. More significantly, ESDI could signal a change in the trans-Atlantic security balance, with a potentially reduced role for the U.S., Turkey's primary supporter in the alliance. This clearly would not serve Turkish interests, especially in light of Ankara's difficult relations with Europe. The language adopted with regard to ESDI at the Washington summit, with important constraints on EU freedom of action and ability to "borrow" NATO military assets, was hailed as a diplomatic victory in Ankara. But the future contours of ESDI, and a common European foreign and security policy more generally, are far from established and will depend heavily on prospective European decisions on defense spending and priorities. The issue of trans-Atlantic roles in European security is likely to remain a key factor in Turkish perceptions and policies.

U.S.–Turkish Relations

As Turkey's relations with Europe deteriorated, relations with the U.S. appeared to enter a new, somewhat more positive phase. Nevertheless, the bilateral security relationship established in the wake of the Gulf

War has been troubled by numerous factors, some emanating from Ankara and Washington, others the product of more general changes in the post-Cold War security environment.

It is often observed—somewhat unfairly—that the U.S. has no Turkey policy in its own right. Rather, policy toward Turkey has been a product of other interests, from Russian recovery to Balkan stability, from the Middle East peace process to the containment of Iran and Iraq. One of the very few positive consequences of mid-1990s political turmoil in Turkey—particularly, the period of the pro-Islamist Necmettin Erbakan's prime ministry and its collapse—was that it forced U.S. policy-makers and analysts to focus on developments in Turkey itself. Indeed, there is an emerging consensus that the future of Turkish relations with the West as a whole, including the U.S., will be driven above all by the evolution of Turkish society and politics. Moreover, this is an area in which U.S. influence is likely to be quite limited.

As Turkey's security concerns expanded and the foreign policy debate became more active, U.S.-Turkish bilateral differences became more pronounced. The problem of divergent security perceptions is central to the future of bilateral cooperation, because much of the value of the strategic relationship flows from the predictability of Turkish policy in regional crises. Turkey's pivotal location and its ability to further U.S. freedom of action in key regions is a theoretical and potentially hollow rationale for cooperation in the absence of shared perceptions and policies. For example, the U.S. ability to use İncirlik air base in southern Turkey for non-NATO contingencies will turn critically on Ankara's own judgment about the consequences of any proposed action for Turkey's own regional objectives.

Many Turks regard with dismay the seeming contradiction between U.S. declarations of interest in Turkey as a vital strategic partner and the inability of successive U.S. administrations to translate this interest into a stable defense relationship. A leading measure of the relationship from the Turkish perspective has been the declining level and quality—and, in 1998, the end—of security assistance. Although Turkish policy-makers are aware of the general trend toward reduced U.S. security assistance worldwide, they tend to view the arms-transfer environment of recent years as a *de facto* embargo engineered by hostile lobbies. Realistic observers are inclined to treat the long-delayed release to Turkey of frigates and other military items as the result of congressional bargaining rather than evidence of fundamental change. Further challenges for arms transfer policy, including likely requests for attack helicopters and main battle tanks, are on the horizon and will inevitably be seen as new tests of the bilateral relationship.

Although the Turkish military has a clear preference for U.S. equipment, the difficulty of completing major transfers with Washington drove Ankara to explore avenues for diversification. The extensive defense-industrial relationship with Israel is a significant development in this regard and has been accompanied by less sophisticated acquisitions from Russia and elsewhere.

U.S. criticism of Turkey's human rights situation, including Ankara's handling of the Kurdish insurgency in the southeast and the circumstances surrounding the end of the *Refah*-led government, also emerged as a source of resentment. Although official U.S. criticism of Turkey on this score was less pronounced than Europe's, human rights and democratization concerns clearly complicated the bilateral relationship at many levels. The diversity of criticism aimed at Ankara since the Gulf War encourages the impression that Turkey has been treated as "part ally, part rogue state."[20]

Turkey's political crises, its troubled security relationship with the U.S., and its uncertain relations with the EU combined to galvanize concern in Washington and Ankara. Turkey's leadership appears interested in repairing the country's image and is inclined to open an active dialogue aimed at redefining bilateral strategic relations to address post-Cold War concerns, including such high-profile issues as energy security. There is also a growing awareness on all sides that a more diverse—that is, less security-heavy—bilateral relationship is likely to be more predictable and sustainable. Yet the overwhelmingly important role of Europe as a long-term economic partner for Turkey, coupled with the similarly overwhelming role of the U.S. as a regional security actor, may place natural limits on this diversification.

Overall Obsevations and Conclusions

Images of Turkey as a bridge or a barrier in security terms have not lost their relevance, but they no longer capture the full scope of the debate about Turkey's strategic role. Three broad observations can be offered with regard to Turkey, its external policy, and the outlook for its security relations with the West.

First, the Turkish external scene was transformed during the 1990s by the greatly expanded range of Turkish security concerns, a more active debate on external objectives, and a trend toward more assertive regional policies. As a consequence, the potential for friction with U.S. and European security partners increased significantly. Even where interests are congruent, differences between Turkey and its partners in policy and approach are now more common and hold the potential to disrupt cooperation in core areas such as NATO policy.

Second, Turkey's post-Cold War, post-Gulf War strategic role is being shaped by the emergence of new transregional challenges that are eroding traditional definitions of the European security space. European, Middle Eastern, and Eurasian security are increasingly interdependent, and Turkey is at the center of this phenomenon. Turkish and U.S. analyses in particular display a similar focus on this trend as a factor contributing to Turkey's strategic significance. As NATO moves to broaden its geographical and functional purview and as security challenges on the periphery come to the fore, interest in Turkey as a new "consumer" of security within the alliance will increase, as will the demands on Ankara for security cooperation. NATO will be the key institution binding Turkey to the West, but vigorous reassertion of NATO's commitment to Turkish security will be required to stem Ankara's fears about erosion of security guarantees.

Finally, long-standing assumptions about Turkey's internal evolution and policy orientation can no longer be taken for granted. In this regard, the most important influence on Ankara's regional behavior may not be the struggle between secularism and Islam, or East versus West in foreign policy terms, but rather the implications of a more assertive Turkish nationalism. Turkey's troubled political relations with Europe bolstered nationalist sentiment and complicated prospects for stability in key areas, not least Cyprus and the Aegean. At the same time the primacy of internal security issues—specifically, the PKK—in the current Turkish calculus suggests a potentially more difficult relationship with security partners whose assessment of these issues may not accord with Ankara's.

Taken together, these observations suggest a future in which Turkey can play a pivotal role as a security partner for the West, but only if Turks are convinced that their own judgments are taken seriously and that cooperation supports Turkey's own more finely gauged national interests. Turkey is emerging as a more important, but also more independent and assertive, actor at the center, rather than the periphery, of Western security debates.

Notes

1   See Ian O. Lesser, "Bridge or Barrier? Turkey and the West After the Cold War," in Graham Fuller, Ian Lesser et al., *Turkey's New Geopolitics: From the Balkans to Western China* (Boulder: Westview/RAND, 1993). An earlier version of this chapter was published as a RAND Report in 1991.
2   Alan O. Makovsky, "Turkey," in Robert Chase, Emily Hill and Paul Kennedy (eds.), *The Pivotal States: A New Framework for U.S. Policy in the Developing World* (New York and London: W.W. Norton, 1999).
3   Greece, Cyprus, Lebanon, Tunisia, and even Spain are often cited as "bridges" between regions. There is also a longstanding intellectual debate about the broader role of the Mediterranean as bridge and barrier.

See Fernand Braudel, *The Mediterranean and the Mediterranean World in the Age of Philip II* (New York: Harper and Row, 1973).

4   Philip Robins, *Turkey and the Middle East* (London: Royal Institute of International Affairs, 1991); Ferenc A. Vali, *Bridge Across the Bosporus: The Foreign Policy of Turkey* (Baltimore: Johns Hopkins University Press, 1971).

5   As of 1999, Turkish officials asserted that Turkey had lost some $35 billion to $40 billion as a consequence of the embargo, an amount beyond the possibility of international compensation. Interview by author, April 1999.

6   "Turkey's General Bir on Issues," *Sabah*, in Foreign Broadcast Information Service Daily Report-West Europe (FBIS-WEU), 98-177, March 29, 1998.

7   Interview by author, April 1999.

8   E.M. Earle, *Turkey, the Great Powers and the Baghdad Railway* (New York: Macmillan, 1924).

9   Geoffrey Kemp and Robert E. Harkavy, *Strategic Geography and the Changing Middle East* (Washington, D.C.: Carnegie/Brookings Institution Press, 1997), pp. 109-153.

10 Ian O. Lesser and Ashley Tellis, *Strategic Exposure: Proliferation around the Mediterranean* (Santa Monica, Calif.: RAND, 1996).

11 Washington Summit Communiqué, NAC-S(99)64 and Strategic Concept document NAC-S(99)65, April 24, 1999.

12 Alessandro Politi, *European Security: The New Transnational Risks,* Chaillot Papers no. 29 (Paris: WEU Institute for Security Studies, 1997).

13 Turkish and U.S. officials (1998-1999), interviews by author.

14 F. Stephen Larrabee, "U.S. and European Policy toward Turkey and the Caspian Basin," in Robert Blackwill and Michael Sturmer (eds.), *Allies Divided: Transatlantic Policies for the Greater Middle East* (Cambridge: MIT Press, 1997).

15 F. Stephen Larrabee, *The Troubled Partnership: Turkey and Europe* (P-8020, Santa Monica, Calif.: RAND, 1998); *Turkey and the European Union: Nebulous Nature of Relations* (Ankara: Foreign Policy Institute, 1996).

16 BBC-1 television, interview with the foreign secretary by David Frost, April 1, 1998, transcript.

17 Timothy Garton Ash, "Europe's Endangered Liberal Order," *Foreign Affairs*, March-April 1998.

18 *Perceptions*, Special Issue on NATO, vol. 4, no. 1 (March-May 1999).

19 Article 5 of the North Atlantic Treaty, NATO's founding document, specifies that an attack on any ally "shall be considered an attack against them all" and requires every ally to "assist" the attacked party by "taking forthwith, individually and in concert with the other parties [allies], such action as it deems necessary, including the use of armed force. . . ."

20 A characterization suggested—but certainly not supported—by my RAND colleague Zalmay Khalilzad.

Contributors

Meliha Benli Altunışık is assistant professor of international relations at Middle East Technical University in Ankara, Turkey.

Tozun Bahcheli is professor of political science at King's College in London, Ontario, Canada.

Clement H. Dodd, an independent scholar, was formerly chairman of the Modern Turkish Studies Programme in the School of Oriental and African Studies, University of London (United Kingdom).

Atila Eralp is director of the Center for European Studies at Middle East Technical University in Ankara, Turkey.

William Hale is reader in politics with reference to Turkey at the School of Oriental and African Studies, University of London (United Kingdom).

George Harris, an independent scholar, is recently retired from the U.S. Department of State.

Kemal Kirişçi is professor of political science and international relations at Bogazici (Bosporus) University in Istanbul, Turkey.

Şule Kut is professor of international relations at Bilgi University in Istanbul, Turkey.

Ian Lesser is a senior analyst at RAND in Washington, D.C.

Alan Makovsky is senior fellow and director of the Turkish Research Program at The Washington Institute for Near East Policy in Washington, D.C.

Andrew Mango is an associate of the Modern Turkish Studies Programme, University of London (United Kingdom).

Sabri Sayarı is executive director of the Institute of Turkish Studies and also teaches at Georgetown University's School of Foreign Service in Washington, D.C.

Duygu Bazoğlu Sezer is professor of international relations at Bilkent University in Ankara, Turkey.

Gareth Winrow is professor of international relations at Bilgi University in Istanbul, Turkey.

Index

A

Abdullah II 48

Abiyev, Safar 100

Abkhazia/Abkhaz(es) 16, 17, 120, 122, 124

Adriatic Sea 76, 83, 102, 117, 125

Aegean Sea 1, 2, 7, 30, 125, 131, 133-36, 139, 141, 142, 145, 146, 148, 149, 150, 164, 183, 191, 192, 210, 214, 215, 220

Afghanistan 119

Albania/Albanian(s) 16, 17, 32, 74-76, 80, 81, 82, 85-87, 88, 90, 98, 125, 137, 138

Albright, Madeleine 9, 152

Algeria 34, 37, 42, 127

Aliyev, Haydar 33, 99, 100, 118, 121, 122, 129

Aliyev, Ilham 122

Anavatan (Motherland) Party (ANAP) 41, 127, 128, 159, 162, 163, 171, 179, 181

Arabs 2, 3, 8, 35, 37, 39, 40, 41, 42, 44, 47, 48, 49, 52, 53, 55, 59, 60, 62, 64, 65, 67, 68, 70, 71, 157, 206, 209

Arafat, Yasir 42, 49

Armenia/Armenian(s) 12, 13, 32, 37, 40, 47, 52, 93, 95, 98, 100, 101, 103, 120, 121, 124, 128, 139, 143, 146, 192, 194, 195, 198, 213

Arsenis, Gerasimos 139

Armenian Secret Army for the Liberation of Armenia (ASALA) 13

Asia 2, 5, 7, 16, 32, 33, 34, 35, 39, 50, 51, 52, 88, 92, 95, 96, 97, 98, 99, 116, 117, 118, 119, 122, 123, 127, 128, 129, 139, 164, 169, 174, 185, 205, 211

Atatürk, Mustafa Kemal 1, 9-12, 14, 15-16, 18, 36, 39, 121, 132, 157, 179, 197

Atatürk Dam 36

Atatürkism/Kemalism/ Kemalist(s) 7, 9, 10, 16, 18, 29, 140, 156

Avrasya incident (1996) 17, 94, 106, 204

Azerbaijan/Azerbaijani(s)/ Azeri(s) 4, 15, 16, 17, 27, 28, 32-34, 47, 50, 51, 52, 93, 95, 98-101, 103, 104, 116, 117, 118, 120, 121-25, 126, 127, 128, 129, 195, 200, 204, 213

Azerbaijan International Operating Company (AIOC) 125, 126, 129

B

Baath Party, Iraqi 39; Syrian 46

Baghdad Pact 13, 33, 39, 47

Baker, James 117

Baku-Ceyhan pipeline 27, 28, 100, 103, 104, 105, 106, 111, 122-26, 128, 129, 139, 196, 198, 200, 209, 213. *See also* Caspian Sea *and* pipelines.

Baku-Novorossiisk pipeline 103, 104, 123, 125, 139. *See also* Caspian Sea *and* pipelines.

Baku-Supsa pipeline 103, 104, 123, 125, 126. *See also* Caspian Sea *and* pipelines.

Balkans 2, 3, 4, 7, 10, 15, 16, 39, 51, 74-89, 92, 97, 102, 116, 131, 137, 138, 139, 185, 193, 203, 207, 208, 210, 213, 214, 215, 217, 218

Balkars 98

Bangladesh 34

Barzani, Mustafa 13
Barzani, Massoud 14, 45
Bashkirs 98
Baykal, Deniz 64, 163
Bechtel 28
Berisha, Sali 74, 76
Berne Declaration 133, 136
Bir, Çevik 48, 66, 69, 120
Birand, Mehmet Ali 160, 167, 172
Black Sea 2, 3, 5, 17, 29, 31, 32, 39, 78, 94, 95, 102, 103, 104, 109, 116, 120, 123, 125, 127, 137, 138, 139, 200, 204, 209
Black Sea Economic Cooperation (BSEC) 3, 32, 34, 78, 81, 138
Black Sea Trade and Development Bank 32
Blue Stream pipeline 32, 95, 109, 127, 128, 200. *See also* Caspian Sea *and* pipelines.
Bosnia/Bosnia-Herzegovina/ Bosniacs (Bosnian Muslims)/ Bosnian 4, 15, 16, 17, 79, 80-85, 87, 88, 93, 98, 137, 138, 164, 193, 204, 208, 213; Bosniac-Croat (*or* Bosnian-Croat) Federation 83, 84, 85, 137
Bosporus 17, 123, 125
BOTAŞ 28, 128, 196
Britain (United Kingdom) 9, 12, 25, 31, 45, 125, 129, 133, 156, 157, 159, 162, 163, 169, 171, 193, 216
Bulgaria 1, 5, 7, 17, 27, 32, 77, 78, 79, 82, 85, 86, 88, 102, 105, 125, 138, 139
Bulgarification 7, 77, 78
Burgas-Alexandroupolis pipeline 105, 139. *See also* Caspian Sea *and* pipelines.

C

Canada 37
Caspian Finance Center 128

Caspian Sea 4, 5, 28, 44, 100, 103, 104, 106, 109, 116, 118, 120-129, 139, 169, 196, 200, 207, 209, 212, 213; energy and other resources in 116, 117-22, 123-26, 128, 129, 139, 169, 207
Caucasus 2, 5, 16, 17, 39, 88, 92, 93, 94, 95, 96, 98-104, 106, 107, 116, 119, 120, 122, 128, 129, 131, 137, 139, 164, 174, 191, 196, 204-206, 209, 210, 211, 213
Cem, İsmail 49, 50, 70, 76, 87, 131, 152, 165, 168, 197
Cemal, Hasan 160
Central America 37
Central Asia 2, 5, 7, 16, 29, 32-35, 39, 50-52, 68, 88, 92, 95, 96, 97-99, 111, 116-23, 127-29, 139, 156, 164, 169, 174, 185, 205, 211
Central Bank, Turkish 21, 23
Central Treaty Organization (CENTO) 33, 39, 192
Ceyhan 27, 100, 122, 124, 128
Chechnya/Chechen(s) 16, 17, 97, 103, 105, 106, 120, 125, 204, 213
Chernomyrdin, Viktor 95, 96
China 16, 17, 33, 117, 119, 129, 203
Chinese Turkestan 16
Circassians 11, 16, 17
Clerides, Glafcos 157, 160, 167, 172, 193
Clinton, Bill 53, 122, 128, 169, 193, 198
coalition governments, Turkish 6, 9, 20, 40, 41, 59, 68-70, 75, 76, 87, 110, 119, 128, 147, 162, 163, 181, 184, 194, 204, 206, 214
Cold War 1-3, 7, 23, 26, 28, 29, 39, 41, 43, 44, 47, 48, 52, 53, 59, 60, 74, 79, 82, 88, 92, 93, 97, 104, 131, 137, 138, 173, 175, 203-5, 218-20

Commonwealth of Independent
 States (CIS) 32, 38, 95, 101, 121
Congress, U.S. 15, 37, 128, 139,
 146, 147, 148, 190, 193-96, 198,
 199, 200
Constantinescu, Emil 79
continental shelf, Aegean 78, 134,
 135, 137
continental shelf, Black Sea 78
Conventional Forces in Europe
 (CFE) Treaty 94, 103, 107, 191
Cook, Robin 216
Cordovez, Diego 168
Council of Europe 143
Crete 81, 146, 193, 207
Crimea 16
Croatia/Croats 79, 80, 83, 84, 85, 88
Cumhuriyet Halk (Republican
 People's) Party (CHP) 41, 163,
 179
customs union, Turkish, with EU
 3, 22, 26, 29, 30, 42, 141, 158-
 160, 163, 166, 168, 173, 175, 177,
 178, 179, 180-84, 186, 208. *See
 also* European Union (EU).
Cyprus 1, 2, 3, 6, 7, 30, 31, 39, 52,
 60, 93, 94, 103, 105, 129, 131,
 133, 139, 140, 141, 142, 143, 145,
 146, 147, 148, 149, 150, 151, 153-
 72, 178, 181-84, 186, 190, 192,
 193, 198, 199, 207, 211, 214, 215,
 220; Republic of Cyprus 139,
 142, 153, 156, 159, 160, 163, 164,
 165, 166, 167, 181, 182, 193;
 Turkish Republic of Northern
 Cyprus (TRNC) 129, 157, 160,
 165, 168, 170, 181; division
 along Green Line 133, 150, 160;
 Turkish Cypriots 6, 140, 141,
 153, 154, 155, 156, 157, 158, 159,
 160, 162, 164, 165, 166, 168, 169,
 170, 171, 178, 182, 186, 193, 198,
 199; Greek Cypriots 30, 31, 52,

93, 94, 103, 105, 133, 141-43,
 146, 151, 153-60, 162, 164-72,
 181, 182, 186, 193, 198, 199;
 Turkish military intervention
 (1974) 3, 30, 153, 154, 155, 156,
 157, 178, 192, 193, 194, 196;
 Treaty of Guarantee (1960) 124,
 155, 158, 162, 165, 168, 206, 211

Ç

Çağlayangil, İhsan Sabri 157, 171
Çetin, Hikmet 41, 62, 85
Çiller, Tansu 41, 49, 63, 67, 69, 75,
 99, 118, 146, 158, 159, 160, 163,
 167, 181

D

D-8 (Developing-8) 16, 34
Daghestan/ Daghestanis 16, 125
Davos process/initiative 133,
 136, 147, 150
Dayton Peace Accords 81, 83, 84,
 137
Demirel, Süleyman 4, 5, 14, 49, 51,
 62, 79, 85, 87, 95, 98, 99, 100, 117,
 118, 126, 129, 131, 144, 157, 158
democratization 77, 79, 173, 185,
 219
Demokratik Sol (Democratic Left)
 Party (DSP) 41, 68, 70, 159, 162,
 163, 165, 171, 192, 197
Democratic Left Party. See
 Demokratik Sol (Democratic
 Left) Party (DSP).
Denktaş, Rauf 6, 157, 158, 160,
 161, 162, 163, 164, 166, 168, 169,
 170
Doğru Yol (True Path) Party
 (DYP) 9, 41, 69, 158, 162, 163,
 171, 181
Dostum, Abdul Rashid 119
drug trade 13, 185, 194, 211
dual containment, U.S. policy of
 53, 214

E

earthquakes 131, 145, 186
East Germany 108
Eastern Europe 23, 107, 175, 181
Ecevit, Bülent 4, 41, 51, 68, 75, 76,
    90, 128, 131, 159, 160, 163, 165,
    178, 179, 182, 192, 194, 197, 199
Economic Cooperation Organiza-
    tion (ECO) 33
Egypt 34, 36, 37, 41, 44, 47, 48, 55,
    64, 67, 127, 195
Elchibey, Ebulfez 52, 120, 121, 122
ENKA 127
enosis (union of Cyprus with
    Greece) 154, 155
Enver Pasha 16, 97
Erbakan, Necmettin 14, 16, 29,
    34, 35, 37, 41, 42, 69, 75, 87, 130,
    179, 195, 197, 218
Erdoğan, Recep Tayyip 200
ethnicity 2, 11, 12, 14, 15, 16, 17,
    18, 30, 33, 76, 77, 79, 80, 81, 82,
    84, 97, 116, 119, 120, 190, 204
ethnic lobbies 17, 30, 204. *See also*
    lobbies/lobbying.
Euphrates River 36, 40, 44, 46, 61,
    63, 64, 139, 192, 212
Eurasia 74, 92, 96, 98, 110, 111,
    185, 207, 209, 210
European Community (EC) 173,
    174, 176, 177-81, 187. *See also*
    European Union (EU).
European Council 151
European Economic Community
    (EEC) 23, 187. *See also* Euro-
    pean Union (EU).
European Investment Bank 26
European Security and Defense
    Initiative (ESDI) 185, 186, 215,
    217
European Union (EU) 2, 3, 9, 22,
    23, 25, 26, 29, 30, 41, 42, 83, 87,
    96, 131, 133, 136, 138, 140-43,

145, 147, 148, 150, 151, 156, 158,
159, 160, 161, 162, 163-70, 171,
173-87, 190, 198, 204, 208, 211,
215-17, 219; *acquis communitaire*
182; *Agenda 2000* 171, 175, 176;
Amsterdam, Treaty of 141;
Ankara Association Agreement
("Ankara Agreement") 141, 187,
208; Association Council 174,
180; Barcelona process 208;
"Copenhagen criteria" 182;
Maastricht Treaty 187; summits:
Cardiff (1998) 183; Copenhagen
(1993); Helsinki (1999) 131, 140,
141, 184-87, 204, 215; Luxembourg (1997) 96, 140, 176,
182-84, 186, 187, 215. *See also*
customs union.
Eximbank, Turkish 33, 108, 109, 117
Eximbank, U.S. 128
exports, Turkish 22, 23, 30, 33, 34,
35, 43, 46, 50, 60, 68, 80, 87, 109,
119, 126, 179, 207, 214

F

Fazilet (Virtue) Party (FP) 29, 43,
171, 200
France 42, 144, 176
fundamentalism, Islamic 4, 51, 54,
63, 64, 65. *See also* Islamism.

G

Gagauz 17, 79, 138
GAMA 127
GAP (Southeast Anatolian
Project) 40, 44, 46, 61, 64
Gee, Robert 128
General Electric 28
Georgia 17, 28, 32, 99, 100, 102,
103, 116, 120, 122, 123, 124, 200
Germany 23, 25, 108, 140, 144,
175, 176, 184, 206, 212, 217
Gligorov, Kiro 87

Golan Heights 55
Gorbachev, Mikhail 23, 108, 111
Greece 1, 3, 6, 7, 11, 26, 30-32, 37,
   46, 47, 52, 64, 66, 71, 74-78, 80,
   84-86, 88, 93, 94, 103, 105, 125,
   131-72, 175, 176, 178, 181-86,
   191-94, 198, 199, 203, 214, 215,
   220
Gül, Abdullah 14
Gülen, Fethullah 69, 119
Gulf War (1991) 3, 5, 6, 43, 45, 46,
   53, 59, 60, 191, 196, 197, 206,
   209, 212, 215, 217, 219, 220
Guluzade, Vafa 100, 121
Gürel, Şükrü 165

H

Hamas 42
Hatay (Alexandretta) issue 36, 46,
   63, 212
Heper, Doğan 15
Hizbollah (Lebanese) 42
Holbrooke, Richard 167, 169, 193,
   198
human rights 18, 66, 81, 85, 139,
   142, 143, 145, 146, 165, 173, 178,
   179, 183, 184, 190, 193, 194, 198,
   199, 201, 216, 219
Hürriyet 161, 171
Husayn, Saddam 3, 5, 40, 45, 199,
   214
Hussein, king of Jordan 48, 49

I

International Monetary Fund
   (IMF) 25
Imia-Kardak 7, 131, 133, 136, 145,
   146, 148, 170, 191, 204
Implementation Force NATO
   (IFOR) 83, 213
imports, Turkish 21, 22, 23, 26, 30,
   33, 34, 50, 60, 68, 109, 119, 209
Indonesia 34

International Civil Aviation
   Organization (ICAO) 135
International Court of Justice
   (ICJ) 85, 135, 136, 140, 183
International Development
   Association (IDA) 25
International Finance Corporation (IFC) 26
International Monetary Fund
   (IMF) 25
Iran 1, 3, 4, 8, 12-16, 23, 27, 28,
   33-35, 40, 41, 42, 43, 44, 45, 50,
   51, 52, 53, 54, 55, 59, 60, 62, 63,
   64, 65, 67, 70, 93, 95, 99, 103,
   104, 109, 116, 117, 118, 122,
   125, 126, 127, 128, 129, 130,
   139, 143, 169, 192, 195, 196,
   200, 207, 208, 209, 210, 214,
   218; revolution 23
Iraq 1, 2, 3, 4, 5, 6, 12, 13, 14, 23,
   27, 33, 35, 36, 39, 40, 42, 43, 44-
   47, 48, 49, 50, 53-55, 59, 60, 61,
   62, 63, 64, 71, 93, 94, 111, 127,
   139, 143, 145, 146, 192, 196, 197,
   199, 201, 206, 208, 209, 210, 213,
   214, 216, 218
Iraqi National Congress 54
Islamic Development Bank 26
Islamism 9, 10, 14, 18, 29, 31, 42,
   53, 66, 69, 84, 145, 180, 192, 200,
   204, 206, 215, 216. See also fundamentalism, Islamic.
Israel 2, 3, 8, 29, 34, 35, 36, 37, 39,
   40, 41, 42, 43, 45, 46, 47, 48, 49,
   50, 52, 53, 55, 59-72, 137, 139,
   146, 159, 198, 199, 206, 208, 209,
   214, 219
Italy 75, 106, 176, 198

İ

İnan, Kamran 162
İncirlik 45, 62, 191, 218
İnönü, İsmet 12, 147, 157, 192

J

Japan 25, 29, 30
Javakhetia 124
Johnson, Lyndon B. 147, 157, 192;
  1964 Johnson letter 147, 192
Jordan 35, 36, 41, 44, 48, 67, 206,
  210

K

Karabekir, Kazım 12
Kardak. *See* Imia-Kardak.
Karimov, Islam 116, 118, 129
Kaya, Burhan 123
Kazakhstan/Kazak 17, 34, 103,
  116, 118, 119, 120, 124, 125, 129
Kemal, Mustafa. *See* Atatürk,
  Mustafa Kemal.
Kemalism. *See* Atatürkism/
  Kemalism/Kemalist(s).
Kenya 7, 131, 144, 198
Khalilzad, Zalmay 221
Khatami, Mohammad 52, 192
Khomeini, Ayatollah Ruhollah 192
Kocharian, Robert 195
Kosovo 17, 76, 80, 81, 87, 88, 93,
  98, 111, 131, 137, 138, 185, 193,
  204, 208, 212, 213
Kournishev, Anatoly 121
Kurds/Kurdish issue 2, 11-14, 35,
  36, 40, 42, 43, 44, 45, 46, 53, 54,
  61, 62, 63, 66, 71, 93, 103, 105,
  106, 120, 124, 131, 139, 142, 144-
  46, 190, 192, 194, 197, 206, 210,
  211, 216, 219
Kurdistan Democratic Party
  (KDP) 14, 45, 54
Kurdistan Workers Party (PKK)
  2, 4, 6, 7, 13, 14, 35, 36, 42, 43,
  45, 46, 51, 52, 54, 55, 61, 62-64,
  65, 66, 71, 93, 94, 106, 120, 124,
  131, 139, 143, 144, 145, 190, 192,
  194, 198, 206, 207, 210, 212, 214,
  215, 216, 220

Kuwait 23, 40, 44, 50, 53
Kyrgyzstan 34, 116, 119, 129

L

Lausanne Treaty of 1923 10, 136,
  142
Law of the Sea 134
Lazistan 14
Lebanon 12, 13, 40, 41, 62, 143,
  210, 220
Lezgi 16
Libya 16, 34, 35, 36, 40, 42, 195, 196
lobbies/lobbying 16, 17, 30, 37,
  60, 76, 121, 128, 139, 146, 148,
  165, 169, 179, 191, 192, 195, 196,
  198, 204, 218. *See also* ethnic
  lobbies.
Lockheed Martin 2
luggage trade/suitcase trade 17,
  22, 23, 32, 38, 109, 119

M

Macedonia 10, 17, 76, 80, 82, 85,
  86, 87, 88, 137, 138
Madrid Communiqué (1997) 148,
  152
mafia, Turkish 122
Mahabad, Kurdish republic of 13
Malaysia 34
Marxism 13
Mediterranean Sea 2, 26, 27, 41,
  64, 93, 94, 100, 102, 104, 116,
  122, 139, 176, 185, 204, 205, 207,
  208, 214, 220
MEP (main export pipeline). *See*
  pipelines.
Mendelson, M. H. 165
Menderes, Adnan 157
Middle East 2-4, 13, 14, 23, 25, 29,
  30, 34, 37, 39, 40-44, 48-55, 59-
  63, 65, 66, 69, 70, 93, 116, 131,
  137, 139, 146, 152, 164, 169, 174,
  185, 191, 194, 204-15, 218, 220

military coup, Turkish (1980) 13, 61

Milliyet 160, 161, 171

Milliyetçi Hareket (Nationalist Movement) Party (MHP) 41, 69, 110, 118, 162, 170, 171

Milosevic, Slobodan 80, 81

Moldova 32, 138

Montreux Convention of 1936 104, 105, 123

Morningstar, Richard 200

Mosul, Ottoman province of 12

Motherland Party. See *Anavatan* (Motherland) Party (ANAP).

Mubarak, Hosni 47

Muslim Brotherhood 42

N

Nagorno-Karabakh 121, 128, 195

Nano, Fatos 75

National Security Council, Turkish 4, 5, 6, 65, 146

nationalism 11, 12, 63, 78, 84, 87, 106, 110, 206, 211, 215, 216

Nationalist Action Party. See *Milliyetçi Hareket* (Nationalist Movement) Party (MHP).

Nationalist Movement Party. See *Milliyetçi Hareket* (Nationalist Movement) Party (MHP).

"near abroad," Russian concept of 32, 98, 101, 103

neo-Ottomanism 84

Netanyahu, Binyamin 42, 66

Nigeria 34, 127

Niyazov, Saparmurat 118, 127

"no-fly" zone (northern Iraq) 6, 42, 83, 191, 197, 201

North Africa 208

North Atlantic Treaty Organization (NATO) 1, 3, 42, 59, 74, 76, 77, 81, 82, 83, 85, 87, 92, 93, 100, 101, 102, 104, 107, 108, 111, 120, 121, 131, 133, 135, 137, 138, 147, 148, 149, 169, 177, 185, 189, 190, 191, 192, 193, 197, 205, 206, 207, 208, 209, 210, 211, 212, 214-18, 219, 220, 221; charter, Article 5 of 205, 216-217, 221; Strategic Concept (1999) 217; Washington summit (1999) 215, 217

O

Operation Deny Flight 83

Operation Northern Watch 6, 45, 53, 54, 145. *See also* Operation Provide Comfort.

Operation Provide Comfort 6, 7, 40, 42, 45, 53, 54, 145. *See also* Operation Northern Watch.

Organisation for Economic Cooperation and Development (OECD) 23, 25, 29, 30, 31, 159, 171

Ottoman Empire 10, 12, 16, 78, 79, 88, 89, 97, 121, 138, 154, 192, 206, 209

Overseas Private Investment Corporation (OPIC) 128

Ö

Öcalan, Abdullah 2, 7, 14, 36, 37, 43, 46, 47, 52, 54, 55, 61, 65, 70, 71, 94, 106, 110, 131, 139, 142, 143, 144, 145, 151, 198, 210-12, 215

Özal, Turgut 5, 15, 21, 30, 36, 40, 41, 53, 59, 60, 65, 95, 98, 108, 117, 118, 138, 147, 150, 158, 161, 162, 174, 178, 179, 191, 195, 206

P

Pakistan 34, 119

Palestine Liberation Organization (PLO) 40, 49, 53, 61

Palestinians 2, 39, 41, 42, 44, 48, 49, 50, 53, 61, 63, 64, 67

pan-Islamism 10, 16
pan-Turkism 11, 52, 118
Papandreou, Andreas 131, 136, 147, 150
parliament, Turkish (*also known as* Turkish Grand National Assembly) 5, 6, 10, 12, 36, 40, 49, 69, 100, 110, 122, 134, 147, 150, 158, 171, 179, 183, 190
Partnership for Peace 76, 92, 102, 120
Patriotic Union of Kurdistan (PUK) 13, 45, 54
Persian Gulf 23, 27, 50, 125, 169
Persian Gulf states 50
pipelines 5, 26, 27, 28, 32, 35, 36, 40, 44, 46, 95, 100, 103, 104, 105, 106, 109, 116, 120-29, 139, 169, 195, 196, 198, 200, 209, 213, 214; main export pipeline (MEP) 100, 103, 104, 121, 122, 123. *See also* Baku-Ceyhan pipeline; Baku-Novorossiisk pipeline; Baku-Supsa pipeline; Blue Stream pipeline; *and* Burgas-Alexandroupolis pipeline.
Pomaks 16
Portugal 178, 181
PSG consortium 28

Q

Qadhafi, Mu'ammar 36
Qasim, Abd al-Karim 39
Qatar 127

R

Rabbani, Burhanuddin 119
Rambouillet conference 76, 81
Refah (Welfare) Party (RP) 9, 18, 29, 41-43, 64, 66, 68-69, 119, 130, 162, 171, 179, 180, 195, 197, 200
refugees 43, 144
Regional Cooperation for Development (RCD) 33

Republican People's Party. See *Cumhuriyet Halk* (Republican People's) Party (CHP).
Rights and Freedoms Movement (Bulgarian) 77
Robins, Philip 33
Romania 5, 17, 32, 79, 88, 102, 125
Russia 1, 2, 3, 4, 7, 10, 13, 16, 17, 22, 23, 26, 27, 28, 29, 31-33, 44, 47, 50, 52, 92-116, 118, 119, 120, 121, 122-24, 125, 126, 127, 128, 129, 133, 139, 160, 164, 167, 191, 193, 196, 200, 203, 204, 206, 207, 209, 210, 211, 213, 216, 218, 219

S

S-300 air defense missiles, Cypriot purchase of 93, 94, 101, 121, 133, 146, 148, 160, 167, 170, 193, 199, 207
Saadabad Pact 13
Sabah 158, 160, 171, 172
Salih, Mohammed 118
Sampson, Nicos 155
sanctions against Iraq 35, 220
Sandjak 138
Saudi Arabia 34, 37, 44, 50
separatism 2, 42, 51, 65, 81, 94, 95, 99, 103, 104, 105, 106, 122, 124, 131, 139, 211, 213, 216
Serbia/Serbian/Serb(s) 15, 80, 81, 83, 85, 88, 93, 102, 137, 138, 212
Sezgin, İsmet 62
sharia 65
Shaykh Said revolt 14
Shevardnadze, Eduard 99, 100, 122
Simitis, Costas 131, 137, 145
Sincan affair 64, 65
Slovenia 79, 80, 87
Social Democratic Populist Party. See *Sosyal Demokrat Halkçı* (Social Democratic Populist) Party (SHP).

Sosyal Demokrat Halkçı (Social Democratic Populist) Party (SHP) 179, 181
South Korea 29
Southeast Anatolian Project. *See* GAP.
Southeast Asia 34
Soviet Union (USSR) 1, 2, 3, 10, 12, 13, 15, 17, 22, 23, 28, 31, 33, 39, 41, 47, 51, 74, 92, 94, 95, 97, 98, 99, 101, 103, 104, 107, 108, 109, 110, 111, 116, 117, 121, 122, 123, 129, 157, 174, 189, 191, 192, 203, 204, 205, 206; territory of former 3, 15, 17, 22, 23, 51, 97, 98, 99, 110, 111, 121, 174, 205, 206
Soysal, Mümtaz 159, 160, 197
Spain 178, 181, 220
Stabilization Force, NATO (SFOR) 83, 213
State Oil Company of Azerbaijan (SOCAR) 122
State Planning Organization (SPO), Turkish 177
suitcase trade. *See* luggage trade/ suitcase trade.
Syria 1, 2, 3, 6, 13, 14, 34, 35, 36, 37, 40, 41, 42, 43, 44-47, 48, 52, 54, 55, 59, 61, 62, 63, 64, 65, 66, 70, 71, 94, 106, 139, 143, 145, 146, 167, 192, 208, 209, 210, 212, 214, 215

T

taksim (division of Cyprus) 154, 155, 157, 181
Talabani, Jalal 13, 45
Taliban 119
Tatarstan/Tatar(s) 17, 97, 98, 118
Tekfen 127
Ter-Petrossian, Levon 33, 195
territorial seas 133, 134, 135, 136, 148

terrorism 1, 13, 14, 40, 42, 48, 49, 55, 62, 64, 66, 106, 131, 144, 145, 185, 190, 194, 204, 207, 210, 211
Thrace, western (Greek), Turkish minority issue in 10, 138, 142-143
Thrace, Turkish 205
Tigris River 44, 46, 55, 61, 212
Trade and Development Agency, U.S. 128
trans-Caspian pipeline (TCP) 123, 128, 200
True Path Party. See *Doğru Yol* (True Path) Party (DYP).
Tunisia 220
Turkic commonwealth, concept of 117
Turkic peoples or republics 3, 10, 15, 16, 31-33, 41, 95, 97, 98, 99, 110, 111, 116-19, 129, 130, 191, 205, 206
Turkic summits 3, 117
Turkish Grand National Assembly. *See* parliament, Turkish.
Turkish International Cooperation Agency (TİKA) 117
Turkish Straits 1, 93, 97, 102, 103, 104, 105, 123, 167, 209
"Turkish model" (for regional states) 117, 118, 174
Turkmenistan/Turkmens 4, 27, 28, 34, 35, 103, 104, 109, 116, 118, 119, 120, 123, 126, 127, 129, 200, 209
Turks, ethnic, in Turkey 11, 14, 18, 118, 144, 157; outside Turkey, 7, 10, 11, 14, 16, 18, 78, 83, 87, 88, 89, 118, 120, 139, 143, 144, 157, 205
Türkeş, Alparslan 69
Türkiye 171
Türkmen, İlter 158

U

Uighurs 17, 119
Ukraine 17, 32, 102, 125
Union of Soviet Socialist Republics (USSR). *See* Soviet Union (USSR).
United Arab Emirates (UAE) 35
United Nations (UN) 35, 40, 42, 48, 53, 54, 60, 83, 86, 137, 140, 155, 156, 157, 159, 161, 162, 164, 165, 166, 168, 170, 183, 196, 199; Security Council 4, 6, 35, 65, 146, 157; UNPROFOR 83, 137
United States of America (U.S.) 1, 2, 3, 4, 5, 6, 8, 9, 16, 25, 26, 27, 28, 29, 30, 31, 35, 36, 37, 40, 42, 43, 45, 47, 48, 50, 52, 53, 54, 55, 59, 60, 62, 63, 64, 67, 69, 83, 85, 89, 92, 93, 99, 100, 103, 104, 108, 109, 111, 117, 121, 122, 123, 124, 125, 126-28, 135, 137, 139, 144, 145, 146, 147-50, 152, 157, 158, 163, 167, 169, 171, 173, 174, 176, 189-201, 203, 204, 205, 206, 207, 209, 210, 213, 214, 215, 216, 217-20
Uzbekistan/Uzbek(s) 118, 119

V

Venizelos, Eleftherios 132
Virtue Party. See *Fazilet* (Virtue) Party (FP).

W

War of Independence, Turkish 9, 10, 11, 12, 16
Warsaw Pact 1, 3, 92, 107, 175
Washington Institute for Near East Policy 1, 2, 4
water dispute, Turkish-Syrian 36, 40, 44, 46, 55, 61, 63, 64, 139, 192, 212
weapons of mass destruction (WMD) 43, 46, 52, 139, 204, 209, 210, 212, 217; proliferation of, 204, 209, 210, 211, 214
Weizman, Ezer 63
Welfare Party. See *Refah* (Welfare) Party (RP).
West-East Motorway (WEM) 86, 89
Western European Union (WEU) 83, 141, 186, 215, 217
World Bank 25
World War I 10, 16, 97, 189
World War II 1, 9, 13, 79

X

Xinjiang 16, 17, 119

Y

Yakutia 118
Yılmaz, Mesut 20, 21, 70, 75, 76, 78, 81, 87, 96, 122, 127, 136, 159, 162, 167, 171
Yugoslavia 2, 74, 76, 79-82, 84, 85, 86, 87, 88, 90, 93, 102, 131, 137, 193

Z

Zhelev, Zhelu 77
Zhivkov, Todor 77, 138